READINGS ON EQUAL EDUCATION
(Formerly *Educating the Disadvantaged*)

ADVISORY PANEL

READINGS ON EQUAL EDUCATION

Volume 13

FORTY YEARS AFTER THE *BROWN* DECISION: IMPLICATIONS OF SCHOOL DESEGREGATION FOR U.S. EDUCATION

Co-Editors
Kofi Lomotey
Charles Teddlie

Managing Editor
John Freeman

AMS PRESS
NEW YORK

Library of Congress Catalogue Number: 77-83137
International Standard Book Number: Set 0-404-10100-3
International Standard Book Number: Vol. 13:0-404-10113-5
International Standard Series Number: 0270-1448

All AMS Books are printed on acid-free paper that meets the guidelines for performance and durability of the Committee on Production
Guidelines for Book Longevity of the Council On Library Resources.

Manufactured in the United States of America

AMS Press, Inc.
56 East 13th Street
New York, N.Y. 10003

CONTENTS

VOLUME 13

VOLUME 14

FOREWORD

FORTY YEARS AFTER THE *BROWN* DECISION: IMPLICATIONS OF SCHOOL DESEGREGATION FOR U.S. EDUCATION

Reginald Wilson

When Reverend Oliver Brown won his case before the Supreme Court on May 17, 1954 — sometimes known as "Black Monday" — it was greeted around the world as the revolution that, indeed, it was. It meant that legal segregation (as established by *Plessy v. Ferguson* in 1896) was finally ended as the law of the land, and it also meant, primarily, that the maintenance of segregated schools was at last declared unconstitutional. Thurgood Marshall, the lead attorney for the plaintiffs, predicted optimistically at the time that segregation in the United States would be "entirely stamped out in no more than five years." William Taylor, former staff chief of the U.S. Commission on Civil Rights, more pessimistically said, "The Court decision led to a great deal of progress and, at the same time, a lot of frustrations about the lack of progress." Taylor, unfortunately, was the more accurate.

Brown v. Board of Education of Topeka was the culmination of years of carefully planned litigation and political maneuvering on the part of African Americans. The first effort was the founding of the Afro-American League (1887–1908), whose support of the Blair Education Bill resulted in its greatest struggle. That bill would have mandated equal federal funding of black and white schools while maintaining segregation; thus, it was acceptable to some Southerners. But it was not acceptable to most Southerners (and a few Northerners), and in 1891, after much debate, it went down to defeat. This defeat had enormous implications for black empowerment in the South and one black spokesman saw that the "failure [of the Blair bill] would be a disaster to the whole country, especially to the black race." But the bill was defeated despite this foreboding and eventually led to the demise of the Afro-American League.

The downfall of the League led to the formation of the National Association for the Advancement of Colored People (NAACP) in 1909. The NAACP maintained as its main objective, however, the same prime motivation as that of the League — the ending of segregated public schooling in the South. But this time its primary strategy would be through the courts rather than through the legislature, which it thought less susceptible to the vagaries of the political process and more open to the presentation of facts rather than being swayed by emotion. Ultimately they were to learn otherwise, but that was a fairly accurate assessment of the federal courts at that point in time.

Charles Hamilton Houston was the main strategist for the legal program of the NAACP. A brilliant magna cum laude graduate of Amherst College and Howard University Law School, he saw that his first strategy was raising a cadre of first-rate lawyers to fight the enormous battle of overturning a 50-year-old precedent of racially segregated schools. His first task, as dean of the Howard University Law School, was to raise the standards and recruit a group of top-flight students to become the shock troops of that battle. Thurgood Marshall, one of those students, led the way with victory after victory culminating in the *Brown* decision.

This book is about what happened to the 40-year fight for school desegregation following *Brown*. In the following chapters it presents in-depth analyses of the various attempts to implement *Brown*, both North and South, urban and rural, and the few successes and many failures along the way.

Janet Schofield does an exhaustive study of the effect of school desegregation on black and white students. John Stanfield explains brilliantly how protest movements changed the mood of the country toward school desegregation. Jim Garvin shows how public housing patterns affected school attendance. Susan Eaton and Gary Orfield explore in-depth how the *Milliken* decision stopped further school desegregation into the suburbs, though several legal challenges were attempted. Charles Glenn explores the explosive Boston busing situation and its consequences that linger bitterly to this day. But the tenor of most of the chapters is a mood of guarded pessimism which characterizes the entire volume and especially the concluding essay by Lomotey and Fossey, aptly titled, "School Desegregation: Why it Hasn't Worked and What Could Work."

The schools in Hartford, Connecticut, are 93% minority. The schools in Detroit, Michigan, are 90% minority. Schools in America that were over 50% black declined from 76.6% in 1968 to 63.6% in 1972, but had risen to 66% by 1992. For Hispanics the picture was even more depressing. Schools that were over 90% Hispanic in 1968 were 23%. By 1992 they were 34% (Orfield, 1993). Despite dramatic gains for blacks in the late 60s and early 70s, the thrust of restrictive court orders, shifting housing patterns, and the ending of desegregation orders have left minorities, especially in urban areas, more segregated than before *Brown*. And even more ironical, desegregation has been more effective in the "massive resistance" South that in the "liberal" North. For example, two of the most segregated cities are Chicago and Detroit. What are we to make of all this?

Hindsight is, of course, perfect. But it is evident now that a purely legal approach to school desegregation was too narrow. Robert Carter, a counsel for the plaintiffs in *Brown*, and now a retired federal judge, said wistfully, "I thought the problem was segregation," in reminiscing about the case. The attorneys did not anticipate the massive resistance that would result both in the North and in the South, nor did they foresee a change in the Court's direction from one of relative openness to one of hostility to changing the status quo. Fair enough, they could not have foreseen these things, but they could have developed a comprehensive plan to offer the courts for rational school desegregation and teacher employment, or a theory for the ultimate, and inevitable, impact that desegregation would have on higher education. But that was not to be, with desegregation being accomplished with the emphasis on busing rather than on quality education, which was the primary motive to begin with. Eventually the strain in philosophy and approach led to a break between black educators and black lawyers. But that is the subject for another essay.

Suffice it to say that in reading this collection of essays one is left with a rich, in-depth knowledge of one of the great moral experiments on which this nation has embarked as it struggles to arrive at its fulfillment of democracy. Now, 40 years after *Brown,* is an appropriate time to explore the consequent triumphs and tragedies that experiment entailed.

ROBERT L. CRAIN is a professor of sociology and education at Columbia University's Teachers College and an expert on school desegregation and race relations. He is first author of *The Politics of School Desegregation* (1969, Doubleday) and co-author of five books, including *Making School Desegregation Work* (Ballinger) and *Stepping Over the Colorline: Black Inner-City Students in White Suburban Schools* (in press, Yale University Press).

SUSAN E. EATON is assistant director of the Harvard Project on School Desegregation and a doctoral candidate at the Harvard Graduate School of Education. She has been the education writer for daily metropolitan newspapers in Massachusetts and Connecticut. She is co-author, with Gary Orfield, of *Dismantling Desegregation: The Quiet Reversal of Brown v. Board of Education*, to be published by the New Press in 1996.

RICHARD FOSSEY is associate professor of education law and policy at Louisiana State University. He received his doctorate in education policy from Harvard University and his law degree from the University of Texas School of Law. Prior to beginning an academic career, he practiced education law in Alaska, where he represented school boards in Inuit, Athabaskan, and other Alaska Native communities. His research interests include education law, school choice, child abuse and neglect, and school reform. Fossey is co-author, along with Michael Clay Smith, of *Crime on Campus: Liability Issues and Campus Administration,* published by Oryx Press and the American Council on Education.

JOHN FREEMAN is a doctoral student and research assistant at Louisiana State University. A former high school social studies teacher and principal, his research interests are school effectiveness and improvement, as well as school law and finance. Freeman also served as Managing Editor for this volume.

ANTOINE M. GARIBALDI is vice president for Academic Affairs and professor of education at Xavier University. He is the author of ten books and monographs and more than 60 chapters and scholarly articles on black colleges and universities, African

American males, minority teacher recruitment and retention, and urban education issues. Some of his recent books are: *The Education of African Americans* (co-edited with Charles Willie and Wornie L. Reed, 1991); *Teacher Recruitment and Retention* (1989); *The Revitalization of Teacher Education Programs at Historically Black Colleges* (1989); *Educating Black Male Youth: A Moral and Civic Imperative* (1988); and, *Black Colleges and Universities: Challenges for the Future* (1984). He received his undergraduate degree magna cum laude from Howard University in 1973 and his Ph.D. in Educational and Social Psychology from the University of Minnesota in 1976.

JIM GARVIN is an assistant professor of educational administration in the Department of Administrative and Foundational Services at Louisiana State University. His primary research interests include schools and communities, urban education, and sociology of education.

CHARLES L. GLENN is professor and chairman of the Department of Administration, Training, and Policy Studies in the Boston University School of Education. Previously he served 21 years as the Massachusetts official responsible for urban education and civil rights in schools, in which capacity he had primary responsibility for requiring and helping 16 cities to implement school desegregation plans. He has published three books and dozens of book chapters on equity issues, urban school reform, parental choice of schools, the education of immigrant and language-minority children and the accommodation of religious conviction in educational systems. Glenn has also been involved extensively with education policy issues in Western and Eastern Europe and has served as a consultant on equity issues to a number of states and large cities.

CHERYL BROWN HENDERSON is one of the daughters of the late Rev. Oliver Brown who was lead plaintiff in the landmark U.S. Supreme Court Case of 1954 — *Oliver L. Brown et al. v. The Board of Education of Topeka*. She has been an educator for 23 years in the positions of public school teacher, guidance counselor, university guest lecturer, and state administrator. She is currently Executive Director of the Brown Foundation for Educational Equity, Excellence, and Research, and co-owner of Brown &

Brown Associates educational consultants. Her recent published writing is an article entitled "Landmark Decision: Remembering the Struggle for Equal Education," *Land and People,* 6(1), Spring 1994.

FREDERICK S. HUMPHRIES has served as a university president for more than twenty years, including 10 years at the helm of Tennessee State University and more than a decade as president of Florida A & M University. He became FAMUs eighth president in 1985 and has since earned national acclaim for his achievements, which helped FAMU become one of the nation's premier institutions of higher learning. In 1992, FAMU became the first university to defeat Harvard University in the recruitment of National Achievement Scholars, the most highly recruited African American scholars in the nation. One of the nation's most honored educators, Humphries serves on numerous boards of distinction in the private and public sectors. He is a 1957 magna cum laude graduate of FAMU with a bachelor's degree in chemistry and a Ph.D. in physical chemistry from the University of Pittsburgh in 1964.

JACQULIN SENSLEY JACOBS earned her doctorate from George Peabody College of Vanderbilt University and is currently employed at Southern University in Baton Rouge. Dr. Jacobs's professional career has been focused on researching, teaching, and informing the educational community about the academic and social needs of children that are culturally different. She has published book chapters, articles in scholarly journals, and made numerous presentations at national conferences on learning styles, multicultural education, test-taking skills, and techniques that work with culturally different children.

SHARON R. JOHNSON is currently the Writing/Reading/Study Skills Component Coordinator of the Thomas J. Edwards Learning Center located at the State University of New York at Buffalo. She is completing her doctoral dissertation in the Department of Education, Organization, Administration, and Policy at the State University of New York at Buffalo. Her research focuses on school desegregation and its legal and social impact on the quality of education for African American children.

KOFI LOMOTEY is chair and an associate professor in the Department of Administrative and Foundational Services in the College of Education at Louisiana State University in Baton Rouge. His research interests include African American principals, independent African-centered schools, issues of race in higher education, and urban education. His recent publications include "African-American Principals: Bureaucrat/Administrators and Ethno-humanists," in M. J. Shujaa (Ed.), *Too Much Schooling, Too Little Education: A Paradox in African-American Life* (1994) and "Social and Cultural Influences on Schooling: A Commentary on the UCEA Knowledge Base Project, Domain I, in *Educational Administration Quarterly, 31*(2) (1995). Lomotey is the editor of the journal *Urban Education* and the National Secretary/Treasurer of the Council of Independent Black Institutions, an umbrella organization for independent African-centered schools. In addition, he serves on the editorial boards of several journals, including *Educational Administration Quarterly* and *Journal for a Just and Caring Education.*

JAMES MEZA, JR. is director of the Accelerated Schools Center and associate professor of educational administration at the University of New Orleans in New Orleans. He served six years as a member of the Southern University System Board of Supervisors and chairperson of the Southern System's Academic Affairs, Faculty, and Personnel Committee. He also served as executive director of the Louisiana State Board of Elementary and Secondary Education.

GARY A. ORFIELD is professor of education, at the Harvard Graduate School of Education. His primary research interests are government policy and minority opportunity. He is co-author, with Susan Eaton, of *Dismantling Desegregation: The Quiet Reversal of Brown v. Board of Education*, to be published by the New Press in 1996.

SHARIBA RIVERS is a graduate student at Louisiana State University in the Department of Administrative and Foundational Services. She is currently working on her Master's Degree with a concentration in Higher Education Administration and serves as a graduate/research assistant for Dr. Kofi Lomotey.

JANET WARD SCHOFIELD is professor of psychology and a senior scientist in the Learning Research and Development Center at the University of Pittsburgh. She has also served as a faculty member at Spelman College. She received a B.A. magna cum laude from Radcliffe College where she was elected to Phi Beta Kappa. She received her Ph.D. from Harvard University in 1972. Professor Schofield is a social psychologist whose major research interest for more than twenty years has been social processes in desegregated schools. She has published more than two dozen papers in this area as well as two books. One of these, *Black and White in School: Trust, Tension or Tolerance?* was awarded the Society for the Psychological Study of Social Issues' Gordon Allport Intergroup Relations Prize.

MWALIMU J. SHUJAA is an associate professor in the area of social and philosophical foundations of education at the State University of New York at Buffalo. The focus of his academic research and writing is in the areas of theory and practice that add clarity to our understandings of (1) the social and cultural tensions that affect schooling and education; (2) the right of all people to cultural and political self-determination; and (3) the complexities of the personal transformations involved in liberating African consciousness from white supremacy ideology. Shujaa's edited book, *Too Much Schooling, Too Little Education: A Paradox of Black Life and White Societies* (published by Africa World Press, 1994), is an attempt to expand the conceptual bases for differentiating schooling and education in societies where the relationships of power between cultural groups are unequal and antagonistic. A second edited book, *Beyond Desegregation: The Politics of Quality in African American Schooling* (published by Corwin Press, 1996), examines the power relations affecting the schooling of people of African descent in the United States. He is also the editor of the journal *Education Policy*, and has been an Executive Officer of the Council of Independent Black Institutions since 1990.

DELORES R. SPIKES is president of the Southern University A & M College System and was directly involved in Louisiana's higher education desegregation case since 1981. She is past chairperson of Council 1890 Presidents, National Association of State Universities and Land Grant Colleges and currently serves as a Commissioner for the Southern Association of Colleges and Schools. She is a member of President Clinton's Advisory Board for Historically Black Universities and ACE/AID representative, University of Northwest in MMabatho, South Africa.

JOHN H. STANFIELD is professor of sociology and professor of African American and African Studies, University of California – Davis.

WILLIAM F. TATE is an assistant professor of curriculum and instruction at the University of Wisconsin–Madison. His research interests include the political and cultural dimensions of mathematics education. "School Mathematics and African American Students: Thinking Seriously About Opportunity-to-Learn Stand-adds," to appear in *Educational Administration Quarterly*, reflects his scholarly interests.

CHARLES TEDDLIE is professor of educational research methodology in the College of Education at Louisiana State University. He also taught at the University of New Orleans and served as Assistant Superintendent for Research and Development at the Louisiana Department of Education. He has published over 60 chapters and articles and co-authored two recent books: *Schools Make a Difference: Lessons Learned from a 10-year Study of School Effects* (1993, Teachers College Press) and *Advances in School Effectiveness Research and Practice* (1994, Pergamon). He serves as the series editor for *Readings on Equal Education, Volumes 13-17*. He received his B.S. cum laude in Psychology from LSU and his M.A. and Ph.D. (1979) from the University of North Carolina in Social Psychology.

J. DALE THORN is assistant professor of mass communications at Louisiana State University in Baton Rouge. A former associate commissioner of higher education in Louisiana, he has written a number of articles on higher education desegregation. He presented a paper on the topic at the 1994 National Conference on Race Relations and Civil Rights, at the Roy Wilkins Center, University of Minnesota. He is indebted to the Freedom Forum Foundation and the LSU Research Council for grants that supported this research.

JEROLD WALTMAN is professor of political science at the University of Southern Mississippi. He is the author of several books, the most recent of which is *American Government: Politics and Citizenship* (1993). He is currently working on a history of the minimum wage.

AMY STUART WELLS is an assistant professor of educational policy at UCLAs Graduate School of Education and Information Studies. Her areas of research include school desegregation, school choice policy, and detracking in racially mixed schools. She is author of *Time to Choose: America at the Crossroads of School Choice Policy* (1993, Hill & Wang) and co-author with Robert L. Crain of *Stepping Over the Colorline: Black Inner-City Students in White Suburban Schools* (in press, Yale University Press).

REGINALD WILSON was named Senior Scholar of the American Council on Education in October, 1988. He joined the Council as Director of the Office of Minority Concerns on October 1, 1981. Prior to that appointment he was, for nearly ten years, President of Wayne County Community College in Detroit. Dr. Wilson is the co-author of *Human Development in the Urban Community*, the editor of *Race and Equity in Higher Education*, and the author of *Civil Liberties and the U.S.* He is also on the editorial board of *The American Journal of Education* and *The Urban Review*.

INTRODUCTION

Kofi Lomotey and Charles Teddlie

Preparing these two volumes was an exciting task for a number of reasons, not the least of which was that the topic has garnered such a tremendous amount of interest in the academic community in the past few years. Several volumes, as well as special issues of journals (e.g., Lagemann, 1995; Shujaa, in press), have been or will be produced, focusing specifically on some aspects of a 40-year retrospective look at the *Brown v. Board of Education* (1954, 1955) Supreme Court decisions. These volumes, then, are important in that they make a significant contribution to this growing body of literature on this vital topic.

In this introduction, we describe the organization of Volumes 13 and 14 (while more details of each section of the volumes — and of the chapters within them precede the specific sections); highlight several themes that run across more than one chapter within the volumes; and discuss, in greater detail, certain aspects of the significance of the volumes. Specifically, with regard to the volumes' significance, we consider the fact that the books' authors: (a) provide a historical focus on the impact of *Brown* across several strata of U.S. society, including all levels of educational desegregation, (b) provide multiple solutions to some of the current problems regarding desegregation in our schools and society, (c) provide specific suggestions for future research in this area, (d) include several late breaking events of interest in both desegregation litigation and enrollment trends, and (e) provide a great deal of reference material, both in terms of the desegregation literature and relevant court cases.

A General Overview of the Volume

These volumes are divided into four sections: In Volume 13 we include The General Implications of Desegregation for U.S. Education and the Impact of Desegregation on Black Colleges. In Volume 14 we include Social and Cultural Effects of School Desegregation and A Look to the Future. Each section is preceded by a "chapter" summarizing the contents of the section. In Section I, Teddlie and Freeman, and then Jacobs, discuss the history of precollegiate and collegiate efforts at desegregation. Schofield and then Eaton and Orfield provide a historical sketch of desegregation efforts on the elementary and secondary levels only. Also, Glenn provides a case study of one of the most well known, and perhaps one of the most explosive, desegregation situations in the U.S. — Boston, Massachusetts. Finally, Fossey discusses the role of the judiciary in the Hartford, Connecticut desegregation case.

In Section II, Garibaldi provides an overview of the impact of *Brown* on Historically Black Colleges and Universities (HBCUs). This is preceded by case studies of the long standing Louisiana (Spikes & Meza) and the Mississippi higher education (Humphries) desegregation cases. These case studies are written from the perspective of authors who are presidents of HBCUs.

Schools are affected by many social and cultural influences. The authors whose chapters appear in Section III look at the relationships between several of these factors and school desegregation. Tate addresses the link between desegregation and the politics of mathematics education in U.S. society. Wells and Crain look at the issue of desegregation from a sociological perspective, examining the effects of desegregation on the ultimate life chances of African American children.

Garvin, in the next chapter in Section III, looks at the relationship between schooling and housing patterns, using a powerful historical case study of New Orleans. Stanfield considers the impact of race on school desegregation in the U.S. which he refers to as a "race-centered nation." Lastly, Thorn looks at the impact of the media on the way in which desegregation's story has been told over the years, focusing specifically on higher education desegregation.

The final section (Section IV) begins with a retrospective look at the *Brown* case, written by Cheryl Brown Henderson (a daughter of Reverend Oliver Brown, the lead plaintiff in the first *Brown* case) and Shariba Rivers. This chapter is followed by a discussion of the future of HBCUs by Waltman. Lomotey and Fossey offer an in-depth analysis of elementary and secondary desegregation efforts and a prescription for improving the disease of disenfranchisement of large numbers of students who are primarily in urban and rural areas, primarily poor, and primarily African American or Hispanic American. In the final chapter, Mwalimu J. Shujaa and Sharon Johnson examine two desegregation strategies and their implications for the quality of schooling experienced by African Americans. The authors focus their discussion on the goals pursued through court-ordered desegregation and those that drive African Americans to organize independent educational institutions.

Themes of these Volumes

No doubt, readers will uncover themes that run throughout the chapters that may be of particular interest to them. We mention a few here that struck us as we prepared the manuscript. First, there is the issue of the relationship between poverty, race, educational outcomes, and housing patterns. This came across powerfully in the Eaton and Orfield chapter, the Garvin chapter, and the Henderson and Rivers chapter, among others.

Second is the notion of the negative impact of the media on the ultimate story that has been told with regard to the nature of desegregation efforts. Thorn addresses this issue in his chapter, specifically looking at higher education. Additionally, Henderson and Rivers talk about this theme in the context of precollegiate desegregation efforts.

A third theme that flows through several chapters is one of pessimism in that the original promises of the *Brown* decision have never been realized at the precollegiate level, the collegiate level, or at any of the other levels of society where they were to have had their most profound impact. Other recent volumes devoted to the *Brown* decision, such as Lagemann (1995), are equally pessimistic. While a few chapters do address successes associated with the *Brown* decision, the overall tone of these volumes is best exemplified by Glenn's discussion of the problems with the desegregation of Boston's public schools, Humphries's description of the continuing unfairness of the treatment of HBCUs within higher education, and Lomotey and Fossey's concern regarding the relationship between power and education.

A fourth theme is that several authors provide clear and strong warnings to educational leaders, political leaders, and to our society in general regarding the continuing failure to live up to the promise of *Brown*. Jacobs suggests that our continued failure to address adequately our educational dilemma will result in: more resegregation, more African American students in inferior schools, more schools of choice that provide little choice for most African American students, more litigation, less support for higher education desegregation, and more conflicts at the local level. Garvin argues that if we do not come to grips with the nature of the relationship between schooling and housing, we will be ill-prepared to address issues of inequity and power in society and in the schools.

Thorn contends that if the media continues to distort the reality of desegregation, the public will continue to be confused about the real story. Humphries suggests that the Mississippi case has implications nationally. He also suggests that higher education desegregation plans should demonstrate respect, not disdain, for African American colleges and universities, culture, and people.

Significance of these Volumes

Readers will, no doubt, find these volumes significant for reasons of their own. For us, these volumes are significant, first, because of their strong historical focus and their implications for our understanding of the story of desegregation. Second, they are significant because of their two-pronged focus on both precollegiate *and* collegiate efforts at desegregating educational institutions. Often, volumes address one or the other educational level, but usually not both.

Third, most of the chapters, while theoretical and analytical, are also prescriptive in terms of offering solutions to our educational dilemma. At least nine of the chapters offer some suggestions for attaining aspects of the *Brown* decision. The following are the chapters that address school improvement issues:

1. Chapter Four. Schofield argues that instead of focusing so much on changing the racial composition of schools, we should

focus on improving the educational opportunities of students—wherever they are in school.

2. Chapter Five. Eaton and Orfield suggest that we gear our efforts toward enabling inner-city children to benefit from the tremendous opportunities that exist within urban centers by developing a strategy. Their specific plan is called metropolitan desegregation and involves the creation of a cross-district (an urban center and one or more suburban districts) desegregation program. Eaton and Orfield contend that such a program may be deemed best when there are not enough students from a particular racial group (usually white) within the urban district to enable desegregation to work.

3. Chapter Six. Glenn argues, in reassessing the Boston case, that fundamental and comprehensive change in the school system should now be the focus of efforts in that city. He also calls for an approach that is less confrontational and involves more informed parental choice than that originally allowed in Boston.

4. Chapter Nine. Spikes and Meza suggest that future court orders should take into consideration: the potential for African American success in higher education, the need to discontinue the practice of making HBCUs appear (and in reality be) inferior, and the need for adequate representation of African Americans in policy discussions around the issue of higher education governance.

5. Chapter Eleven. Garibaldi cites several of the assets of HBCUs (e.g., tutoring and remedial assistance, monitoring by faculty, small classes, and promoting graduate and professional opportunities) as indicative of what we can do in all institutions to improve upon the success of African American students.

6. Chapter Thirteen. Tate calls for, in a rather straight forward manner, the elimination of ability grouping, tracking, and unequal funding of school districts.

7. Chapter Sixteen. Stanfield urges the establishment of citizen advocacy groups and transracial coalitions to challenge states, local governments, media, political parties, and other citizens' groups to contribute to more equitable education for all students.

8. Chapter Twenty. Waltman calls for a federally controlled board to insure the survival and development of HBCUs.

9. Chapter Twenty-one. Lomotey and Fossey recommend: culturally equitable pedagogy; effective, competent, and passion-

ate educators; making schools safe and nurturing; and addressing issues of inequality in society and in schools.

A fourth contribution of these volumes is the inclusion of several late-breaking events of interest in both desegregation litigation and behavioral data:

1. Developments in the resolution of the higher education desegregation cases in Louisiana (*United States v. Louisiana,* 1994) and Mississippi (*Ayers v. Fordice,* 1995). (Chapters Two, Three, Nine, Ten, and Seventeen.)

2. A 1995 Supreme Court ruling in a University of Maryland case involving a scholarship program limited to African Americans stating that the university could not reinstate the scholarship program because it was race-based (*Kirwan v. Podberesky,* 1995). (Chapter Two.)

3. A 1995 ruling in Connecticut regarding metropolitan school desegregation in the Hartford city-suburban area (*Sheff v. O'Neill,* 1995). (Chapters Five and Seven.)

4. A 1995 Supreme Court ruling concerning a Kansas City desegregation case which makes it more difficult for federal judges to order city school desegregation plans designed to attract white students from the suburbs (*Missouri v. Jenkins,* 1995). (Chapter One.)

5. Data on desegregation at both the elementary-secondary level through 1991–92 (Chapter Five) and higher education level through 1993 (Chapter Two).

Fifth, some of the authors in these volumes offer suggestions for future research. These include Stanfield, who calls for African Americans, specifically, to address the question: what do we want to achieve with desegregated schools? desegregation? assimilation? pluralism? or some combination of the above? Garibaldi implies that there is a need for case studies of some HBCUs in order for other institutions to learn about some of the efforts that have been successful with African American students in these institutions.

One final note of interest regarding the significance of these volumes concerns the amount of reference material that is made available to readers, both in terms of the desegregation literature and relevant court cases. While not a handbook regarding *Brown* and U.S. desegregation, several of the chapters in these volumes provide exhaustive scholarly references and legal citations regarding specific aspects of these issues.

1. Schofield, in Chapter Four alone, cites over 200 references from desegregation and other literature.

2. Chapter Two has many references particular to the higher education desegregation literature ranging from the mid-1930s through the mid-1990s.

3. Chapters Five, Six, and Seven contain similar references for elementary-secondary desegregation.

4. As for case law, Jacobs in Chapter Three references over 50 desegregation cases, while Chapter Two has several case citations relevant to higher education and Chapter Five has similar citations for elementary-secondary desegregation court cases.

All in all, the authors in these volumes provide a plethora of information for scholars and students of the study of desegregation in higher education and in elementary and secondary schools.

We would like to acknowledge our wives, Nahuja and Susan for providing continuous support and wisdom. We would also like to pay tribute to our children, Shawnjua, Juba, Mbeja, Katie, and Timmy. They are our inspiration for the future.

We are indebted to John Freeman, a graduate student at LSU, who served as the Managing Editor for these volumes. His patience, diligence, and focus on specificity were priceless. Thanks also to Melonee Wicker and Cyn. D. Reynaud, staff members in our department, for their technical assistance. We also appreciated the editorial assistance of Shariba Rivers and Janis Simms, two graduate students in our department.

References

Lagemann, E. C. (Ed.). (1995). *Brown* plus forty [Special issue]. *Teachers College Record, 96*(4).

Shujaa, M. J. (Ed.). (In press.) *Beyond desegregation: Perspectives on the quality of African American schooling.* Thousand Oaks, CA: Corwin Press.

Table of Legal Cases

Ayers v. Fordice, 112 S.Ct. 2727 (1992).

Brown v. Board of Education, 347 U.S. 483, 74 S.Ct. 686, 98 L.Ed. 873 (1954).

Brown v. Board of Education, 349 U.S. 294, 75 S.Ct. 53, 99 L.Ed. 1083 (1955).

Kirwan v. Podberesky, 63 U.S.L.W. 3832 (U.S. May 22, 1995).

Sheff v. O'Neill, No. CV89-0360977S (1995) Conn. Super. LEXIS 1148.

United States v. Louisiana, No. 80-3300 (USD/ED, 1994).

CHAPTER 1

HISTORICAL PERSPECTIVES ON SCHOOL DESEGREGATION:
AN INTRODUCTORY OVERVIEW

Charles Teddlie and Kofi Lomotey

Section I, Historical Perspectives on School Desegregation, contains six chapters reviewing different aspects of the impact of the *Brown* decision and subsequent litigation and federal laws on the desegregation of elementary-secondary and higher education in the U.S. Chapter Two is concerned primarily with higher education (although some data on high school completion rates are included), while both the elementary-secondary and higher education levels are discussed in Chapter Three. The authors of Chapters Four, Five, and Seven address general issues in elementary-secondary education, while the focus in Chapter Six is on the desegregation of the Boston public school system.

In Chapter Two, Charles Teddlie and John Freeman describe five distinct periods in higher education desegregation, which became a reality in the U.S. with the *Brown* and subsequent *Hawkins* court decisions in the mid-1950s:

1. The NAACP's initial desegregation campaign from 1933–53 focused on eliminating segregation in graduate and professional schools in order to set precedents for ultimately desegregating education at all levels of U.S. society.

2. The NAACP achieved ultimate victory in the courts during the 1954–63 period, culminating with the *Brown* (1954,

1

1955) and *Hawkins* (1956) decisions. Yet actual desegregation of higher education institutions was greatly delayed over the next decade by massive white resistance, particularly in the South.

3. Federal legislative acts, such as Title VI of the Civil Rights Act of 1964 and the Higher Education Act of 1965, contributed to a dramatic rise (greater than 200%) in African American enrollment in higher education, especially in formerly segregated colleges and universities, during the 1964–73 period.

4. The period from 1974–84 was characterized by stagnation in African American enrollment in higher education due to a variety of factors: declining student aid and increasing fees, the introduction of reverse discrimination concerns, the failure of the federal government to pursue aggressively Title VI regulations, etc.

5. African American enrollment in colleges and universities increased moderately (greater than 30%) across the board during the 1985–95 period as the final Title VI higher education cases were being decided. Few closures or mergers of institutions have resulted from these cases.

In Chapter Three, Jacqulin Jacobs examines desegregation litigation and the position that the Court has taken since the *Brown* ruling in 1954. She explains that segregation-related litigation in this country has ranged from sustained unenforced desegregation, intense desegregation-enforcement efforts, a period of calm and moderate activity, to a movement toward resegregation. In this chapter, she focuses on how the courts have softened their stance on desegregation and given school districts more autonomy and freedom in developing desegregation plans. Jacobs also addresses such controversial issues as busing and attendance zones.

Jacobs concludes that the U.S. government is allowing local boards and governments to make decisions regarding ensuring equitable educational systems. According to her, these local policymakers, as evidenced by their past and present behavior, have proven that they are either incapable of, or unwilling to, design fair and equitable desegregation plans. Jacobs suggests that the consequences of continuing such a system will be (a) a slow trend toward resegregation, (b) disproportionate numbers of African American students in inadequate schools, (c) more freedom of choice programs that fail to meet the needs of minority students, (d) more local, federal, and Supreme Court suits, (e) decreased social support for desegregation in higher education, and (f) increased confrontation at local levels.

In Chapter Four, Janet Schofield explores the impact of school desegregation on elementary and secondary school students. She suggests that research *does* indicate that desegregation has had some positive effects on the reading skills of African American children, although that effect is not substantial. On the other hand, she notes that such is not the case with these students' mathematics skills, which generally seem unaffected by desegregation.

Schofield argues that evidence has begun to accumulate suggesting that desegregation may favorably influence college graduation, future income, and employment patterns. According to Schofield, evidence regarding the role of desegregation on intergroup relations is inconclusive and inconsistent. In summary, she states that viewing racially and ethnically heterogeneous schools as having the potential to improve student outcomes and focusing more attention on the actual nature of the students' experiences to assure that they are fruitful should make it possible to improve outcomes for students.

Susan Eaton and Gary Orfield discuss the struggle for desegregated school systems since the *Brown* decision in 1954. They argue, in Chapter Five, that although 40 years have passed, racially and ethnically segregated schools are a fact of everyday educational life all across the U.S. They further note that for the first time since the *Brown* decision, national data indicate that school segregation is on the rise for African American students and has been steadily increasing for Hispanic American students for decades.

Using Norfolk, Virginia and Hartford, Connecticut as examples, the authors demonstrate two patterns whereby this resegregation has occurred. The Connecticut example is extended to describe the concept of "metropolitan school desegregation" which the authors consider to be the best alternative for desegregation at this time. Eaton and Orfield also argue that there is greater support among the public for desegregation (and for busing to achieve it) than is commonly reported, citing extensive data collected from several Harris and Gallup polls to support their conclusions.

Eaton and Orfield conclude that although *Brown's* power has been stripped considerably, the struggle to achieve the decision's ideals continues. They argue that school desegregation is a strategy that seeks not only to bring the races together for improved relations, but also to break up concentrations of poverty that accompany racial stratification. They add that education advocates should focus upon efforts that would allow economically disadvantaged urban children to take advantage of the economic growth and opportunity that exists within their own metropolitan area.

One of the most controversial issues to hit the education scene has been and continues to be "busing." In Chapter Six, Charles Glenn discusses the implementation of busing in Boston. Glenn, who was appointed as the first director of the Massachusetts desegregation program, explores the antagonistic attitudes and practices regarding the first stage of mandatory desegregation in Boston which began in 1974. He then traces these efforts through the years.

Glenn later makes suggestions for what could have been done to improve the process. These suggestions include seeking areas of agreement with school officials rather than operating in a climate of mistrust, and working with, rather than against, the desire of parents and teachers to make decisions about how children are educated. Glenn adds that Boston education officials, along with teachers and parents, should have used the desegregation crisis to push for fundamental and comprehensive changes in the school system.

Richard Fossey, in Chapter Seven, expands upon the Hartford desegregation case in discussing the potential of establishing large regional districts to address the issues of desegregation and equity in resources and the impact of these issues on inner-city schools. While contradicting the current literature concerning decentralization of authority and the restructuring movement, Fossey makes valid points concerning the ability of regional school districts' ability to address some of the issues plaguing schools in general and metropolitan schools in particular.

Authors in this section, while addressing general issues regarding desegregation, have spent considerable space describing particular "cases" which are illustrative of general trends. These cases include:

1. The Hartford, Connecticut metropolitan desegregation case (*Sheff v. O'Neill*, 1995), which is examined in detail in

Chapters Five and Seven, with information going back more than 20 years.

2. The resegregation of the Norfolk, Virginia school system is also examined in Chapter Five.

3. The highly publicized Boston desegregation experience is chronicled in detail in Chapter Six by one of the principal players in the case.

4. The Mississippi higher education case is discussed in several places in this volume, including Chapters Two and Three in this section and Chapters Nine and Ten later in the volume.

5. The relationship (legal and otherwise) that exists between two land grant state universities in Louisiana (Southern University and Louisiana State University) is discussed in Chapters Two and Three and later in Chapter Nine.

6. The Maryland case (*Kirwan v. Podberesky*, 1995) regarding a scholarship for African American students only and the Supreme Court decision concerning it is discussed in Chapter Two.

These case studies present specific information that illustrates the general points being made in the chapters. Several of these specific cases appear to have considerable relevance for the future of desegregation at both the elementary/secondary (e.g., the Hartford case) and the higher education levels (e.g., the Mississippi desegregation and Maryland scholarship cases).

As the manuscript for this volume was being sent to the publisher, the Supreme Court ruled in another case that may have relevance to the further desegregation of elementary/secondary education (*Missouri v. Jenkins*, 1995). This ruling involved a long-standing desegregation case in Kansas City in which a federal court judge had ordered the spending of approximately $1.5 billion on a desegregation program aimed at attracting more white students from suburban areas to city schools with predominantly African American student populations. The success of this program had been mixed, with non-minority enrollment in the schools below 25% at the time of the ruling.

The Supreme Court ruling (in a 5–4 vote) stated that such desegregation plans could be imposed only if a judge determined that *both* urban and suburban schools still showed signs of prior segregation. This ruling has the effect of making it more difficult for federal judges to order city school desegregation plans designed to attract white suburban students (Asseo, 1995; Will,

1995), because suburban school systems would have to be found in violation of the constitutional rights of African Americans.

Justice Clarence Thomas, commenting separately on the decision, stated that the district court had improperly focused on "a theory of injury that was predicated on black inferiority." He stated further that "It never ceases to amaze me that the courts are so willing to assume that anything that is predominantly black must be inferior." Thomas further stated that "This position rests upon the idea that any school that is black is inferior and that blacks cannot succeed without the company of whites."

While it is unclear what impact this particular ruling will have on other desegregation cases across the country, it is clear that the Supreme Court is now less likely to consider race as a defining criterion on a number of important issues, including affirmative action and the make-up of congressional districts.

This 5–4 ruling was another example of a turn toward a more conservative Supreme Court judiciary in the mid-1990s. This more conservative Court appears to be saying that it is time "to put race aside" (Conservative justices gaining control of court, 1995).

References

Asseo, L. (1995, June 13). Court cuts desegregation powers. *The Baton Rouge Morning Advocate*, p. 5-A.
Conservative justices gaining control of court. (1995, July 3). *The Baton Rouge Morning Advocate*, p. 2-A.
Will, G. F. (1995, June 26). From Topeka to Kansas City. *Newsweek*, p. 66.

Table of Legal Cases

Brown v. The Board of Education of Topeka, Kansas, 347 U.S. 483, (1954).
Florida ex rel Hawkins v. Board of Control, 47 So.2d 608 (1950), mot. denied, 53 So.2d 116 (1951), cert. denied., 342 U.S. 877 (1951), *vacated*, 347 U.S. 971 (1954), recalled, vacated, 350 U.S. 413 (1956).
Kirwan v. Podberesky, 63 U.S.L.W. 3832 (U.S. May 22,1995).
Missouri v. Jenkins, Case No. 93-1823, (Decided June 12, 1995).
Sheff v. O'Neill, No. CV89–0360977S (1995) Conn. Super. LEXIS 1148.

CHAPTER 2

With All Deliberate Speed:
An Historical Overview of the Relationship Between the *Brown* Decision and Higher Education

Charles Teddlie and John Freeman

Introduction

The landmark case of *Brown v. The Board of Education of Topeka, Kansas* (1954, 1955) is arguably the most famous decision in the history of the United States Supreme Court (McDearman, 1989). Although essentially a combination of five lower court cases involving suits to seek the admission of African American children to all-white public schools in four states, plus the District of Columbia, *Brown* was in reality the culmination of an organized legal campaign conducted by the National Association for the Advancement of Colored People (NAACP) for over 20 years. The ultimate impact of *Brown* was the rejection of the "separate but equal" doctrine of *Plessy v. Ferguson* (1896) and the end of legally sanctioned racial segregation in public schools and eventually American society as a whole.

Although specifically addressing elementary and secondary education, the legacy of the *Brown* decision to desegregation in

7

higher education is profound, since the *Brown* decision was eventually extended to higher education in the *Florida ex rel Hawkins v. Board of Control* decision in 1956. Without the *Brown* decision, there would have been no *Hawkins* decision, no 1964 Civil Rights Act, no threat of loss of federal funds to segregated colleges and universities under Title VI, and no *Adams* litigation to force Title VI enactment. *Brown* was the basic legal tool that was used by the U.S. Congress and the federal court system to set these events in motion. With this background in mind, our objective in this chapter is to provide an historical overview of these relationships through five specific historical periods:

1. 1933–53 — The NAACP's initial desegregation campaign focused on graduate and professional schools for the purpose of attacking racial segregation in education.

2. 1954–63 — The NAACP achieved numerous victories in the courts, culminating with *Brown* and *Hawkins*. It was also during this period that white resistance to court-ordered desegregation slowed the process, leading the federal government to enact legislation to enforce compliance with court-ordered desegregation.

3. 1964–73 — Title VI of the Civil Rights Act of 1964 and the Higher Education Act of 1965 threatened to withhold federal monetary support to any institution that practiced discrimination in admission standards. These laws contributed to a dramatic rise in African American enrollment in formerly segregated colleges and universities.

4. 1974–84 — The *Regents of University of California v. Bakke* (1978) decision (which introduced the concept of "reverse discrimination"), along with the "salutary neglect" of the Nixon and Reagan administrations regarding the enforcement of affirmative action, combined to slow the progress of desegregation in higher education. This period also witnessed resistance to the dismantling of historically black colleges and universities (HBCUs) that were threatened by the implementation of court-ordered desegregation in higher education.

5. 1985–95 — The *Adams* cases regarding Title VI regulations and the ongoing higher education desegregation court cases in states such as Louisiana, Mississippi, and Alabama had an impact on the legal status of higher education desegregation, while African American enrollment in colleges and universities increased moderately across the board.

The 1933–53 Period: The Journey Through the Wilderness
Litigation Prior to World War II

To initiate a discussion of desegregation in higher education, 1933 is an appropriate starting date, since it was in that year that the first lawsuit by an African American seeking admission to an all-white university was heard. This North Carolina state court case was also the first to be pursued by the NAACP, with financial assistance from the Garland Fund (Ware, 1984).

The story surrounding the organization of the NAACP's legal campaign to end segregation is relevant to the events of this time period. In 1922, Charles Garland donated his entire fortune to establish the American Fund for Public Service. Known as the Garland Fund, this organization sought to address legal and social problems confronting African Americans by dedicating $100,000 toward the establishment of a unified legal effort designed to attack segregation in education, transportation, housing, voting, and forced labor (Hill & Greenberg, 1955).

Nathan Margold, a Harvard Law School instructor and former Assistant U.S. Attorney for New York, was hired in 1930 to direct this legal campaign and under his guidance a plan was devised to achieve the stated goals of the Garland Fund. The plan consisted of the following three elements: (a) to file a large number of taxpayers' suits designed to win equality in elementary schools by creating a severe economic burden that would force states to give up segregation, (b) to launch an immediate attack on segregation as being unconstitutional when it involved inequality, and (c) to begin segregation lawsuits against graduate and professional schools, particularly law schools (Hill & Greenberg, 1955).

Unfortunately, the Great Depression significantly reduced the value of the securities held by the Garland Fund before the plan could be fully implemented. In 1934, a committee composed of members of the Garland Fund and the NAACP met and readjusted their plan of attack in keeping with their now depleted funds. By 1936, the Garland Fund had expended all of its revenues and in 1939 the NAACP created the Legal Defense and Education Fund (LDEF) to generate the money needed to finance its legal campaign.

Meanwhile, Margold left the program and Charles Hamilton Houston, vice-dean of the Howard University Law School, was selected as his replacement. The grandson of enslaved Africans, Houston was admitted to Amherst College at the age of 15 and upon graduation entered Harvard Law School, where he became an honor student and editor of the *Harvard Law Review*. As vice-dean at Howard, Houston developed the law school into one of the finest in the country with a goal of producing a legion of African American attorneys who would wage the inevitable legal battles against segregation. Although he died shortly before *Brown* was decided, his importance to this event is best described by William H. Hastie, an early member of the NAACP legal team and later a judge in the Federal Court of Appeals, who said of Houston upon his death, ". . . . he led us through the legal wilderness of second-class citizenship. He was truly the Moses of that journey" (Hill & Greenberg, 1955, p.57).

Houston chose to concentrate on the third element of the Margold Plan, sensing that there would be an advantage to attacking segregation in graduate and professional schools. He felt that inequality could be more easily proven at this level, since many states did not provide separate graduate and professional schools. Houston also felt that whatever the outcome (i.e., whether African Americans gained admission to white schools, or new African American graduate and professional schools were created) more African American leaders would be educated than ever before (Hill & Greenberg, 1955).

As stated earlier, it was in 1933 that the first lawsuit on behalf of an African American student seeking admission to an all-white professional school was initiated when Hastie was dispatched by the NAACP to seek admission for an African American student to the University of North Carolina. The case ended abruptly when the president of the North Carolina Negro College, the plaintiff's alma mater, refused to certify his scholastic record. Because of that action, the merits of the segregation issue were not addressed and the plaintiff's case was dismissed (Ware, 1984).

Two years later, the case of *Pearson v. Murray* (1936), was decided in the Maryland state courts. The plaintiff, Donald Murray, was a graduate of Amherst College, but had been denied admission to the University of Maryland Law School because of his race. The state of Maryland did not have a separate African American law school, so it was argued by the NAACP that since no "separate, equal" law school existed in Maryland, the University of Maryland had to allow Murray to be admitted. In an effort to avoid such a result, University of Maryland officials offered Murray a scholarship to attend any law school that would accept him — in another state. Murray held fast and continued to claim his right to attend a state-supported school in Maryland.

Although the case did not reach the United States Supreme Court, the Maryland Court of Appeals answered two critical questions in the application of the separate but equal doctrine found in *Plessy*. The first concerned equality and the court stated that Maryland's offer of an out-of-state tuition scholarship was inadequate to prove equality as a matter of dollars and cents, because Murray would still have to bear the cost of living away from home. The second question dealt with the proper remedy and "since in Maryland now the equal treatment can be furnished only in the one existing law school, the petitioner, in our opinion, must be admitted there." Based upon these findings, Murray was admitted to the University of Maryland Law School. Ironically, the attorney who represented the state in its attempt to bar Murray's admission hired him upon his graduation (Hill & Greenberg, 1955).

Murray proved to be a major victory for the NAACP and a sweet victory for the young Howard University Law School graduate and Houston protege who handled the litigation in the case. Thurgood Marshall had been denied admission to the same law school five years earlier and now this particular case began a series of events that would culminate in 1967 with his appointment as the first African American Supreme Court Justice.

After the victory in *Murray*, Marshall decided to follow the same tactics as prescribed by Houston and challenge the legality of "separate but equal" by concentrating on graduate and professional schools. He felt confident that judges would be able to understand that "separate" law schools were not "equal" law schools and by achieving a small number of victories at this level, a foundation of precedents would be created to attack the "separate but equal" doctrine in all other educational institutions (Davis & Clark, 1992).

There was also a pragmatic reason for opting to focus on graduate and professional schools. Marshall believed there would be less resistance to African American and white students attending the same graduate schools than there would be at the public school level. Marshall said:

Those racial supremacy boys somehow think that little kids of six or seven are going to get funny ideas about sex and marriage just from going to school together, but for some equally funny reason, youngsters in law school aren't supposed to feel that way. We didn't get it, but we decided if that was what the South believed, then the best thing for the moment was to go along. (Davis & Clark, 1992, p. 12)

The *Murray* case was soon followed by the case of *Missouri ex rel Gaines v. Canada* (1938), the first case initiated by the NAACP to reach the Supreme Court. Like Murray, Lloyd Gaines was denied admission to the University of Missouri Law School even though there was not a separate African American law school in Missouri. In a vote of seven to one, the Supreme Court held that Gaines must be offered a legal education in Missouri, and that in the absence of a separate equal school in the state, he had the right to attend the "white" law school. While reversing the state court and ordering that Gaines be admitted to the University of Missouri Law School, the Supreme Court continued to recognize the validity of "separate-but-substantially equal," which was an illusory term the Court used to indicate that separate institutions did not have to be equal in every way. There was a standard below which the state could not fall in terms of separate facilities or institutions. However, in Missouri, the state did not attempt to provide a separate law school, so the admission of Gaines to the "white" law school did not contradict *Plessy*.

Soon after the decision, Gaines disappeared under mysterious circumstances and was unable to take advantage of the Court's decision (Blaustein & Ferguson, 1962). Immediately, the state of Missouri established a separate African American law school and a subsequent Missouri case resulted in the establishment of a separate African American journalism school as well. While *Gaines* can be considered a victory for the NAACP, in reality the decision did not affect the segregated status of higher education.

Post-World War II Litigation

The war years interrupted the actions of the LDEF until 1948 when another desegregation case reached the Supreme Court. In the case of *Sipuel v. Board of Regents of the University of Oklahoma* (1948) an African American student sought admission to the University of Oklahoma Law School and was denied admission because of her race. She filed a lawsuit seeking admission to the school based upon the precedent established in *Gaines* and the U.S. Supreme Court ruled that since there was not a separate African American law school in Oklahoma, Sipuel should be admitted to the all-white law school based upon the Equal Protection Clause of the 14th Amendment. The Court further stated that she had the right to an education at the same time as any other individual in the state, thus preventing the state of Oklahoma from delaying her admission until a separate African American law school could be hurriedly created.

Two years later, in the case of *Sweatt v. Painter* (1950), an African American student sought admission to the University of Texas Law School. Texas did not have a separate law school for African Americans, so based on the precedent of *Gaines*, a lower state court ordered that Texas extablish a law school for African Americans. The law school was quickly established in the basement of an African American college in Houston and two African American attorneys in the area were hired as the faculty. The school was woefully inadequate and Sweatt again challenged the system by seeking admission to the University of Texas Law School.

Sweatt represented a different problem for the Supreme Court. The decision in *Gaines* and *Sipuel* relied on the constitutionality of separate-but-equal. However, in *Sweatt*, the plaintiff maintained that the schools were not equal and that he should be allowed to attend the University of Texas Law School. After hearing the arguments, the Court determined that the African American law school was not equal to that of the University of Texas because of limitations in curriculum, faculty, educational atmosphere, and professional development. *Sweatt* raised a constitutional question as to whether separate education facilities for both African Americans and whites could ever be equal. On the same day that *Sweatt* was decided, the case of *McLaurin v. Oklahoma State Regents for Higher Education* (1950) was also decided. In this case, the plaintiff was admitted to the University of Oklahoma as a doctoral student in the College of Education, based upon the precedent established in *Sipuel*. However, after being admitted, he was required to sit and study in designated sections for African Americans in the classrooms, library, and dining hall. The Court said that if a state chooses not to establish a separate-but-substantially equal school for African Americans, it cannot segregate them after they are admitted to the all-white school. In the majority opinion for the *McLaurin* decision, Chief Justice Vinson stated, "There is a vast difference — a Constitutional difference — between restrictions imposed by the state which prohibit the intellectual commingling of students and the refusal of individuals to commingle where the state presents no such bar" (Bartholomew, 1974, p. 189).

Throughout its history the Supreme Court has resisted ruling on a constitutional issue unless that issue was present in the case being heard. In *Gaines, Sipuel, Sweatt,* and *McLaurin,* the Court felt that it could make equity decisions that did not require a reexamination of the "separate-but-equal" doctrine of *Plessy.* However, the importance of *Sweatt* and *McLaurin* lies in the fact that they addressed the equity issue in terms of the effects on students and their educational opportunities, rather than in terms of equality of revenues.

The 1954–63 Period: *Brown* Withstands
Resistance and Extends to Higher Education

The *Brown* case, decided four years after *Sweatt* and *McLaurin,* rested upon a realistic view of education and provided the opportunity for the Supreme Court to address the ultimate question: Is racial segregation in public schools unconstitutional per se (Blaustein & Ferguson, 1962)? The Court referred to the cases involving graduate and professional schools where the entire learning process was weighed in deciding whether there was equality. This required balancing not only tangible, but intangible factors, such as benefits of association with fellow students, as well as, the prestige and traditions of the educational institutions in question. This process would now be utilized in determining the equality of K–12 education.

In the *Brown* cases, teams of professional educators and social scientists were introduced as expert witnesses to prove that segregation was detrimental to the educational well-being of African American students and that it was an inherent violation of the Equal Protection Clause of the 14th Amendment. Presented with an eloquent argument by Thurgood Marshall, the Court was persuaded to rule that segregation and equality cannot coexist. Racially separate schools have "a tendency to retard the educational and mental development of Negro children and to deprive them of some of the benefits they would receive in a racially integrated school system" (Hill & Greenberg, 1955, p.120). Since the 14th Amendment requires equality, it follows that "in the field of public education the doctrine of separate but equal has no place" (Hill & Greenberg, 1955, p. 120). With Chief Justice Earl Warren writing the majority opinion, the Court declared that segregation of public schools in the United States must end.

The Warren Court was aware of the complexities involved in implementing the *Brown* decision in 1954 and delayed granting specific relief to the parties involved in the case. In a prudent move, the Court invited the U.S. Attorney General and the Attorneys General of all the states to submit their ideas concerning the implementation of the decision. In what became known as *Brown II* (1955), the Court stated that consideration should be given to "the public interest," as well as "the personal interest of the plaintiffs." Therefore, the Court ordered that the lower courts should fashion remedies that would allow desegregation to take place with "all deliberate speed." Although often criticized for allowing too much flexibility in implementation, *Brown II* was the Court's way of allowing the local federal courts to settle individual complaints on a case-by-case basis with the intent of maintaining equity for all concerned.

Reactions to the *Brown* decisions were mixed. In some border states compliance was almost immediate, while in the deep South, the decision was met with great hostility by white citizen groups that were formed to use economic blackmail to fight the Court's mandate (Blaustein & Ferguson, 1962).

State legislatures throughout the region passed desperate measures in hopes of circumventing the decision. On January 19, 1956, the Alabama state senate approved nullification of the Supreme Court decision. Although the issue of nullification was decided 100 years earlier, this relic of pre-Civil War states' rights advocacy demonstrates how desperate the segregationists had become. Similarly, on February 1, 1956, the Virginia legislature adopted a resolution of interposition, challenging the Supreme Court's authority to outlaw segregation in the state's public schools and a month later closed its public schools and amended state law to permit the use of state money for private schools. On March 12, 1956, 101 Southern senators and representatives published a manifesto against school desegregation and encouraged the states to resist the *Brown* decisions "by all lawful means" (Blaustein & Ferguson, 1962).

Although the earlier college desegregation cases provided a foundation for *Brown*, it would take another Supreme Court case, in 1956, to apply that decision to colleges and universities and in effect bring an end to segregation in all public schools. In the case of *Florida, ex rel. Hawkins v. Board of Control* (1956), a group of African American students had sought admission to the University of Florida Law School. The state of Florida had an African American law school at Florida A & M University, so, Hawkins and the other students were denied admission to the University of Florida based on *Plessy*.

The time sequence is very important in this case. The original state court lawsuit was filed in 1950, but after the appeals process, the U.S. Supreme Court did not hear the case until one week after the *Brown* decision, on May 24, 1954. The Court ordered the decision of the Florida Supreme Court vacated and remanded the case to be reconsidered in light of the *Brown* decision. The Court was providing an open invitation to Florida to apply *Brown* to this college case.

The Florida Supreme Court unanimously agreed that in principle its state universities must admit all qualified applicants regardless of race. However, the University of Florida urged a delay in admitting Hawkins to its law school, arguing that Chief Justice Warren had urged a delay in desegregation due to the "social complexities" involved. On this principle, five of the seven judges on the state supreme court took the view that there was no duty to admit Hawkins "immediately or at any particular time in the future."

The case again reached the U.S. Supreme Court in 1956 and the Court clarified its decision in *Brown* by stating that "we did not imply that decrees involving graduate study present the problems of public elementary and secondary schools." Therefore, the case was remanded to the Florida court again with clear instructions: "As this case involves the admission of a Negro to a graduate professional school, there is no reason for delay. He is entitled to prompt admission under the rules and regulations applicable to other qualified applicants." With this decision, *Hawkins* succeeded in extending the *Brown* decision to all public schools and added that there was no need for delay in desegregating colleges and universities.

The resistance to desegregation continued unabated over the remaining years of the fifties, reaching a zenith on September 24,

1957, when President Dwight Eisenhower called out the national guard to enforce the desegregation of the Little Rock, Arkansas school system. Not since the end of the Civil War had this country witnessed federal troops used against its own citizens. Serious incidents of opposition to desegregation occurred at several major Southern universities, including the University of Alabama in 1956, the University of Georgia in 1961, and the University of Mississippi in 1962. When the army secured James Meredith's enrollment at the University of Mississippi after Governor Ross Barnett had physically barred him twice, the era of "mob violence" against higher education desegregation drew to a close (Sansing, 1989; Synnott, 1989). The next era was to be characterized by the utilization of federal legislation to force the implementation of the *Brown* and *Hawkins* decisions.

African American Enrollment in Higher Education Through 1954
As a point of reference for data contained in the rest of this chapter, some information regarding African American enrollment in higher education through 1954 will be given. It should be noted that accurate figures regarding the number of African Americans enrolled in institutions of higher education prior to the mid-1950s is scarce and the figures quoted here were the best estimates available to us. According to data first published in 1903 by the eminent African American historian, W. E. B. DuBois, there was a total of 2,304 "Negro college graduates" *up to the year 1899* in the United States (DuBois, 1989/1986). Of this total, he indicated that 83% were from "Negro colleges" and the remaining 17% were graduates from white colleges.

Utilizing U.S. Commissioner of Education data, Anderson (1989/1988) reported that in the year 1900 there were 3,880 African American college and professional students enrolled in the Southern states and the District of Columbia; of this number 2,168 (56%) were enrolled in "Negro colleges". By the year 1915, Anderson (1989/1988) reported that there were "2,474 African American students enrolled in collegiate grades in the Southern states and the District of Columbia" (p. 455). Anderson noted that the figures for African American college students in the southern states and the District of Columbia increased to 13,860 by the academic year 1926–27 and to 29,269 by 1935. Anderson did not report data for African Americans enrolled outside the Southern states during this period of time, but it was a limited number.

Bowles and DeCosta (1989/1971) estimated that there were 63,000 African American undergraduates enrolled in "Negro colleges" in the South in 1954, with another 45,000 enrolled in Northern colleges. Thus, according to their figures, the total enrollment of African Americans in 1954 was at least 108,000. As will be noted in the next section, these figures multiplied rapidly in the next 20 years.

The 1964–73 Period: Desegregation in Higher Education
During the First Decade After the Civil Rights Act
The Legacy of the Brown Decision for Higher Education
As noted in the previous section, the judgment of the *Brown* case was extended to higher education through the *Hawkins* case in 1956. The *Brown* and *Hawkins* cases set the stage for the passage of the historic 1964 Civil Rights Act, which finally resulted in significant desegregation in higher education during the next decade. The *Brown* decision set into motion this historic civil rights legislation and a series of court actions that ensured African Americans access to all public institutions of higher education by the early 1970s.

The 1964 Civil Rights Act empowered the U.S. Attorney General to bring lawsuits for African American plaintiffs and prohibited under Title VI the spending of federal funds in segregated colleges and universities. The threat of the withdrawal of federal funds to institutions of higher education who maintained segregation became a reality with the passage of the Higher Education Act of 1965 (Synnott, 1989).

In the 1970s, the filing of a series of cases known collectively as the *Adams* litigation encouraged first the Department of Health, Education, and Welfare (DHEW) and later the U.S. Department of Education (USDE) to actively implement Title VI (Williams, 1991). These cases addressed complex issues such as (a) the "disestablishment" of dual systems of higher education, (b) the desegregation of student enrollment, faculty, staff and governing boards, and (c) the submission of plans and monitoring procedures (Trent, 1991). This *Adams* legislation has been the primary point of departure for the desegregation of higher education in the U.S. over the past 20 years. This will be described in more detail in following sections of this chapter.

Title VI of the 1964 Civil Rights Act

Federal legislators passed the 1964 Civil Rights Act in order to enhance the implementation of the *Brown* decision (Trent, 1991). De jure segregation persisted in several states at the time of the passage of the 1964 Civil Rights Act, and Title VI of the act specifically prohibited the spending of federal funds in higher education institutions that continued to discriminate on the basis of "race, color or national origin" (Blaustein & Zangrando, 1968; Trent, 1991).

In 1964, only around 300,000 African Americans were enrolled in higher education institutions in the U.S., compared to 4.7 million whites (NCES, 1987; Williams, 1991). According to Williams (1991), the federal government recognized this inequity in educational opportunity and utilized Title VI of the 1964 Civil Rights Act to afford African Americans greater opportunities to attend institutions of higher education. Although Williams argues that the promise of federal intervention to accomplish "greater equity" has never been fully realized, there was a dramatic increase in the number of African Americans attending institutions of higher education from the mid-1960s through the mid-1970s.

In 1964 African Americans constituted only about 6% of the total number of students attending institutions of higher education; by 1974 that percentage had increased to 8.4% (NCES, 1976). More dramatically, during that period of time the number of African Americans enrolled in colleges and universities increased more than 200% (from approximately 300,000 to over 900,000). While enrollment at HBCUs also increased during that time, most of the gains in African American enrollment came at predominantly white institutions, and much of that gain was directly attributable to the 1964 Civil Rights Act and the 1965 Higher Education Act.

Sudarkasa (1988) and Colon (1991) have observed that federal legislation (including the 1964 Economic Opportunity Act and the 1972 amendments to the Higher Education Act) greatly extended the opportunity of African American and other racial minority groups to attend predominantly white institutions of higher education. Without financial assistance, many of these economically disadvantaged students would not have been able to attend higher education institutions, in spite of their newly gained access to them.

Despite these dramatic gains in access and in enrollment, many in the African American and academic communities (e.g., Colon, 1991; Sudarkasa, 1988; Trent, 1991; Williams, 1991) were concerned that the federal government and the courts did not enforce Title VI regulations as vigorously as they should have during the decade following the 1964 Civil Rights Act. As that enforcement became even more sluggish during the next decade (1974–84), the NAACP began using the *Adams* litigation to encourage the federal government to bring states in compliance with Title VI.

The Impact of Desegregation on HBCUs, 1964–73

It is impossible to tell the story of the desegregation of U.S. institutions of higher education without discussing their impact upon HBCUs and the subsequent reactions of those institutions. The landmark *Brown* and *Hawkins* decisions were bound to have a large effect on HBCUs, but in 1955–56 it was difficult to predict what that impact would be. In fact, in the mid-1950s there were few educational policymakers or administrators who were even considering the possible impact of *Brown* on HBCUs since desegregation was the primary issue of the time.

While the NAACP considered the desegregation of higher education to be in the best interest of African Americans, it proved to be a threat to the only viable option most African Americans traditionally had to receive higher education before the 1960s: the HBCUs. Myers (1989) summarized the implicit mission of higher education desegregation following the 1964 Civil Rights Act as an attempt to shift the education of African Americans from HBCUs to predominantly white institutions. Interested observers began to realize that the goals of shifting African American students to predominantly white institutions and increasing the white enrollment at HBCUs could ultimately lead to the merging or closing of many HBCUs. In retrospect, the *Brown* decision and the resultant 1964 Civil Rights Act posed potential threats to HBCUs in three specific areas, (a) the potential loss of enrollment at HBCUs, (b) the potential merger of HBCUs with predominantly white institutions of higher education, and (c) the potential closing of HBCUs due to their inability to compete in the larger market place defined by desegregated state higher education systems.

When the NAACP began to challenge the "separate but equal" doctrine of *Plessy*, the legal strategies required challenging the quality of the HBCUs. The NAACP argued in those cases that the education received in HBCUs was not equal to that received in predominantly white institutions due to the longstanding inequity in financial support for the segregated institutions. While the legal strategy was successful, it had the unfortunate side effect of damaging the credibility and image of HBCUs (Preer, 1982; Trent, 1991).

As noted by Willie (1991a), the HBCUs came under further attack from unexpected quarters during the period immediately following the passage of the 1964 Civil Rights Act. For example, Jencks and Riesman (1967) in an article in the *Harvard Education Review* lumped all HBCUs together and described them as an "academic disaster area" (p. 26). Thus, individuals writing in a well-known liberal educational journal were attacking the HBCUs as a group, not distinguishing among the great variety of institutions in the category. While their arguments were in support of further desegregation at the higher education level, the impact on the HBCUs was negative, having the effect of perpetuating inappropriate stereotypes (Weinberg, 1991).

These attacks on the perceived quality of the HBCUs foreshadowed a dilemma still facing those interested in the higher education of African Americans: should the argument be made that HBCUs have such deficiencies that African Americans need further access to predominantly white institutions, *or* should the quality of HBCUs be defended, thus possibly promoting strategies that might reinforce segregation? A compromise strategy of increasing funding at HBCUs so that more white students would attend (and thus desegregate) them emerged during the mid-1970s and into the 1980s, unfortunately at a time of declining higher education revenues. A further complication regarding this strategy was that many HBCU administrators did not want to attract too many white students to their institutions. They were concerned that this would detract from their historical mission of providing African Americans access to higher education.

The 1964 Civil Rights Act required that predominantly white colleges and universities implement affirmative action programs to attract more African Americans. Enrollment figures indicate that this in fact happened: before the 1960s, 80% of African American students attended HBCUs, but by the end of the 1960s, 80% of African American students were attending predominantly white institutions of higher education (Lomotey, 1991). It should be noted that many of these African American students were attending junior colleges, as they are today (NCES, 1994).

Despite these trends, HBCUs *also* continued to enroll more African American students during the decade immediately following the passage of the 1964 Civil Rights Act. From the mid-1960s to mid-1970s enrollments at HBCUs increased, concurrent with the rapidly increasing African American enroll-ment at white institutions (Myers, 1989). Garibaldi noted that total enrollment at the nation's 105 HBCUs increased 60% from 129,444 in 1966 to 212,574 in 1977 (Blake, Lambert, & Martin, 1978; Garibaldi, 1991a). While this increase was significant, it constituted but a small portion of the greater than 200% increase in the total African American higher education student population that occurred during that time period.

A result of the potential threats to HBCUs noted above was the formation in 1969 of the National Association for Equal Opportunity in Higher Education (NAFEO). NAFEO represents over 100 HBCUs in the U.S. According to Myers (1989), NAFEO was organized to "articulate the need for a higher education system where race, income, and previous education are not determinants of either the quantity or quality of higher education" (1989, p.83). NAFEO was formed in a period of time in which some of the smaller and less financially sound HBCUs were closing. For instance, Myers (1989) provided a list of 14 HBCUs that are now closed, and that list is only partial. By the mid-1970s, such closures became less frequent, partially due to changing federal policy regarding HBCUs, which was mandated through the *Adams* litigation. This litigation required that the role of HBCUs be specified within state systems of higher education.

For HBCUs the decade following the 1964 Civil Rights Act can be characterized by the following (a) a substantial (but less than proportionate) increase in African American enrollment, (b) the closure of some economically marginal HBCUs, and (c) the growing realization among some in the African American academic community that the role of the HBCUs must be pro-tected. HBCUs became just one of many alternatives for higher education available to African Americans during this period.

The 1974–84 Period: The Impact of *Adams, Bakke,*
and Other Factors on Desegregation in Higher Education

The original *Adams* case and the *Bakke* case were first filed in the early 1970s. *Adams* was filed to encourage Title VI compliance that would lead to greater African American access to higher education, while *Bakke* introduced the notion of "reverse discrimination," which claims that certain "set aside" programs deny whites equal access to higher education guaranteed under Title VI. These two cases were primary factors impacting higher education desegregation during the 1974–84 period.

The Adams Litigation

The *Adams* litigation encompasses several separate court cases (e.g., *Adams v. Richardson,* 1973; *Adams v. Weinberger,* 1975; *Adams v. Califano,* 1977; *Adams v. Bell,* 1982) brought by the NAACP to assure that the USDE (initially the DHEW) would execute its duties to secure compliance with Title VI requirements. Under the presidencies of Nixon/Ford (1968–76) and Reagan/Bush (1980–92), there is evidence that a policy of "nonenforcement of desegregation laws and policies" was adopted (Dentler, 1991; Trent, 1991; Williams, 1991). The initial *Adams v. Richardson* suit sought to change President Nixon's desegregation policy by requiring that DHEW institute enforcement proceedings in documented cases of noncompliance with Title VI, conduct additional reviews, monitor compliance and respond to state plans for desegregation of institutions of higher education (Williams, 1991).

This litigation was successful in encouraging the federal government to enforce Title VI regulations. By the mid-1970s, the governors of ten states (Arkansas, Florida, Georgia, Louisiana, Maryland, Mississippi, North Carolina, Oklahoma, Pennsylvania, and Virginia) were sent letters requiring them to submit desegregation plans to the federal government (Williams, 1991). In 1981, an additional eight states were notified of Title VI noncompliance (Alabama, Delaware, Kentucky, Missouri, Ohio, South Carolina, Texas, and West Virginia).

Guidelines for the desegregation of higher education were finally established in 1977 upon order of the *Adams v. Califano* case. Among these guidelines were, (a) the proportion of African American and white high school graduates entering institutions of higher education shall be equal, (b) there shall be an annual increase in the proportion of African Americans in predominantly white institutions, and (c) there shall be an increase in the proportion of white students attending HBCUs (Williams, 1991). Similar goals were established for faculty and staff.

The Bakke Decision

The *Bakke* case also appeared at the beginning of this time period, having been originally filed in 1973; it was not settled until 1977. In this case, Allan Bakke, a white applicant, claimed that administrators at the University of California (Davis) Medical School had denied him access to their institution solely on the basis of his race. He sought relief under the Equal Protection Clause of Title VI, specifically claiming that the medical school had "set aside" 16 places for underrepresented minorities and that they had denied whites access to those places. A divided Supreme Court decided in Bakke's favor (Trent, 1991), introducing the term "reverse discrimination" into the civil rights lexicon.

Pettigrew (1979) concluded that the *Bakke* decision would have a "chilling effect" on affirmative action and minority access. He further concluded that *Bakke* can be viewed as an excuse that administrators at educational institutions could use to "avoid, resist, or stop" doing what they did not want to do (Williams, 1991).

Immediately following the *Bakke* decision, there was a decline in the absolute number of African Americans attending higher education institutions from a peak in 1980 through the mid-1980s. Some analysts believe that *Bakke* contributed to that decline (Trent, 1991), but it is more likely that *Bakke* was simply a manifestation of a larger issue: the continued resistance of institutions and individuals to the affirmative action components of compliance with Title VI (such as "set asides"). Trent (1991) concluded that the mediating effects of *Bakke*, (i.e., the threats of similar suits and a more conservative judiciary) had indeed combined to have a chilling effect on minority access by constraining affirmative action efforts.

Other Factors Contributing to Static African American Enrollment in Higher Education, 1974–84

While the first decade after the 1964 Civil Rights Act was characterized by large increases in African American enrollment in higher education, the second decade (1974–84) *was not*. As indicated in Table 2.1, the absolute number of African American students enrolled in higher education remained relatively constant

Table 2.1 Enrollment in Higher Education by Type of Institution and Ethnicity (White, Black), Selected Years, 1976–1984.

Year/ Ethnicity	Total Enrollment	Four Year Institution	Two Year Institution	% Two Year Institution
1976 Total	10,970	7,090	3,880	35.4%
White	9,061	5,984	3,077	34.0%
Black	1,032	603	429	41.6%
% Black	9.4%	8.5%	11.1%	NA
1980 Total	12,038	7,548	4,490	37.3%
White	9,791	6,259	3,532	36.1%
Black	1,101	633	468	42.5%
% Black	9.1%	8.4%	10.4%	NA
1984 Total	12,235	7,708	4,527	37.0%
White	9,815	6,301	3,514	35.8%
Black	1,076	617	459	42.9%
% Black	8.8%	8.0%	10.1%	NA
% Change 1976-84 Total	11.5%	8.7%	16.7%	1.6%
% Change 1976-84 White	8.3%	5.3%	14.2%	1.8%
% Change 1976-84 Black	4.3%	2.3%	7.0%	1.3%

Note. Enrollment numbers are indicated in thousands. The white and black numbers do not add up to the total number because other ethnicities are not included. These figures were taken from *Trends in Enrollment in Higher Education, by Racial/Ethnic Category: Fall 1982 through Fall 1992* (NCES, 1994) and *Minorities in Higher Education: Thirteenth Annual Report,* published in 1995 by the ACE.

from the mid-1970s through the mid-1980s. This period can be characterized as one of stability in overall African American enrollment in higher education, with signs of actual decline in some areas. Since white enrollment in higher education increased during this period, the proportion of the total number of students who were African American *declined* from 9.4% in 1976–78 to 8.8% in 1982–84 (Garibaldi, 1991a; NCES, 1976, 1984, 1994).

Several authors (e.g., Garibaldi, 1991a; Trent, 1991; Willie, 1991b) considered this trend particularly disturbing given the fact that the proportion of African American high school graduates *increased* during this same time period. For instance, between 1974 and 1984 the number of African American students who graduated from high school increased by 39% and the high school completion rate increased by 7.6% (from 67.1% to 74.7%). During the same time period, the high school graduates' enrolledin-college rate declined from 34% in 1976 to 27% in 1984. (See Table 2.2)

Moreover, as indicated in Table 2.1, the percentage of total enrollment that was African American *declined* in 1974–84 at both four-year institutions (from 8.5% to 8.0%) and two-year institutions (from 11.1% to 10.1%). Garibaldi (1991a) described these trends as follows: "Thus, rather than capitalizing on the increasing size of the age cohort and the higher numbers graduating from high school, college participation rates of today's generation of African American youth have regressed significantly in . . . proportional representation on college campuses" (p. 94).

Many authors were interested in uncovering the reasons for the drop in African American participation rates in higher education that occurred from 1980 through 1985, after the large gains that had been made in the 1965–1975 period. Willie (1991b) pointed out two basic contradictions that occurred during this time for African American students: their high school graduation rate went up as their college progression rate declined (as documented in Tables 2.1 and 2.2) and the proportion of African American students needing financial aid to go to college increased as the amount of available aid declined. Several reasons were given for the decline in African American participation rates in higher education enrollment in the early to mid-1980s, including the following:

1. The aforementioned *decline in the availability of financial aid* for college education (Carter-Williams, 1989; Garibaldi,

Table 2.2 High School Completion Rates and College Progression Rates by Ethnicity (White, Black), Selected Years, 1974–1984.

Year/ Ethnicity	High School Graduates	Completion Rate (%)	# Enrolled in College	% Enrolled in College
1974 Total	20,725	80.7%	6,316	30.5%
White	18,318	82.7%	5,589	30.5%
Black	2,083	67.1%	555	26.6%
1976 Total	21,677	80.5%	7,181	33.1%
White	19,045	82.4%	6,276	33.0%
Black	2,239	67.5%	749	33.5%
1980 Total	23,413	80.9%	7,400	31.6%
White	20,214	82.6%	6,423	31.8%
Black	2,592	69.7%	715	27.6%
1984 Total	22,870	81.6%	7,591	33.2%
White	19,373	83.0%	6,256	33.7%
Black	2,885	74.7%	786	27.2%
Change 1974-84 Total	2,145	0.9%	1,275	2.7%
Change 1976-84 White	1,055	0.3%	667	3.2%
Change 1976-84 Black	802	7.6%	231	0.6%

Note. Enrollment numbers are indicated in thousands. The white and black numbers do not add up to the total number because other ethnicities are not included. These figures were taken from *Minorities in Higher Education: Thirteenth Annual Report,* published in 1995 by the ACE.

1991a; Solmon & Wingard, 1991: Willie, 1991b). Carter-Williams (1989) analyzed these declines especially in terms of the availability of Pell grants.

2. *Inflationary increases in the costs* of attending colleges and universities (Garibaldi, 1991a; Solmon & Wingard, 1991).

3. *Higher attrition rates in the first years in college* due to poor preparation in elementary/secondary education. As noted by (Garibaldi, 1991b), this has been a real problem in colleges and universities that do not provide nurturing environments for African Americans.

4. Some evidence of a post-*Bakke reverse discrimination* effect (Trent, 1991).

5. The beginning of the *dismantling of equal opportunity and affirmative action programs* based on the "color-blind" doctrine of the Reagan administration (Deskins, 1991).

6. *Failure of the federal government to aggressively pursue the Title VI* requirements for further desegregation (Trent, 1991; Williams, 1991).

7. The *failure of many African American students to view a college education as "a worthwhile investment"* (Garibaldi, 1991a).

Despite the decreases in participation rate in higher education during this period, Trent (1991) presented a compelling analysis that segregation actually continued to decline in higher education during the period from 1976 to 1984. Using the Coleman segregation index (Becker, 1978), Trent argued that segregation specifically decreased in undergraduate public education institutions during that period. This was especially the case for the Southern region of the country, a trend that Trent attributed to Title VI and the *Adams* litigation, that encouraged the recruitment of African American students to institutions that had been deliberately segregated historically.

Trent further concluded that whatever amount of desegregation occurred in the 1976 to 1984 period, it was *not* accompanied by net gains in African American enrollment. In fact, the only regional college/university group that succeeded in increasing both their enrollment *and* in decreasing their segregation index during this period was the traditionally white public colleges in the South. This was the major group of colleges identified in the *Adams* litigation, so some tangible success for the *Adams* cases can be inferred from these data (Trent, 1991).

The NAACP's continued *Adams* litigation appeared to be the major driving force behind Title VI compliance during the Reagan administration. On several occasions during this time period, the NAACP used the *Adams* litigation to get the federal courts to pressure the Office of Civil Rights (OCR) at the USDE to implement Title VI compliance. For instance, the *Adams v. Bell* case in 1982 resulted in a ruling that Arkansas, Georgia, Florida, Virginia, Oklahoma, and North Carolina had faulted on Title VI compliance with regard to their community college systems (Williams, 1991).

Despite these occasional victories in federal courts, there is a general consensus that Title VI compliance was severely curtailed during the Reagan years (Dentler, 1991; Trent, 1991; Williams, 1991). The OCR at the USDE and the Department of Justice's Civil Rights Division had their desegregation activities virtually shut down. Dentler (1991) summarized his views with regard to the Reagan administration and desegregation as follows:

> With the advent of the Reagan administration, however, a quarter of a century of slow, often disenchanting, and uneven movement toward compliance with *Brown* drew to a close . . . . There were, in other words, just a few brief years — a decade at most (1966 to 1976) — during which the far-reaching policy of *Brown* had a direct impact on the learning opportunities of African American students. (pp. 34–35)

The Impact of Desegregation on HBCUs, 1974–84

Statistical analyses indicate that HBCUs lost around 24,000 students from the mid-1970s through the mid-1980s, a period of time in which African American participation rates in higher education declined throughout higher education (Trent, 1991). As noted above, HBCUs were now just one of several avenues for higher education available to African American students and these institutions were just beginning to formulate a response to the threat to their enrollments from predominantly white institutions and junior colleges.

Some members of the African American academic community began to actively defend the continuing role of the HBCUs during this period. For example, Myers (1989) concluded that "The historically black colleges, indeed, though segregated and underfunded, have succeeded in producing a solid middle-class among blacks" (p. 3). Also, Garibaldi (1984, 1991a) discussed at length the role of the HBCUs in training professionals in a variety of occupations and in graduating a disproportionate share of African Americans. (See Chapter Eleven for more details.) While these specific statements from Myers and Garibaldi were published after the 1974–84 period, these were the arguments that began to be increasingly articulated during that period.

The 1985–95 Period: Trends in
Enrollment and Litigation Since 1985

A new trend can be found in African American higher education enrollment figures in the years since 1985. As indicated in Table 2.3, total higher education enrollment increased by over 14% from 1986 to 1993, while African American enrollment increased by over 30% during that same period of time. While not as dramatic as the increases in African American enrollment from the 1964–1973 period, these recent increases have reversed the trends of the 1974–1984 period. Moreover, these increases since 1985 have been especially pronounced in four-year institutions where the percent of African Americans increased almost 32%, compared to an overall 12% increase in total enrollment at those institutions during this period.

An especially encouraging trend since 1985 has been the increase in the percentage of the total higher education enrollment that is African American from 8.7% in 1986 to 9.9% in 1993. This reverses the decline in the percentage of the total higher education enrollment that was African American that occurred during the previous decade (from 9.4% in 1976 to 8.8% in 1984). Thus, the trend in the percentage of the total higher education enrollment that is African American has been curvilinear over the past two decades, with a peak in 1976–78 at 9.4%, a valley in 1986–88 at 8.7% and a peak again in 1993 at 9.9%. This curvilinear trend is also evident in the percentage of the four-year-institution total enrollment that is African American, with a peak in 1976–78 at 8.5%, a valley in 1986 at 7.9% and a peak in 1993 at 9.3%.

The 1993 data presented in Table 2.3 are especially encouraging because they represent the highest enrollment and percentage of total enrollment figures that African Americans have ever had for higher education institutions in general and for four-year institutions. These recent gains in African American percentage

Table 2.3 Enrollment in Higher Education by Type of Institution and Ethnicity (White, Black), Selected Years, 1986–1993.

Year/ Ethnicity	Total Enrollment	Four Year Institution	Two Year Institution	% Two Year Institution
1986 Total	12,504	7,824	4,680	37.4%
White	9,921	6,337	3,584	36.1%
Black	1,082	615	467	43.2%
% Black	8.7%	7.9%	10.0%	NA
1990 Total	13,820	8,579	5,240	37.9%
White	10,723	6,769	3,954	36.9%
Black	1,247	723	524	42.0%
% Black	9.0%	8.4%	10.0%	NA
1993 Total	14,306	8,740	5,566	38.9%
White	10,605	6,643	3,961	37.4%
Black	1,410	811	599	42.5%
% Black	9.9%	9.3%	10.8%	NA
% Change 1986-93	14.4%	11.7%	18.9%	1.5%
% Change 1986-93	6.9%	4.8%	10.5%	1.3%
% Change 1986-93	30.3%	31.9%	28.3%	-0.7%

Note. Enrollment numbers are indicated in thousands. The white and black numbers do not add up to the total number because other ethnicities are not included. These figures were taken from *Trends in Enrollment in Higher Education, by Racial/Ethnic Category: Fall 1982 through Fall 1992* (NCES, 1994) and *Minorities in Higher Education: Thirteenth Annual Report,* published in 1995 by the ACE.

of total higher education enrollment are across the board, not limited to certain types of institutions. These recent data also indicate that Garibaldi's (1991) conclusion that African Americans were not " . . . capitalizing on the increasing size of the age cohort and the higher numbers graduating from high school . . ." (p. 94), is not as relevant in 1995 as it was in 1985.

Data from Table 2.4 appear to confirm this cautiously optimistic assessment. The percent of high school graduates' enrolled-in-college rate for African Americans increased from a low of 26.1% in 1985 to around 33% for 1990 and 1993. Interestingly, the changes in the overall trends for whites and African Americans in both high school completion rates and high school graduates enrolled-in-college rates are very similar over the 1985-93 period:

1. For both groups there has been a slight decline in high school completion rate from 1985-93 (-0.2% for whites; -0.8% for African Americans).

2. For both groups there has been an increase in high school graduates enrolled-in-college rates from 1985–93 (7.4% for whites; 6.7% for African Americans).

These 1985–93 data indicate that if students can get through high school, it is more likely that they will proceed on to college. That was *not* the case for African American students in 1974–84 when a 7.6% increase in high school completion rate was translated into a negligible increase (0.6%) in the high school graduates enrolled-in-college rate.

Other noticeable trends since 1985 include the following:

1. The percentage of African Americans (74.8% in 1993) that graduate from high school is still less than that of white Americans (83.4%) and the gap *has not decreased over the 1985–93 period.* (See Table 2.4 for more detail.)

2. The percentage of African American high school graduates that enroll in colleges or universities is still less than that for white Americans and the gap *has not decreased over the 1985–93 period.* Thus, the guideline established in the 1977 *Adams v. Califano* case, that the proportion of African American and white high school graduates entering institutions of higher education shall be equal, has yet to be realized. In fact,there has been a trend in the *opposite direction* since 1974: (a) In 1974 (see Table 2.2), 30.5% of white high school graduates enrolled in college, while 26.6% of African Americans did, for a gap of 3.9% between the

Table 2.4 High School Completion Rates and College Progression
Rates by Ethnicity (White, Black), Selected Years, 1985-1993.

Year/ Ethnicity	High School Graduates	Completion Rate (%)	# Enrolled in College	% Enrolled in College
1985 Total	22,349	82.4%	7,537	33.7%
White	18,916	83.6%	6,500	34.4%
Black	2,810	75.6%	734	26.1%
1990 Total	20,311	82.3%	7,964	39.1%
White	16,823	82.5%	6,635	39.4%
Black	2,710	77.0%	894	33.0%
1993 Total	19,772	82.0%	8,193	41.1%
White	16,196	83.4%	6,763	41.8%
Black	2,629	74.8%	861	32.8%
Change 1985-93 Total	-2,577	-0.4%	656	7.7%
Change 1985-93 White	-2,720	-.02%	293	7.4%
Change 1985-93 Black	-181	-0.8%	127	6.7%

Note. Enrollment numbers are indicated in thousands. The white and black numbers do not add up to the total number because other ethnicities are not included. These figures were taken from *Minorities in Higher Education: Thirteenth Annual Report,* published in 1995 by the ACE.

two groups, and (b) In 1993 (see Table 2.4), 41.8% of white high school graduates enrolled in college, while 32.8% of African Americans did, for a gap of 9% between the two groups.

3. While segregation indices are not available for recent years, it is likely that the current level of segregation is equal to or lower than that measured in 1984. While the federal government has continued to downplay higher education desegregation, affirmative action programs persist at many predominantly white institutions.   4. The remaining Title VI compliance cases are being settled without the closure or merger of institutions. (This issue is discussed in the last section of this chapter, as well as in Chapters Nine and Ten.)

5. HBCUs have continued to attract their proportionate share of African American students after a slight decline in enrollment from the mid-1970s through the mid-1980s.

6. "Reverse discrimination" cases have been relatively rare since the *Bakke* decision. Nevertheless, resentment of affirmative action programs persists at higher education institutions and at the national political level. With the Republican victories in the 1994 congressional elections, the affirmative action debate has grown more confrontational, with some legislators calling for a re-appraisal of all affirmative action programs including those in higher education.

The impact of a 1995 U.S. Supreme Court ruling in a University of Maryland case (*Kirwan v. Podberesky*, 1995) involving a scholarship program limited to African Americans has yet to be determined. An Hispanic American student filed the case contending that he did not qualify for the scholarship because he was not African American. The university, with the support of the Clinton administration, argued that the scholarship had been developed to address the lingering effects of past discrimination because the university had barred African Americans until the 1950s and had remained virtually all-white until the 1970s (Stone, 1995). In fact, the scholarship program had been developed while the university was negotiating with the federal government regarding Title VI violations.

The Supreme Court rejected this argument stating that the university could not reinstate the scholarship program because it was exclusively for African Americans. The application of this ruling to other regions of the country (beyond its point of origin in the Fourth U.S. Circuit Court of Appeals) and to other scholarships that are exclusively earmarked for African Americans was unknown at the time of the publication of this volume. Nevertheless, the resolution of this case is another example of the judiciary's increasing opposition to race-based scholarships or awards.

The Impact of Desegregation on HBCUs Since 1985
The impact on HBCU enrollment and graduation rates.

The overall downturn in the participation rate of African American students in higher education from the mid-1970s through the mid-1980s appears to have been a short-lived phenomenon. Similarly, the decline in the number of African American students attending HBCUs that occurred at the same time has now been reversed. As noted in Table 2.5, there was an increase of 31.4% in the number of African Americans attending HBCUs in the 1984–93 period. This percentage is almost identical to the overall increase in African American students enrolled in all higher education institutions during this period of time (see Table 2.3).

It may be concluded that HBCUs *have continued to enroll their share of African American students throughout the entire 30-year period from the passage of the 1964 Civil Rights Act.* In fact, some analysts have concluded that HBCUs graduate a disproportionate share of African American students due to a more positive campus culture or ethos (Davis, 1991; Garibaldi, 1991a, 1991b). For instance, Garibaldi reported that even though HBCUs enroll less than 20% of all African Americans in college, they produced 37% of all bachelor and 30% of all master degrees awarded to African Americans through the mid-1980s, citing data from an American Council on Education (ACE) publication (Carter & Wilson, 1989). (This Garibaldi (1991b) article on the role of HBCUs in African American education is reprinted as Chapter Eleven of this volume.)

More recent information from the same data source (U.S. Department of Education) indicates different percentages, but HBCUs' proportionate share of degrees is still significant. According to a 1995 report from ACE, "Four-year HBCUs enrolled 28% of African Americans attending four-year institutions in 1992. Not surprisingly, African Americans earned 27.6% of their bachelor's degrees at these institutions that year" (Carter & Wilson, 1995, p. 17).

Table 2.5 Enrollment at HCBUs by Ethnicity, Selected Years,
Fall 1983 to Fall 1993.

Year	Enroll-ment	Black	White	Other	% Black
1984	216,050	175,110	23,450	17,490	81.1%
1986	213,114	176,610	22,784	13,720	82.9%
1987	217,670	182,020	23,227	12,423	83.6%
1988	230,758	192,848	25,767	12,143	83.6%
1989	238,946	199,974	26,962	12,010	83.7%
1990	248,697	207,547	29,601	11,549	83.5%
1991	258,509	213,904	31,085	13,520	82.7%
1992	277,261	224,946	36,203	16,112	81.1%
1993	284,247	230,078	37,375	16,794	80.9%
% Change 1984-93	31.6%	31.4%	59.4%	-3.9%	-0.2%

Note. The numbers in the other column were determined by subtracting the number of black and white students from the total number of students. These figures were taken from *Minorities in Higher Education: Thirteenth Annual Report,* published in 1995 by the ACE.

According to Garibaldi, the discrepancy between these two sets of percentages is simply due to the fact that the total number of HBCU graduates was analyzed in comparison to the total number of African American baccalaureates during those years. For example, in 1985, ACE reports that there were 20,887 HBCU graduates; of that number, 16,326 were African Americans. The total number of African Americans receiving baccalaureates that year was 57,473. Therefore, HBCUs awarded undergraduate degrees to 28% of all African American baccalaureate recipients. A similar percentage has occurred over the last few years even though HBCUs enroll slightly more than 15% of all African Americans in institutions of higher education. Garibaldi states:

> As the disaggregation of data by the U.S. Department of Education becomes even more refined as shown in the 1995 ACE report (e.g., the partialing out of enrollment of all students, but African Americans particularly, at two-year and four-year colleges), it will be easier to notice the substantial contributions which HBCUs continue to make to the undergraduate production of African Americans in comparison to the other 3,500 colleges and univeristies in this country. (A. M. Garibaldi, personal communication, August 26, 1995)

Garibaldi has also contended (Garibaldi, 1991b) that HBCUs enroll and graduate a larger proportion of African American students who might *not be eligible* to enroll at some other institutions of higher education, due to low ACT and SAT scores or other factors. For many of these students with low college entrance test scores, their choice for higher education often comes down to two-year institutions or HBCUs, if there are any within the student's geographical area. These two-year institutions are often dead ends for students wishing to complete a bachelor degree. Using this logic, it may be concluded that *HBCUs graduate a disproportionate number of African American undergraduate students who have academic or economic disadvantages* and little access to other institutions of higher education. Beyond these definitional considerations, however, there have been some changes in graduation rates at other institutions that have affected the role of HBCUs.

According to ACE data for the years 1983–84 through 1991–92 (Carter & Wilson, 1995), the percentage of bachelor degrees awarded to African Americans by HBCUs remained consistently between 27% and 29% of the total awarded by all institutions. Thus, HBCUs have kept pace with the general increases in African American undergraduate enrollment and graduation rates over the past decade described in the previous section of this chapter. At the graduate level, however, the number of master's degrees awarded by HBCUs remained about the same from 1984–85 through 1991–92 (at around 2,500 per year). During the same time period, the total number of master's degrees awarded to African Americans from all institutions increased from around 14,000 in 1985 to over 18,000 in 1992.

Accordingly, the percentage of master's degrees awarded to African Americans by HBCUs declined from 18% to 15% of the total awarded by all institutions during that time period. A decline was also reported in the percentage of first-professional degrees awarded to African Americans by HBCUs during this same time period (Carter & Wilson, 1995).

The role of HBCUs in producing African American students with advanced degrees appears to be diminishing somewhat as the absolute number of such students continues to rise modestly, while the number produced by HBCUs stays about the same. Unless states begin to place more graduate and professional programs at HBCUs, or increase those institutions' capacity to produce graduates within existing programs, the role of HBCUs in this academic arena will continue to slowly decline.

In many states, an expansion of the graduate role of HBCUs is unlikely, often because they would duplicate existing programs at predominantly white state universities. A recent example of the reluctance of state higher education officials to grant new programs to HBCUs concerns two land grant universities in Baton Rouge, Louisiana (Southern University [an HBCU] and Louisiana State University [LSU, a predominantly white institution]). When Southern University officials requested a new "land grant center" (together with additional programs), they were turned down by the state Board of Regents, due to the potential duplication of programs already in existence at LSU (Regents nix, 1995).

In general, however, it may be concluded that one of the threats to HBCUs noted above (the potential loss of enrollment) has not been realized to date in an absolute sense. While the HBCUs have not gained a proportionate share of African American students during the 30 years following the 1964 Civil Rights Act, they have continued to grow at a steady pace that has in fact increased in recent years. Also, HBCUs have continued to fulfill their historic purpose of educating a disproportionate share of those African Americans who come from economically and educationally impoverished backgrounds.

The resolution of recent desegregation cases involving HBCUs.

As a result of the *Adams* litigation, Title VI was amended in a variety of ways, including the requirement that the role of HBCUs be specified within the various state systems. In particular, the state desegregation plans were to specify how the role of the HBCUs would be strengthened (Trent, 1991). The courts ruled that the special needs of HBCUs should be considered in state desegregation plans and that an "undue burden" of desegregation should not be placed on the HBCUs. According to Myers (1989), "this began a process of policy formulation to enhance historically black colleges" (p. 8).

Such enhancements under Title VI included capital outlay projects (e.g., physical facilities construction) and the placement of new degree programs at HBCUs (Williams, 1991). Title VI also required that HBCUs be enhanced so that they could attract students of all racial populations; this goal has been partially realized for white students (see Table 2.5). While such enhancements have benefitted some HBCUs, states have often delayed court-mandated improvements at these institutions. As noted above, many authors (e.g., Williams, 1991; Willie, 1991b) believe that Title VI was never properly enforced. Williams (1991) concluded that Title VI enforcement became a "regulatory charade" during the late 1980s, and this charade often included the failure of states to enhance HBCUs as ordered by the federal courts.

Recent settlements such as that in Mississippi (see Chapter Ten) and similar cases in Louisiana (see Chapter Nine) and Alabama (where negotiations are still underway) seem to underscore Williams's (1991) point. Observers of these cases have been speculating over the past few years with regard to the impact that the settlement of one case would have on the others, and vice versa. In these cases, there had been consideration of the merger and/or closure of HBCUs and predominantly white institutions of higher education. The closure and merger of HBCUs were two of the threats noted above that were a potential result of the *Brown* and *Hawkins* decisions. For instance, consideration in the Louisiana case was given to the merger of certain programs and the creation of a single board of higher education in the state, thereby eliminating the separate Southern University system (the only separate HBCU system in the country).

Also, consideration was given in the Mississippi case to the merger of institutions and the closure of HBCUs. In 1992, the Supreme Court ruled on the *U.S. v. Fordice* (*Ayers v. Fordice*) case from Mississippi, a case that could have the same implications for desegregation at the higher education level as *Brown* had for elementary-secondary education, according to several authors writing in this volume (e.g., Humphries, Chapter Ten; Spikes & Meza, Chapter Nine; Thorn, Chapter Seventeen). Commenting upon dual systems of higher education for the first time, the Supreme Court ruled that states with such systems of higher education had to either justify the continuation of these systems, or eliminate them. According to Thorn (Chapter Seventeen), the Supreme Court "all but invited" Mississippi to close some of its predominantly segregated colleges, indicating that maintaining all eight public universities was a financial waste. The Supreme Court remanded the case back to the federal district court in Mississippi for determination of specifics regarding its implementation.

Part of the state's subsequent plan for desegregating Mississippi higher education involved merging Mississippi Valley State University (MVSU, an HBCU) and Delta State University into a new entity to be named Delta Valley State University, closing the MVSU campus and making Alcorn State University (an HBCU) an administrative unit of Mississippi State University. The only other such merger to have occurred to date was that of the University of Tennessee at Nashville and Tennessee State University, an action that has caused some controversy and generated mixed results (see Waltman, Chapter Twenty).

In 1995, Judge Neal Biggers of the U.S. District Court for Northern Mississippi ruled in the case, nixing the closure or merger of any of the Mississippi schools (Hardwell, 1995). His ruling called for state college officials to look for methods to desegregate MVSU, to allocate $30 million to enhance programs at HBCUs, to redistribute programs at the graduate level primarily to the advantage of Jackson State University (another HBCU) and to come up with a common set of admission standards for all its public institutions of higher education. His ruling further stated that Mississippi could close higher education institutions if it could prove that such action was economically advantageous. Judges Biggers's ruling, which is certain to be appealed back to the Supreme Court, failed to use the desegregation criterion to eliminate predominantly segregated schools, but allowed the state to use the "financial wastefulness" argument for closing certain schools. It is unlikely that the state will close any of their higher education institutions.

A similar determination was made in 1994 in the Louisiana case (*U.S. v. Louisiana*). In this case, the U.S. District Court left the predominantly African American Southern University system in place and called for the expenditure of more monies at LSU for desegregation efforts and at Southern University to enhance certain programs. In this case, a new wrinkle was added: the proposed establishment of a new junior college to be jointly administered by Southern University (an HBCU) and LSU (a predominantly white institution) in Baton Rouge. (See Chapter Nine for details).

Thus, the potentially revolutionary effects of higher education desegregation cases in states such as Mississippi and Louisiana are *not* being realized as these cases are now being decided. While a strict interpretation of Title VI regulations may have called for mergers or closures, the ultimate settlements now being negotiated are less radical in nature, requiring that some extra monies be spent at HBCUs (or at predominantly white institutions to attract more African American students), but little else.

The role of the HBCUs and the NAACP in this latest chapter of the desegregation of higher education is interesting. HBCUs have for several years been alarmed about the threat of closings or mergers, claiming that the demise of their institutions would put into jeopardy the future education of many African Americans. The NAACP has had a longstanding policy that desegregation was good for African Americans, and this has occasionally put them at odds with the HBCU proponents. There is some evidence that this NAACP policy may now be changing. As noted in Chapter Seventeen, the NAACP in 1994 opposed the closure of MVSU in Mississippi as a consequence of the higher education desegregation case there. This action put the NAACP in opposition to the Supreme Court's "suggested resolution" of Mississippi's higher education desegregation issues.

Despite this apparent recent change in policy, the NAACP and organizations such as NAFEO have historically held contradictory points of view with regard to the roles of HBCUs. These viewpoints reflect the dilemma described above which first surfaced with the NAACP's legal strategies to desegregate graduate and professional schools in the 1945–54 period. (Both Thorn in Chapter Seventeen and Waltman in Chapter Twenty also discuss this rift between HBCUs and the NAACP.) To point out inequalities in the education received at predominantly white institutions and HBCUs was an argument for desegregation (the traditional NAACP point of view). To defend the quality, accomplishments, and unique role of HBCUs (the traditional HBCU point of view) was an important argument against closure or merger, but could also be used to perpetuate segregation. Enhancement of HBCUs in conjunction with compliance of the desegregation components of Title VI was a compromise of the 1970s and 1980s that has seldom been properly implemented and has failed to satisfy many observers. The current resolution of the higher education desegregation cases in Louisiana and Mississippi appears to reflect the federal court's growing awareness of the importance of HBCUs in the higher education of African Americans.

Overall Trends in African American Enrollment
in Higher Education, mid-1960s through mid-1990s

The overall trends in African American enrollment in higher education since 1964 can be broken down into three periods:

1. The 1964–73 period marked by a greater than 200% increase in the number of African American students enrolled in higher education as Title VI regulations were first enforced.

2. The 1974–84 period in which African American participation in higher education stagnated in terms of absolute numbers and declined in terms of percentage of total enrollment, due to a variety of factors such as increasing costs, declining student aid, the failure to enforce vigorously Title VI regulations and concern over reverse discrimination.

3. The 1985–93 period characterized by a 30% increase in African American enrollment in higher education that was fueled by an increase in the percentage of African American high school graduates enrolling in college.

There has been a curvilinear trend in the percentage of the total higher education enrollment that is African American over the past two decades, with high percentages being registered in 1976 and 1993 and a low percentage occurring in 1986. Data simply comparing the 1974 higher education enrollment with 1993 enrollment tends to obscure this curvilinear trend (see Table 2.6).

Looking just at these two data points (1974 and 1993), one might conclude that African Americans have experienced concurrent, moderate increases in both high school completion rate (7.7%) and in percentage of high school graduates enrolled in

Table 2.6 High School Completion Rates and College Progression Rates by Ethnicity (White, Black), for 1974 and 1993
Only.

Year/ Ethnicity	High School Graduates	Comple- tion Rate (%)	# Enrolled in Col- lege	Progres- sion Rate (%)
1974 To- tal	20,725	80.7%	6,316	30.5%
White	18,318	82.7%	5,589	30.5%
Black	2,083	67.1%	555	26.6%
1993 To- tal	19,772	82.0%	8,193	41.4%
White	16,196	83.4%	6,763	41.8%
Black	2,629	74.8%	861	32.8%
Change 1974-93 Total	953	1.3%	1,877	10.9%
Change 1974-93 White	-2,122	0.7%	1,174	11.3%
Change 1974-93 Black	546	7.7%	306	6.2%

Note. Enrollment numbers are indicated in thousands. The white
and black numbers do not add up to the total number because other
ethnicities are not included. These figures were taken from *Trends
in Enrollment in Higher Education, by Racial/Ethnic Category:
Fall 1982 through Fall 1992* (NCES, 1994) and *Minorities in
Higher Education: Thirteenth Annual Report,* published in 1995
by the ACE.

college (6.2%) over the past two decades. One might conclude
from this that as the high school graduation rate increased, so did
the percentage of high school graduates enrolled in college in a

linear fashion. This interpretation would obliterate the two con-
flicting trends noted above, (a) an increase in African American
high school completion rate that *was not* accompanied by an
increase in percentage of high school graduates enrolled in college
(1974–84) and (b) a decline in African American high school
completion rate that *was* paradoxically accompanied by an increase in the percentage of high school graduates enrolled in
college (1985–93).

In a previous section, various reasons for the 1974–84 trends
were enumerated, but thus far few analysts have attempted to explain the most recent trends in African American high school
completion rates and college participation rates. It appears that
more African American high school students are now "valuing the
importance" of a college degree, as opposed to the trend in the
mid-1980s. This may be due partially to the fact that the "first
wave" of African Americans who gained access to higher education under Title VI now have children who are of college age.

Research indicates that the educational level of parents is a
good predictor of the scholastic attainment of their children. It
could be that these college-educated African American parents are
better able to convince their children of the importance of a
college education due to its importance in their own lives. Certainly, college-educated African Americans have greater personal
awareness of college/university systems and requirements than
most of their parents had. They can now pass this information on
to their children, making them more knowledgeable consumers of
higher education services and de-mystifying the experience for
them.

Due to demographic trends, some colleges may be more
actively recruiting African American students (and other ethnic
minorities) as the pool of white high school graduates continues
to decline. Competitive market forces in the past 20 years have
led to a "corporate revolution" in the management of U.S. colleges
and universities, as the 3,300 institutions of higher education in
the country attempt to find their "market niche" (Best, 1988; Trow,
1988). Thus, many institutions of higher education have altered
their entrance requirements and broadened their recruiting nets to
attract more students that come from previously underserved
segments of the population. This market-driven approach has
been a major factor in the continuing "democratization" that has
occurred at many U.S. colleges and universities. For instance, in

1985 the University of California at Berkeley admitted a freshman class made up of a majority (52%) of minority (African American, Hispanic, Asian) group members (Trow, 1988).

These market trends toward greater recruitment of African American students may explain part of the upturn in their total enrollment over the past ten years. It could be that market forces, rather than moral imperative, will be the primary driving force behind continuing increases in African American enrollment in higher education as we approach the twenty-first century.

"Redeeming the American Promise"

Despite the encouraging enrollment trends noted since 1985, it must be concluded that the desegregation of higher education has not occurred as thoroughly or as quickly as originally hoped. In a report published in 1995 entitled *Redeeming the American Promise*, the authors concluded that colleges were still largely segregated in 12 of the 19 states that set up segregated higher education systems after the Civil War (Applebome, 1995; Healy, 1995; Southern Education Foundation, 1995). In these 12 states, the Southern Education Foundation concluded that HBCUs and two-year community colleges remained the destination for most African American (and other minority) students, while the flagship and research institutions were overwhelmingly populated by white students. Among other results from the study were the following:

1. Only 9% of African American freshmen enrolled in their state's largest and most prestigious institutions in this study. For eight of the 12 states in the study, less than 10% of African American freshmen enrolled in these institutions.

2. Almost 30% of African American freshmen enrolled in HBCUs, while 42% enrolled in two-year institutions in this study. For four of the 12 states in the study, more than 40% of the African American freshmen enrolled in HBCUs (Louisiana, Maryland, North Carolina, Virginia). For another four of the 12 states in the study, more than 45% of the African American freshmen enrolled in two-year institutions (Alabama, Florida, Georgia, Mississippi).

3. The study concluded that higher education financial aid is now more oriented toward middle- and upper-middle- income students than toward low-income students. More federal money in the mid-1990s is being spent on loans than grants, while the opposite was true in the 1970s.

Thus, while the overall trends for total enrollment across the entire country indicate some progress in African American participation in higher education since 1985, little progress has been made in breaking down the segregation of certain types of institutions in particular parts of the country. The partial title of this chapter "with all deliberate speed" is, therefore, ironic given the slow and erratic pace with which institutions of higher education have been desegregated. This is particularly true since the phrase in the *Brown II* decision in 1955 referred only to elementary/secondary education.

The *Hawkins* decision in 1956, on the other hand, clearly stated that the desegregation of graduate education did *not* present the same problems as did public elementary/secondary schools and that these programs could be desegregated immediately. Thirty-six years later in 1992, African Americans earned only around 5% of the total number of master's degrees and first-professional degrees awarded in the U.S. (Carter & Wilson, 1995). It appears that little speed has been clocked to date in the country's efforts to truly desegregate either its graduate or undergraduate educational systems.

References

Alexander, K. (1980). *School law*. St. Paul, MN: West Publishing Co.

Anderson, J. O. (1989). Training the apostles of liberal culture: Black higher education, 1900–1935. In L. F. Goodchild & H. S. Wechsler (Eds.), *ASHE reader on the history of higher education* (pp. 455–477). Needham Heights, MA: Ginn Press. (Reprinted from *The education of blacks in the South, 1860–1935*, 1988. Chapel Hill, NC: University of North Carolina.)

Applebome, P. (1995, May 18). Segregation in higher education persists, study of 12 states says. *The New York Times*, p. 1–A.

Bartholomew, P. C. (1974). *Summaries of leading cases on the Constitution*. Tatowa, NJ: Littlefield, Adams, & Co.

Becker, H. J. (1978). *The measurement of segregation: The dissimilarity index and Coleman's segregation index compared*. Baltimore, MD: The Johns Hopkins University, Center for Social Organization of Schools.

Best, J. H. (1989). The revolution of markets and management: Toward a history of American higher education since 1945. In

L. F. Goodchild & H. S. Wechsler (Eds.), *ASHE reader on the history of higher education* (pp. 491–497). Needham Heights, MA: Ginn Press. (Reprinted from *History of Education Quarterly*, 1988, *28*, 177–189.)

Blake, E., Lambert, L., & Martin, J. (1978). *Degrees granted and enrollment trends in historically black colleges: An eight year study*. Washington, DC: Institute for Services to Education.

Blaustein, A. P., & Ferguson, Jr., C. C. (1962). *Desegregation and the law: The meaning and effect of the school segregation cases*. New York: Vintage Books.

Blaustein, A. P., & Zangrando, R. L. (1968). *Civil rights and the American Negro*. New York: Trident Press.

Bowles, F., & DeCosta, F. A. (1989). 1954 to the present. In L. F. Goodchild & H. S. Wechsler (Eds.), *ASHE reader on the history of higher education* (pp. 545–558). Needham Heights, MA: Ginn Press. (Reprinted from *Between two worlds: A profile of Negro higher education*, 1971, pp. 61–80. New York: McGraw-Hill Book Co.)

Carter-Williams, M. (1989). The eroding status of blacks in higher education: An issue of financial aid. In W. D. Smith & E. W. Chunn (Eds.), *Black education: A quest for equity and excellence* (pp. 107–126). New Brunswick, NJ: Transaction Publishers.

Carter, D. J., & Wilson, R. (1989). *Eighth annual status report: Minorities in higher education*. Washington, DC: American Council on Education.

Carter, D. J., & Wilson, R. (1995). *Thirteenth annual status report: Minorities in higher education*. Washington, DC: American Council on Education.

Colon, A. (1991). Race relations on campus: An administrative perspective. In P. Altbach & K. Lomotey (Eds.), *The racial crisis in American higher education* (pp. 69–88). Albany, NY: State University of New York Press.

Davis, M. D., & Clark, H. (1992). *Thurgood Marshall: Warrior at the bar, rebel on the bench*. New York: Carol Publishing Co.

Davis, R. B. (1991). Social support networks and undergraduate student academic-success-related outcomes: A comparison of black students on black and white campuses. In W. R. Allen, E. G. Epps, & N. Z. Haniff (Eds.), *College in black and white: African American students in predominantly white and in historically black public universities* (pp. 143–160). Albany, NY: State University of New York Press.

Dentler, R. (1991). School desegregation since Gunnar Myrdal's *American dilemma*. In C. V. Willie, A. M. Garibaldi, & W. L. Reed (Eds.), *The education of African Americans* (pp. 27–50). Boston: William Monroe Trotter Institute, University of Massachusetts at Boston.

Deskins, D. A. (1991). Winners and losers: A regional assessment of minority enrollment and earned degrees in U.S. colleges and universities. In W. R. Allen, E. G. Epps, & N. Z. Haniff (Eds.), *College in black and white: African American students in predominantly white and in historically black public universities* (pp. 17–40). Albany, NY: State University of New York Press.

DuBois, W. E. B. (1989). The talented tenth. In L. F. Goodchild & H. S. Wechsler (Eds.), *ASHE reader on the history of higher education* (pp. 478–487). Needham Heights, MA: Ginn Press. (Reprinted from *Writings,* 1986, pp. 842–861. New York: Literary Classics of the United States, Inc.)

Garibaldi, A. M. (Ed.). (1984). *Black colleges and universities: Challenges for the future.* New York: Praeger.

Garibaldi, A. M. (1991a). Blacks in college. In C. V. Willie, A. M. Garibaldi, & W. L. Reed (Eds.), *The education of African Americans* (pp. 93–99). Boston: William Monroe Trotter Institute, University of Massachusetts at Boston.

Garibaldi, A. M. (1991b). The role of historically black colleges in facilitating resilience among African American students. *Education and Urban Society, 24*(1), 103–112.

Hardwell, S. (1995, March 8). Judge nixes Mississippi college merger plan. *The Baton Rouge Morning Advocate,*   p. 1–A.

Healy, P. (1995, May 26). States urged to make new efforts to end persistent segregation. *The Chronicle of Higher Education,* p. 29–A.

Hill, H., & Greenberg, J. (1955). *Citizen's guide to desegregation: A study of social and legal change in American life.* Boston: The Beacon Press.

Jencks, C., & Riesman, D. (1967). The American Negro college. *Harvard Educational Review, 37,* 3-60.

Lomotey, K. (1991). Conclusion. In P. Altbach & K. Lomotey (Eds.), *The racial crisis in American higher education* (pp. 263–268). Albany, NY: State University of New York Press.

McDearman, K. M. (1989). *Brown v. Board of Education.* In R. W. Wilson & W. Ferris (Eds.), *Encyclopedia of Southern culture* (pp. 819–820). Chapel Hill, NC: University of North Carolina Press.

Myers, Jr., S. L. (1989). *Desegregation in higher education.* New York: National Association for Equal Opportunities in Higher Education.

National Center for Educational Statistics. (1976). *The condition of education 1976: A statistical report.* Washington, DC: U.S. Government Printing Office.

National Center for Educational Statistics. (1984). *The condition of education 1984: A statistical report.* Washington, DC: U.S. Government Printing Office.

National Center for Educational Statistics. (1987). *Higher education general information surveys, 1964–1986.* Washington, DC: U.S. Government Printing Office.

National Center for Educational Statistics. (1994). *Trends in enrollment in higher education, by racial/ethnic category: Fall 1982 through Fall 1992.* Washington, DC: U.S. Government Printing Office.

Pettigrew, T. F. (1979). The effects of the *Bakke* decision: An initial look. In *Working papers: Bakke, Weber, and affirmative action.* New York: Rockefeller Foundation.

Preer, J. L. (1982). *Lawyers v. educators: Black colleges and desegregation in public higher education.* Westport, CT: Greenwood Press.

Regents nix SU request for land-grant center. (1995, May 25). *The Baton Rouge Morning Advocate*, p. 1–B.

Sansing, D. (1989). James Meredith. In R. W. Wilson & W. Ferris (Eds.), *Encyclopedia of southern culture* (p. 220). Chapel Hill, NC: University of North Carolina Press.

Solmon, L. C., & Wingard, T. L. (1991). The changing demographics: Problems and opportunities. In P. Altbach & K. Lomotey (Eds.), *The racial crisis in American higher education* (pp. 19–42). Albany, NY: State University of New York Press.

Southern Education Foundation. (1995). *Redeeming the American promise.* Atlanta, GA: Author.

Stone, A. (1995, May 23). Court kills blacks-only scholarship. *USA TODAY*, p. 1–A.

Sudarkasa, N. (1988). Black enrollment in higher education: The unfulfilled promise of equality. In *The state of black America*. New York: National Urban League.

Synnott, M. G. (1989). Desegregation. In R. W. Wilson & W. Ferris (Eds.), *Encyclopedia of southern culture* (pp. 248–249). Chapel Hill, NC: University of North Carolina Press.

Trent, W. T. (1991). Student affirmative action in higher education: Addressing underrepresentation. In P. Altbach & K. Lomotey (Eds.), *The racial crisis in American higher education* (pp. 107–134). Albany, NY: State University of New York Press.

Trow, M. (1989). American higher education: Past, present, future. In L. F. Goodchild & H. S. Wechsler (Eds.), *ASHE reader on the history of higher education* (pp. 616–626). Needham Heights, MA: Ginn Press. (Reprinted from *Educational Researcher*, 1988, 13–23.)

Ware, G. (1984). *Hocutt*: Genesis of *Brown*. *Journal of Negro Education*, *52*, 227–233.

Weinberg, M. (1991). The civil rights movement and educational change. In C. V. Willie, A. M. Garibaldi, & W. L. Reed (Eds.), *The education of African Americans* (pp. 3–6). Boston: William Monroe Trotter Institute, University of Massachusetts at Boston.

Williams, J. B. (1991). Systemwide Title VI regulation of higher education, 1968–88: Implications for increased minority participation. In C. V. Willie, A. M. Garibaldi, & W. L. Reed (Eds.), *The education of African Americans* (pp. 110–122). Boston: William Monroe Trotter Institute, University of Massachusetts at Boston.

Willie, C. V. (1991a). The social and historical context: A case study of philanthropic assistance. In C. V. Willie, A. M. Garibaldi, & W. L. Reed (Eds.), *The education of African Americans* (pp. 7–26). Boston: William Monroe Trotter Institute, University of Massachusetts at Boston.

Willie, C. V. (1991b). Summary and recommendations. In C. V. Willie, A. M. Garibaldi, & W. L. Reed (Eds.), *The education of African Americans* (pp. 177–196). Boston: William Monroe Trotter Institute, University of Massachusetts at Boston.

Table of Legal Cases

Adams v. Bell, Civil Action No. 70-3095 (D.D.C. 1982).

Adams v. Califano, 430 F.Supp. 118, (D.D.C. 1977).

Adams v. Richardson, 356 F.Supp. 92 (D.D.C. 1973).

Adams v. Weinberger, 391 F.Supp. 269 (D.D.C. 1975).

Ayers v. Fordice, 112 S.Ct. 2727 (1992).

Brown v. The Board of Education of Topeka, Kansas, 347 U.S. 483, (1954).

Brown v. The Board of Education of Topeka, Kansas, 349 U.S. 294, (1955).

Florida ex rel Hawkins v. Board of Control, 47 So.2d 608 (1950), mot. denied, 53 So.2d 116 (1951), cert. denied., 342 U.S. 877 (1951), *vacated*, 347 U.S. 971 (1954), recalled, vacated, 350 U.S. 413 (1956).

Kirwan v. Podberesky, 63 U.S.L.W. 3832 (U.S. May 22,1995).

McLaurin v. Oklahoma State Regents for Higher Education, 339 U.S. 637 (1950).

Missouri ex rel Gaines v. Canada, 305 U.S. 337 (1938).

Pearson v. Murray, 169 Md. 478, 182 Atl. 590 (1936).

Plessy v. Ferguson, 163 U.S. 537 (1898).

Regents of University of California v. Bakke, 438 U.S. 265, 98 S.Ct. 2733 (1978).

Sipuel v. Board of Regents of the University of Oklahoma, 332 U.S. 631 (1948).

Sweatt v. Painter, 339 U.S. 629 (1950).

United States v. Fordice, 60 U.S.L.W. 4773 (1992).

United States v. Louisiana, No. 80-3300 (USD/ED, 1994).

CHAPTER 3

SEGREGATION, DESEGREGATION, AND RESEGREGATION

Jacqulin Sensley Jacobs

Introduction

Since the *Brown* ruling in 1954, segregation-related litigation in this country has ranged from sustained unenforced desegregation, intense desegregation enforcement efforts, a period of calm and moderate activity, and a movement toward resegregation. My purpose in this chapter is to show how the courts have softened their stance on desegregation and given school districts more autonomy and freedom in developing desegregation plans.

I will examine desegregation litigation and the position that the Court has taken within the following time spans:

1. From 1954 to 1964, the Supreme Court established powerful mandates, but the enforcement efforts did not coincide with the strong language as set forth in the *Brown* decision.

2. From the mid 1960s to the late 1970s, litigation was numerous and the courts were aggressive in their enforcement efforts.

3. The decade of the 1980s represented a time of sustained desegregation with minimal court interventions.

4. In the early 1990s the courts have relinquished their position as enforcer to become a referee of sorts, giving local school boards more power to determine the ways and means to settle desegregation disputes.

Mandated But Rarely Enforced

The landmark case of *Brown v. Board of Education* (1954) (*Brown I*) held that segregation in public schools violated the Equal Protection Clause of the Fourteenth Amendment. It concluded that further litigation was needed to formulate decrees on how the districts should be desegregated. The *Brown* decision did not apply to school districts in the District of Columbia because Washington, DC is not a state. In *Bolling v. Sharpe* (1954) the Supreme Court held that since the Constitution prohibits states from segregating public schools, it would not be fair to impose a lesser duty on the federal government. The Court held that racial discrimination in DC schools violated the Fifth Amendment's due process clause and thereby ordered the desegregation of these schools. The *Brown* case overturned the separate but equal doctrine and the apartheid system that existed in educational and other social institutions.

Complications brought on by the *Brown* case were most likely foreseen by the Supreme Court when it rendered its decision (Alexander & Alexander, 1985). The courts were faced with sorting out a system that would allow for the desegregation of public schools. In *Brown v. Board of Education* (1955) (*Brown II*) the opinions of the state and federal attorneys general were heard. The court declared that consideration should be given to "public interest of the plaintiffs" and the "personal interest of the plaintiffs."

After viewing this dichotomy, the court decided that implementation of *Brown I* should take place with "all deliberate speed." The Supreme Court's decision allowed the local federal district courts to settle complaints on a case-by-case basis with regard to equality for all involved. Today some believe that the *Brown* decision allowed too much flexibility while others claim that not enough flexibility was allowed.

Immediately after the *Brown* decision, state and local boards devised schemes to evade the orders as decreed by the courts. In Arkansas, under an approved desegregation plan, African American students were ordered to integrate a previously all white school. State officials reacted to the plan by passing laws to perpetuate segregation. On the day the students were to start school, the state dispatched its national guard to forbid the students from entering the school grounds. Accompanied by federal troops, the students were finally admitted to the school.

However, their presence at the school interrupted the schooling process. Subsequently, the federal district court granted the school district's request to suspend the desegregation plan and ordered the African American students back to the segregated schools. The decision was reversed by the Eighth Circuit. The U.S. Supreme Court agreed with the State's Court of Appeals.

After *Cooper v. Aaron* (1958), the court was involved in two cases from Louisiana. In *United States v. State of Louisiana* (1960), the state attempted to avoid desegregation. The Louisiana legislature proposed and enacted various measures that were opposed in federal district court. The court ordered an injunction that nullified the state legislature's enactments. When appealed to the Supreme Court, it was decided that the state did not have exclusive control over the field of public education.

The Louisiana legislature passed a series of laws designed to prevent desegregation in New Orleans after a federal court ordered it to desegregate. The federal courts declared the statutes unconstitutional. The state believed that it had exclusive control over education and sought a stay. The U.S. Supreme Court denied the stay and dismissed the state's contention in *Bush v. Orleans School Board* (1960). These cases illustrate the vigor with which states and local boards opposed the desegregation mandates of the Supreme Court.

Cooper v. Aaron (1958), *United States v. State of Louisiana* (1960), and *Bush v. Orleans School Board* (1960) were the only cases heard by the Supreme Court between the *Brown* decision and 1964. It is important to note that these cases involved one or a very few African American students petitioning for the right to attend predominately white schools. By 1964, only 2.3% of African American students attended predominately white schools, and most of this desegregation was concentrated in the South (NCES, 1988). After this period of gradual desegregation and sustained resistance, the courts and the federal government became more intent on enforcing desegregation laws.

Intense Litigation and Enforcement
During the period of intense litigation and enforcement, the Johnson administration had the Civil Rights Act passed and the mood and sentiments in the country at this time were conducive to enforcing the rights of individuals and minority groups. With this

type of atmosphere prevalent, the courts were very deliberate and forceful regarding the orders handed down.

The great majority of the school systems still operated a dual system of education and when ordered to desegregate, the local boards, city governments, and state legislators were still intent on operating business as usual. For example, when Prince Edward County School System in Virginia was ordered to desegregate, the system resisted. The state passed laws that closed all schools that were desegregated. A "freedom of choice" program was passed after the legislation was struck down by Virginia courts. The U.S. Court of Appeals, Fourth Circuit, ordered the end of discriminatory practices in the district. The county then refused to levy taxes for the next school year. As a result, the public school system was closed for three years during which time private schools operated and students received vouchers from the state. A federal district court ruled that the development of private schools was an attempt to prevent desegregation and demanded that the public schools reopen. The county and school board requested a stay from the district court. The district court refused, but the court of appeals reversed the district court's decision. The U.S. Supreme Court reversed the appellate court's decision and reinstated the district court's ruling. The Court remanded the case to the district court and ordered it to enter a decree ensuring that African American children would receive an equal education in public schools along with whites (*Griffin v. County School Board*, 1964).

The definition of "all deliberate speed" was upheld in *Alexander v. Holmes County Board of Education* (1969). In 1969, the segregated status of Mississippi African American children was challenged. The U.S. Court of Appeals, Fifth Circuit, gave the school districts more time to desegregate under the standard of allowing "all deliberate speed" as affirmed in *Brown II*. The U.S. Supreme Court overruled the decision and ordered the immediate termination of the segregated system.

After the *Alexander* case the court took on cases to clarify the meaning of the decision. In one case, the U.S. Court of Appeals, Fifth Circuit, deferred student desegregation in several school districts. The Supreme Court reversed the court of appeals ruling and stated that its *Alexander* decision had been misconstrued by the appeals court. The Court stated that the burden of proof of segregation should be shifted to the defendant school districts. This meant that if the school districts or segregation challengers could show a chance of trial success, the district must provide immediate relief from unconstitutional segregation. The Court stated that the term "all deliberate speed," meant no more than eight weeks.

The Memphis School District developed a plan to desegregate the system schools. The parents in Memphis believed that the system was already operating a unitary system and that therefore, there was no need to develop plans. The parents filed suit and the lower court ruled that the system was operating a dual system. The court of appeals ruled against the lower court in favor of the parents. In *Northcross v. Board of Education* (1971), the Supreme Court agreed with the lower court and applied *Alexander v. Holmes County Board* (1970) which ruled that when systems are operating segregated schools, they must implement plans for a unitary system immediately.

During the 1960s, school districts attempted to use "freedom of choice" programs to avoid desegregation, but those efforts were turned down by the courts. In *Green v. County School Board* (1965), New Kent County in Virginia was operating two separate school systems within its district. Fifty percent of the population was African American. The county continued the dual schools even after the Court ruled in *Brown II* that Virginia statutory and constitutional provisions requiring racial segregation were unconstitutional. The county adopted a "freedom of choice" program when the federal government threatened to cut off its aid. The program allowed students to choose the school they wanted to attend. The district gained approval from the federal district court to operate the "choice" program. The Court of Appeals, Fourth Circuit, approved the plan also. After the plan was implemented, 85% of the county's African American students still attended an all African American school. The Court held that the "freedom of choice" plan was constitutionally unacceptable because of *Brown II*. *Brown II* required that the burden of desegregation be placed on the district, and not on parents and children as was the case with the New Kent County plan.

In *Monroe v. Board of Commissioners* (1968) and *Raney v. Board of Education* (1967), school districts also adopted the "freedom of choice" strategy, but the Court referred to the *Green* case. The problem with this method was that no white students enrolled in African American schools and only a few African American students were accepted into the white schools.

Another method used to achieve desegregation was attendance zones. This method redraws school attendance zones to increase the number of African Americans attending white schools. In *Dowell v. Board of Education* (1969) a federal court approved an Oklahoma school district desegregation plan which included redrawing attendance zones. The court ordered the school district to submit plans within two months. Students intervened in the lawsuit and asked the U.S. Court of Appeals, Tenth Circuit, to stay implementation on the boundaries. The court of appeals granted a stay to the students. The U.S. Supreme Court reversed the decision because the school system had the burden of desegregation at once.

In *McDaniel v. Barresi* (1971) the U.S. Supreme Court decided that school districts may draw attendance zones according to race to achieve a desegregated school system. The *Pasadena City Board of Education v. Spangler* (1976) decision declared that once a school district has complied with an approved plan, it is not constitutionally mandatory to make adjustments to reach the "no majority" of minority students attendance requirements. Pasadena, California high school students and their parents sued the school district for operating a racially segregated school system. A federal district court ordered the school district to submit a desegregation plan which could assure that there would be no school with a majority of minority students. The school system appealed to the district court stating that the term "majority" was ambiguous. The court denied the order holding that because of shifting populations within the school system, several schools had violated the requirements of desegregation. The court stated that the school system had to abide by the "no majority" requirement. The school system appealed and the Supreme Court ruled that the school system had a justifiable grievance as to the ambiguity of the term "no majority" and were entitled to modification of the district court's original order. In *Vetterli v. United States District Court* (1977), the decision was upheld that there would be a "no majority" provision in the court decision.

Probably the most controversial method used to achieve desegregation has been busing. Busing of students met opposition from several states. *Swann v. Charlotte-Mecklenburg Board of Education* (1971) granted busing as being legal for the purpose of achieving desegregation. The ruling came as a result of a plan that was adopted for the desegregation of 29 elementary schools in

Augusta, Georgia. A challenge was made to busing on the grounds that #803 of the Education Amendments of 1972 required a stay of the judgment where transportation was provided to achieve racial balance. Supreme Court Justice Powell held that desegregation-ordered busing was not initiated for the purpose of reflecting the racial composition of the school system, but for the purpose of eliminating a dual school system. The Supreme Court's decision surrounding *North Carolina State Board of Education v. Swann* (1971) declared that busing based on race was a necessary and legal manner in which to carry out desegregation.

In *Bustop, Inc. v. Board of Education of City of Los Angeles* (1978), the court refused to grant a stay of the busing order handed down by the California Supreme Court. A California court ordered the Los Angeles Board of Education to implement a desegregation plan that involved reassigning more than 60,000 students. The plan paired racially imbalanced white and minority schools using busing in order to achieve desegregation. The California Court of Appeals reversed the decision. The California Supreme Court overruled the Court of Appeals' decision basing its decision on the California Constitution rather than on U.S. constitutional grounds. The parents appealed to the U.S. Supreme Court. The Court refused to grant the stay because the case rested on the California Constitution, as the California Supreme Court had previously ruled. The Court's ruling indicated that busing is a viable and accepted means of achieving desegregation.

Brown I's desegregation mandate required the desegregation of faculty as well as students. In the case *Rogers v. Paul* (1965), the Supreme Court revealed that students had the right to challenge faculty segregation because it denied them equal opportunities in education. The *U.S. v. Montgomery Board of Education* (1962) ruling ordered the Montgomery, Alabama school district to hire African American teachers at a ratio of 1:6 African American to white. *Davis v. Board of School Commissioners* (1971) held that the desegregation of faculty must be achieved in conjunction with the desegregation of students.

In the case of *Bradley v. School Board* (1965/1974), important decisions resulted in regard to faculty ratio. The U.S. Supreme Court ruled that faculty allocation plans were entitled to full hearings because of the relation of faculty in proportion to desegregation. The court also awarded attorney fees to those challenging segregation.

As evidenced by the number of cases that reached the Supreme Court and rulings that insisted that the burden of desegregation is clearly the responsibility of local schools, this period documented the Court's finest hour as the ultimate enforcer. Several strategies were presented to the Court as means of achieving desegregation, but the Court stood firm on its stance and many of the strategies were rejected. This was a time when the Court declared that gradualism was over and that districts must act with a sense of urgency. Another very interesting fact about this period is that in 1968 13% of the nation's African American students attended predominately white schools, and by 1980 that percentage had risen to 37%. The percentage of white students attending predominately white schools decreased from 78% in 1968 to 61% in 1980 (Orfield, 1982).

Desegregation: Sustained, But Fragile

Individuals that are observant of the desegregation movements in this country have observed a change in the attitudes of the courts and the federal government regarding desegregation. Bell (1980) states that "the once supportive Supreme Court has lost its early enthusiasm for implementing what is likely its best known decision" (p. 8). The desegregation movement experienced attacks on court ordered desegregation by national leaders, including past presidents, and the federal government. Orfield very eloquently sums up this period:

> Four of the five Administrations since 1968 have been openly hostile to urban desegregation orders and the Carter Administration (the single exception) took few initiatives. There have been no important positive policy proposals supporting desegregation from any branch of government since the passage of the Emergency School Aid Act desegregation assistance program in 1972 (repealed in 1981). Civil Rights advocates had to devote most of their energy to preventing a rollback of what had already been achieved. In spite of many large battles in the courts and elsewhere over the segregation of black students, the regional and national statistics are virtually unchanged.

> The Justice Department, which sued scores of major school districts for comprehensive desegregation plans under previous administrations, devoted its energy

in the 1980s primarily to limiting or ending existing plans and resisting new mandatory orders. The policy of the Reagan Administration was that mandatory orders which produced the surge in southern desegregation in the 1965–72 period were wrong, that mandatory busing should be ended, and that the courts should drop older orders and let the school officials return to neighborhood schools even if they were segregated. The Justice Department went to the Supreme Court to unsuccessfully argue that the state of Washington should be able to dissolve Seattle's desegregation plan, it dropped a major city-suburban desegregation case in metropolitan Houston and it asked the courts to end supervision of desegregation in more than a hundred southern districts. Justice Department officials encouraged districts to dismantle their plans, with department leaders constantly asserting that the plans had failed. This kind of dramatic, high visibility leadership was naturally expected to have consequences. Many assumed that it meant that the era of busing and court-ordered desegregation was over. This data discloses no substantial changes in the trends under way before Reagan took office.

Although overall national statistics make it appear that nothing much has happened since 1972, there has been some regression in some areas and further desegregation in others, trends which have roughly balanced each other. The rapid decline in white enrollment since the 1970s and the increase in blacks mean that the demographic trends were moving toward less black contact with whites, but this trend was apparently countered by efforts that produced a slight positive movement toward more desegregation, in spite of political attacks. (Orfield, 1983, p. 29)

Resegregation

Federal district courts were given the authority in *Brown II* to oversee school district plans. The Supreme Court has given these courts a great deal of discretionary authority over school desegregation plans. The courts have recently interpreted cases that had similar characteristics with previous cases in a very different manner and tone. In the past the courts were very specific and strict in providing the kind of directions school systems should take. The schools were required to attain all of the criteria set forth in various court rulings. The standard for achieving unitary status was clearly stated in the *Green* case. However, in recent cases the courts are accepting desegregation plans that would have been vigorously rejected in the past.

Freeman v. Pitts is a continuing case that started in 1969. The DeKalb County School System (DCSS) in Georgia was found illegally segregated and placed under judicial supervision. Various measures were taken to allow the district to become desegregated. Their request was based on the premise that they had achieved four of the six criteria set out in *Green v. County School Board* (1968). The four factors met were student assignment, transportation, physical facilities, and extra-curricular activities. The two factors not met were faculty assignment and resource allocation (the court used a non-*Green* factor to examine the relationship for compliance, the quality of education). The district court relinquished control of the areas which it had found were unitary and retained control of the others. The U.S. Court of Appeals disagreed that the "incremental" approach should be used. The Court held that unitary status in some categories could not justify the relinquishing of judicial control until all conditions had been met. The U.S. Supreme Court ruled that the *Green* ruling does not need to be applied as construed by the court of appeals. By relinquishing control in areas deemed to be unitary, a court and school district may concentrate on the areas in need of further attention. The Court held that the "incremental" approach was constitutional and that a court may declare that it will order no further remedy in any areas which are found to be unitary *(Freeman v. Pitts*, 1992). In the *Green* case the Court stated that all categories must have demonstrated compliance before unitary status could be achieved.

In the *Board of Education of Oklahoma City Public Schools v. Dowell* (1991) the U.S. Supreme Court stated that supervision of local districts by federal courts was meant only as a temporary remedy for discrimination. School districts themselves must come forward with plans to ensure the continuation of desegregation initiatives. The school system was determined unitary in 1977 by a federal court.

The following cases are representative of the court rulings of the 1990s. School authorities have broad discretion to implement educational policy, including the power to prescribe a ratio of white to minority students that reflects the composition of the overall school district; this discretionary authority also includes the power to assign faculty to achieve a racial ratio reflecting the racial composition of the system's teachers (*Jacobson v. Cincinnati Board of Education*, 1992).

When a school board sought to compel the state to fund remedial and compensatory programs to eliminate the lingering effects of segregation, the burden of proof was shifted to the board based on the school system's achievement of unitary status (*School Board of Richmond v. Baliles*, 1987). If a school district which had previously maintained a dual system was found to have achieved unitary status, it was under no obligation to eliminate all of the vestiges of discrimination absent a showing that its actions were intentionally discriminatory (*Price v. Austin Independent School District*, 945 F.2d 1307 (5th Circuit, 1991)). A suit will have to be filed on this system to prove that it is operating a dual system. The ruling in this case is reflective of the type of decisions made by the courts today.

A proposed settlement of a desegregation suit which included the development of magnet schools together with backup provisions in those schools was a fair, reasonable, and adequate solution to charges of segregation raised against the school district (*Parents for Quality Education v. Fort Wayne Community Schools Corp.*, 1990). The "freedom of choice" programs that were rejected by the courts during the 1960s and 1970s because they did not achieve desegregation are being accepted by the courts. Magnet schools are considered "freedom of choice" programs.

A city school district's refusal to reestablish a four-year vocational education program at its predominately black vocational school was legitimate where there was little evidence that offering primarily academic courses to ninth and tenth graders would expand or improve the school's image; also, the proposed program would have done little to increase white enrollment at the school (*Liddell v. Board of Education of St. Louis*, 1987).

U.S. v. Fordice (1992) is the first time that the U.S. Supreme Court has dealt with desegregation of higher education. There is a set of universities for whites and another set for blacks in Mississippi. In 1975, a group of private citizens, who were joined by the United States, brought suit against state officials charging that they violated the Fourteenth Amendment's Equal Protection Clause and Title VI of the Civil Rights Acts of 1964. In 1981, the state issued mission statements classifying the three white institutions as "comprehensive" universities, classifying one of the African American universities as an "urban" university and characterizing the two remaining African American universities as "regional" institutions. The universities remained racially identifiable. After the trial, the federal district court stated that the duty to desegregate does not contemplate restricting student choice or the achievement of racial balance. State policies should be racially neutral, developed in good faith, and must not contribute to the racial identifiability of each institution. The U.S. Court of Appeals, Fifth Circuit affirmed. The United States and the private citizens sought review from the Supreme Court.

The U.S. Supreme Court held that the district court had applied the wrong legal standards in declaring that it had complied with the Equal Protection Clause. If a state has practices that contribute to prior segregation practices, even if policies have been eliminated that contributed to segregation, the policy violates the Equal Protection Clause. Because the district court did not ask questions, the Court of Appeals erred in affirming. The Supreme Court declared that given Mississippi's past history, several surviving aspects of Mississippi's dual system were constitutionally suspect. The use of higher minimum ACT composite scores at the white institutions, along with the state's refusal to consider high school grade performance, was suspect. The unnecessary duplication of programs at black and white institutions was suspect. The mission statement's reflection of previous policies to perpetuate racial separation was suspect. Finally, the state's operation of eight universities had to be examined to determine if it was educationally justifiable. The state would have to justify all of these decisions as sound education policy.

Nineteen Southern and border states had segregated higher education systems. Many of these states had been charged by the courts for running segregated universities before the Mississippi ruling. Most of the states cleared were subject to lower standards than those set by the Supreme Court. The standards used to clear those states were rejected by the Supreme Court. Halpern, along with other experts, believes that one or more of the higher education orders will end up back in the Supreme Court.

An appeals court rejected a lower court's determination that Louisiana's higher education system was segregated, even though the state had dual campuses that are racially identifiable in three cities. After the *Fordice* ruling, experts believed historically black colleges (HCBUs) in close proximity would be closed. Orfield (1994) says the Supreme Court requires states to end racially identifiable institutions, not just to improve conditions at HBCUs. He believes helping HBCUs is admirable, but it does not help the masses of African American students. The vast majority of African American students attend predominately white institutions.

Conclusion

The idea of the courts and federal policymakers as the protectors and enforcers of the rights of minorities is slowly diminishing. The courts and the federal government are allowing local boards and governments to decide on the ways and means of ensuring that all members of our society have equal access to a quality education. These local policymakers, as evidenced by their past and present behavior, have proven that they are either incapable or unwilling to design equitable desegregation plans.

Asking local authorities to develop adequate school desegregation plans as suggested by the Supreme Court is like asking the fox (the defendant school board) found guilty of stealing chickens (operating racially segregated schools) to develop a plan to secure the chicken house against further theft (to plan a unitary system) (Willie, 1980).

Our present course of negative sentiments toward desegregation suggests the following consequences:

1. A slow trend toward resegregation.

2. A disproportionate number of minority students in inadequate schools.

3. More "freedom of choice" programs that fail to meet the needs of minority students.

4. More local, federal, and Supreme Court suits.

5. Decreased public support for desegregation in higher education.

6. Increased confrontations at local levels.

References

Alexander, K., & Alexander M.D. (1985). *American public school law.* St. Paul, MN: West Publishing Co.

Bell, D. (1980). *Shades of Brown: New perspective on school desegregation.* New York: Teachers College Press.

Jaschik, S. (1994). Education Department to use 1992 Supreme Court case in judging formerly segregated state systems. *The Chronicle of Higher Education, 60,* 23–36.

Jaschik, S. (1994). Whither desegregation? *The Chronicle of Higher Education, 60,* 21, 33–37.

National Center for Education Statistics (1988). *Digest of Education Statistics.* Washington, DC: U.S. Department of Education.

Orfield, G. (1983). *Public school desegregation in the United States 1968–1980.* Washington, DC: Joint Center for Political Studies.

Willie, C. V. (1984). *School desegregation plans that work.* Westport, CT: Greenwood Press.

Table of Legal Cases

Alexander v. Holmes County Board of Education, 396 U.S. 1990 S. Ct. 29, 24 L.Ed. 2d 19 (1969).

Board of Education of City of Los Angeles v. Superior Court, 448 U.S. 1343, 101 S.Ct. 21, 65 L.Ed. 2d 1166 (1980).

Board of Education of Oklahoma City Public Schools v. Dowell, 498 U.S. 237, 111 S.Ct. 630, 112 L.Ed. 2d 715 (1991).

Bolling v. Sharpe, 347 U.S. 497, 74 S.Ct. 693, 98 L.Ed. 884 (1954).

Bradley v. School Board, 382 U.S. 103, 86 S.Ct. 224, 15 L.Ed. 2d 187 (1965).

Bradley v. School Board, 416 U.S. 696, 94 S.Ct. 2006, 40 L.Ed. 2d 476 (1974).

Brown v. Board of Education, 347 U.S. 483, 74 S.Ct. 686, 98 L.Ed 873 (1954).

Brown v. Board of Education, 349 U.S. 294, 75 S.Ct. 53, 99 L.Ed. 1083 (1955).

Bush v. Orleans School Board, 364 U.S. 500, 81 S.Ct. 260 (1960).

Bustop Inc. v. Board of Education of City of Los Angeles, 439 U.S. 1380, 99 S.Ct. 40, 58 L.Ed. 2d 88 (1978).

Carter v. West Feliciana School Board, 396 U.S. 290, 90 S.Ct. 608, 24 L.Ed. 2d 477 (1970).

Columbus Board of Education v. Pencik, 443 U.S. 449, 99 S.Ct. 2941, 61 L.Ed. 2d 666 (1978).

Cooper v. Aaron, 358 U.S. 1, 78 S.Ct. 1401, 3 L.Ed. 2d 5 (1958).

Cranford v. Board of Education, 458 U.S. 527, 102 S.Ct. 3211, 73 L.Ed. 2d 948 (1982).

Dandridge v. Jefferson Parish School Board, 404 U.S. 1219, 92 S.Ct. 18, 30 L.Ed. 2d 23 (1971).

Davis v. Board of School Commissioners, 402 U.S. 33, 91 S.Ct. 1289, 28 L.Ed. 2d 577 (1971).

Drummon v. Acre, 409 U.S. 1228, 93 S.Ct. 18, 34 L.Ed. 2d 33 (1972).

Dayton Board of Education v. Brinkman, 433 U.S. 406, 97 S.Ct. 2766, 53 L.Ed. 2d 851 (1977).

Dayton Board of Education v. Brinkman, 443 U.S. 526, 99 S.Ct. 2971, 61 L.Ed. 2d 720 (1979).

Dowell v. Board of Education, 396 U.S. 269, 905 S.Ct. 415, 24 L.Ed. 2d 414 (1969).

Evans v. Newton, 382 U.S. 296, 86 S.Ct. 486, 15 L.Ed. 2d 373 (1966).

Freeman v. Pitts, 503 U.S., 112 S.Ct. 1430, 118 L.Ed. 2d 108 (1992).

Gilmore v. City of Montgomery, 417 U.S. 556, 94 S.Ct. 2416, 41 L.Ed. 2d 304 (1974).

Gomperts v. Chase, 404 U.S. 1217, 92 S.Ct. 16, 30 L.Ed. 2d 30 (1971).

Goss v. Board of Education, 373 U.S. 683, 83 S.Ct. 1405, 10 L.Ed. 2d 632 (1963).

Green v. County School Board, 391 U.S. 430, 88 S.Ct. 689, 20 L.Ed. 2d 716 (1968).

Griffin v. County School Board, 377 U.S. 218, 84 S.Ct. 1226, 12 L.Ed. 2d 256 (1964).

Guey Heung Lee v. Johnson, 404 U.S. 1215, 92 S.Ct. 14, 30 L.Ed. 2d 19 (1971).

Hills v. Gautreaux, 425 U.S. 284, 96 S.Ct. 1538, 47 L.Ed. 2d 792 (1976).

Jacobson v. Cincinnati Board of Education (1992).

Keyes v. School District I Denver Colorado, 413 U.S. 189, 93 S.Ct. 2686, 37 L.Ed. 2d 548 (1973).

Liddell v. Board of Education of St. Louis, 822 F.2d 1446 (8th Cir. 1987).

McDaniel v. Barresi, 402 U.S. 39, 91 S.Ct. 1289, 28 L.Ed. 2d 582 (1971).

Milliken v. Bradley, 418 U.S. 717, 94 S.Ct. 311, 41 L.Ed. 2d 1069 (1974).

Milliken v. Bradley, 433 U.S. 267, 97 S.Ct. 2749, 53 L.Ed. 745 (1977).

Missouri v. Jenkins, 491 U.S. 274, 109 S.Ct. 2463, 105 L.Ed. 2d 229 (1989).

Missouri v. Jenkins, 495 U.S. 38, 110 S.Ct. 1651, 109 L.Ed. 2d 31 (1990).

Monroe v. Board of Commissioners, 391 U.S. 450, 88 S.Ct. 1706, 20 L.Ed. 2d 733 (1968).

North Carolina Board of Education v. Swann, 402 U.S. 43, 91 S.Ct. 1284, 28 L.Ed. 2d 586 (1971).

Northcross v. Board of Education, 397 U.S. 232, 90 S.Ct. 891, 25 L.Ed. 2d 246 (1970).

Parents for Quality Education v. Fort Wayne Community Schools Corp., 728 F. Supp. 1373 (N.D. Ind. 990).

Pasadena City Board of Education v. Spangler, 427 U.S. 424, 96 S.Ct. 2697, 49 L.Ed. 2d 599 (1976).

Price v. Austin Independent School District, 945 F.2d 1307 (5th Cir. 1991).

Raney v. Board of Education, 391 U.S. 443, 88 S.Ct. 1697, 20 L.Ed. 2d 27 (1967).

Rogers v. Paul, 382 U.S. 198, 86 S.Ct. 358, 15 L.Ed. 2d 265 (1965).

School Board of Richmond v. Baliles, 829 F.2d 1308, (4th Circuit 1987).

Swann v. Charlotte-Mecklenburg, 402 U.S. 1, 91 S.Ct. 1267, 28 L.Ed. 2d 554 (1970).

Turner v. Fouche, 396 U.S. 346, 90 S.Ct. 532, 24 L.Ed. 2d 567 (1970).

U.S. v. Fordice, 505 U.S. 112 S.Ct. 2727, 120 L.Ed. 2d 575 (1992).

U.S. v. Montgomery Board of Education, 395 U.S. 225, 89 S.Ct. 1670, 23 L.Ed. 2d 263 (1968).

U.S. v. Scotland Neck Board of Education, 407 U.S. 484, 92 S.Ct. 2214, 33 L.Ed. 2d 751 (1979).

U.S. v. State of Louisiana, 364 U.S. 500, 81 S.Ct. 260, 5 L.Ed. 2d 245 (1960).

Vetterli v. U.S. District Court, 435 U.S. 1304, 98 S.Ct. 1219, 55 L.Ed. 2d 751 (1979).
Washington v. Seattle School District Number 1, 458 U.S. 457, 102 S.Ct. 3187, 73 L.Ed. 2d 896 (1982).
Winston-Salem Forsyth Board of Education v. Scott, 404 U.S. 1221, 92 S.Ct. 1236, 31 L.Ed. 2d 441 (1971).
Wright v. Council of City of Emporia, 407 U.S. 451, 92 S.Ct. 2196, 33 L.Ed. 2d 51 (1972).

CHAPTER 4

REVIEW OF RESEARCH ON SCHOOL DESEGREGATION'S IMPACT ON ELEMENTARY AND SECONDARY SCHOOL STUDENTS

Janet Ward Schofield

The Goals of This Review

The *Brown v. Board of Education* decision was based on the constitutional principal of equal protection (Read, 1975; Wisdom, 1975). Yet for most majority and minority group members alike, the most immediate and pressing concern has been how desegregation is likely to affect children — especially their own children. This widespread concern about the impact of desegregation and the controversy over what its effects might be have led to a substantial amount of research. Some research explores desegregation's impact on a wide array of outcomes such as residential desegregation, community protest movements, and employment patterns for teachers and administrators from various ethnic groups. However, there is much more research on the impact of desegregation on students themselves — most notably on their

This chapter was originally published as "Review of Research on School Desegregation's Impact on Elementary and Secondary School Students" by J. W. Schofield, in *Handbook of Research on Multicultural Education* by J. A. Banks and C. A. M. Banks (Eds.), 1995, New York: Macmillan. Copyright 1995 by Macmillan Publishers. Reprinted by permission.

academic achievement and on relations between students from different ethnic and racial groups. It is this kind of work which is the focus of this review.

I preface discussion of this work with a brief consideration of methodological and other problems which typify research in this area. For a more detailed discussion of this topic, I refer the reader to Schofield (1991).

Poor methodology can either mask real effects or suggest false ones and researchers working in this area face a myriad of design and measurement problems. A major difficulty in assessing the impact of desegregation on students is that resegregation within formally desegregated schools is common (Desegregation Studies Unit, 1977). Although longitudinal studies of desegregation's impact have a distinct advantage over cross-sectional studies, they too frequently have serious problems. For example, many longitudinal studies employ no control group. Rather, they simply measure a group of students before and after desegregation, which makes it difficult to know how much of the change found is due to desegregation and how much is due to other factors. Desegregation studies are also often plagued by self-selection problems at the institutional and the individual level that limit one's ability to draw accurate conclusions.

In sum, any review of the literature on the effect of desegregation on outcomes such as academic achievement or intergroup attitudes must face the reality that much of the research is flawed in one way or another (Schofield, 1991). In addition, a great deal of this research was conducted and published some time ago, in the 1970s, the decade in which most desegregation plans were implemented. However, it does appear possible to draw some conclusions. Because the amount, quality, and typical problems of research on different outcomes of desegregation differ markedly, I have not adopted one set of standards which will be applied across the board to determine whether a study is sound enough to be utilized in this review. Rather, in each section I provide the reader with information on the data base on which the conclusions in that section rest.

The Effect of School Desegregation
on Academic Achievement

There has been a great deal of research on the academic impact of school desegregation. An obvious reason for this was the expectation that school desegregation would enhance the achievement of minority pupils which has clearly lagged behind that of whites (Arias, 1986; Carrasquillo, 1991; Howard & Hammond, 1985; Pearl, 1991; Valencia, 1991). The reasons given for this expectation have been many and varied. Some are relatively straightforward, like the idea that the relatively superior facilities and better educated staffs available in many previously all-white schools should enhance achievement. Others are more complex and psychologically oriented. For example, a number of social scientists have put forward variations on a theory that Miller (1980) has called the lateral transmission of values hypothesis — the idea that minority groups coming into contact with whites, who are often from more middle-class backgrounds, would be influenced by their middle-class peers' stronger orientation toward achievement (Coleman et al. 1966; Crain & Weisman, 1972; Pettigrew, 1969b). Research has not lent credence to this notion (Maruyama & Miller, 1979; Maruyama, Miller, & Holtz, 1986; McGarvey, 1977; Miller, 1980; Patchen, 1982). However, there are enough remaining, plausible ideas about why and how desegregation might influence minority group achievement to make the issue worthy of investigation.

Although research on desegregation's impact on achievement has focused primarily on African American students, a number of studies have also addressed its impact on white students. Very little information is available about the impact of desegregation on Hispanic American students' achievement, although this topic has begun to receive some attention.

School Desegregation and African American Math and Reading Achievement
The past 15 years have seen a large number of reviews of the literature on desegregation and the achievement of African American students (Armor, 1984; Bradley & Bradley, 1977; Cook, 1984; Crain, 1984a; Krol 1978; Mahard & Crain, 1983; Miller & Carlson, 1984; Stephan, 1978, 1984; St. John, 1975; Walberg, 1984; Weinberg, 1977; Wortman, 1984). Since only a handful of studies on this topic have been conducted since the most recent of the reviews (Bennett & Easton, 1988; Carsrud, 1984; Gable & Iwanicki, 1986; Pride & Woodward, 1985) and their results are generally consistent with earlier research, these reviews will constitute the basis for the discussion presented here. However, it

is important to note that there has been considerable debate over whether standardized tests, which are used to assess achievement in virtually all of the studies included in this review, are a valid indication of African American students' achievement (Fleming, 1990; Hilliard, 1990).

The earliest of the reviews just cited was conducted by St. John (1975) who examined over 60 studies of desegregation and African American achievement. She included at least four different kinds of desegregation in her review — desegregation occurring through demographic changes in neighborhoods, school board rezoning of districts or school closings, voluntary transfer of pupils, and total district desegregation. Although St. John classified studies by their design features, she did little or no selection of studies on methodological criteria. St. John (1975) concluded that "adequate data has not yet been gathered to determine a causal relation between school racial composition and academic achievement" (p. 36). The data did make it clear, however, that neither African American nor white children suffer academically due to desegregation. Finally St. John found some indication that younger African American children, especially those of kindergarten age, tend to benefit more academically from desegregation than older ones.

Weinberg (1977) reviewed 23 studies of African American achievement in interracial schools and another 48 studies of desegregated schools — that is, those in which the interracial nature of the student body was a consequence of a conscious policy designed to end segregation. Like St. John, he did not select studies on strict methodological criteria. He concluded that the majority of studies of both kinds indicated improved minority achievement, although a substantial proportion reported no effect. Again there was no evidence of academic harm. Stephan's (1978) review came to a similar but not identical conclusion. He reported that the majority of studies suggested no impact, but that a substantial number suggested positive outcomes.

Bradley and Bradley (1977) concur with Weinberg that a majority of the studies conclude that desegregation has positive effects on the achievement of African American students. However, they note that each of the studies showing positive effects suffers from methodological problems. (However, they also criticize most of the studies showing no effect.) Thus they conclude that the evidence suggests no effect or a positive one.

One other feature of this review should be noted. Interestingly, all of the studies of open enrollment plans and "central schools" — desegregated schools in small cities which house all of a system's students in given grades — show positive effects. In contrast, relatively few of those in which desegregation was achieved by school closing or busing show gains. However Bradley and Bradley (1977) do not interpret these patterns as having any real significance because the number and quality of studies varies so much from one type of desegregation to another.

Krol (1978) was the first to apply meta-analytic techniques to the literature in this area. Meta-analysis provides a statistical method for combining results from different studies (Glass, McGaw, & Smith, 1981; Hunter, Schmidt, & Jackson, 1982; Rosenthal, 1978; Schmidt, 1992). Thus, Krol (1978) differs from the other reviews in that it yields statistical estimates of desegregation's impact. Krol concluded overall that the average effect of desegregation on African American achievement is .16 standard deviations, which can be understood more meaningfully as from 1½ to 3 months gain per academic year. (The amount of gain depends on the kind of test.) The subset of studies with good control groups yielded a more modest estimate of .10 of a standard deviation in gain. Although these estimates are both positive they are not statistically significant — that is, typical canons of quantitative analysis would not allow one to conclude that there is an unambiguous positive impact of desegregation on achievement from these data.

The last of the pre-1984 reviews was a meta-analysis authored by Mahard and Crain (1983). These reviewers examined a group of 93 studies including, atypically, some in which *ability* measures, such as IQ, rather than measures designed to tap achievement were the dependent variable. The mean effect size in this review was .08, very similar to that produced by Krol for the "better studies." However, these reviewers argue that this underestimates desegregation's real potential since this estimate is based on studies which included students who transferred from segregated to desegregated systems as well as those of students who experienced only desegregated education. Examining 23 studies which compared the achievement of desegregated African American students in kindergarten and first grade with that of their segregated peers, Mahard and Crain found a much larger effect, .25 of a standard deviation, roughly one-third of a grade level. Also they note that studies using measures of ability, like IQ, found improvement similar to those which utilized achievement measures (Mahard & Crain, 1983).

In 1984 the National Institute of Education commissioned meta-analytic review papers from seven scholars to examine the impact of school desegregation on African American academic achievement. These individuals agreed on a set of methodological criteria to be used in selecting a core group of studies for their analyses. Then each proceeded to conduct a meta-analysis and to write a paper detailing his conclusions. Three of the reviews are precisely what one would expect from the foregoing description, although individual authors tended to add or delete a few studies from the core group of 19 (Armor, 1984; Miller & Carlson, 1984; Stephan, 1984). Although Walberg (1984) presents the results of a meta-analysis of the core studies, his emphasis is on comparing the impact of desegregation with other educational policies or practices. Wortman (1984) reports a meta-analysis on a group of 31 studies which he felt were worthy of inclusion as well as one performed on the basic 19. Crain's (1984a) review challenges the wisdom of selecting only 19 studies for review on a number of cogent grounds. Cook's (1984) paper examines the six others and asks what overall conclusions flow from the project as a whole. Thus I will focus on Cook's paper, referring to the others where necessary. However, before turning to that I will discuss an important issue raised by Crain's paper.

Crain's major point is that the panel's procedures led them inadvertently but systematically to underestimate desegregation's effect. Specifically, the panel selected longitudinal studies, rejecting cross-sectional survey studies as methodologically inferior. They also rejected all longitudinal studies which used different pre- and post-tests. However, use of these inclusion criteria almost automatically results in exclusion of virtually all of the studies of desegregation conducted with kindergartners and first graders, since pretests for these age groups measure "readiness" as opposed to achievement which is measured by the posttests. Crain demonstrates that studies of children of these grade levels, no matter what their design, yield both larger estimates of desegregation's impact and more consistently positive results than studies with other age groups. Furthermore, he argues that these studies are representative of the kind of desegregation most children experience, pointing out that most desegregation plans desegregate children from kindergarten or grade one on up. This means that in the early years of a desegregation program, when research is most likely to be carried out, older children enter desegregated schools having prior experience with segregated education. Their experience is thus quite different from that of the children who follow them, who will start in desegregated rather than in segregated schools just as the kindergarten and first grade students in the rejected studies did.

Cook (1984) concedes that Crain has raised an important issue, but fails to concur that the panel has made a fundamental error. He points out that a number of the studies Crain discusses stem from one voluntary desegregation program, and thus questions the generality of Crain's conclusions. In addition, he notes some possible technical problems in Crain's analysis. I am inclined to give more credence to Crain's concerns than Cook does for two reasons. First, it seems to me eminently plausible that transferring from a segregated to a desegregated school might cause some adjustment problems which would not occur if one started school in a desegregated environment. If one wants to know the effect of desegregated schooling in general, it seems unwise to focus on students who have had to make a transition, especially if the study measuring desegregation's impact is carried out very close to the time of transition. Secondly, the technical criticisms which Cook raises with regard to Crain's work do not seem to me to challenge Crain's basic conclusion. In sum, Crain's paper raises the real possibility that the panel underestimated the academic impact of desegregation. This caveat should be kept in mind as I proceed next to summarize the results of the panel's work.

Cook (1984) ends his paper with several conclusions based on his own analyses and his examination of the other commissioned papers. Since these conclusions seem to be a fair summary of the project's overall outcome, I will structure the following discussion around them. First, consistent with every other review of which I am aware, Cook concludes that desegregation does not undermine African American achievement. None of the individual 1984 papers even suggested a negative impact of desegregation on African American achievement.

Secondly, Cook concludes that on the average desegregation did not lead to an increase in the mathematics achievement of African American students, a conclusion consistent with that of Armor (1984), Miller & Carlson (1984), and Stephan (1984).

Wortman reported a small positive effect on math in the core studies and larger one on his set of 31 studies. Crain (1984a) and Walberg (1984) do not deal with the distinction between reading and mathematics gains in any detailed way.

In contrast to the situation with mathematics, Cook concludes that desegregation does increase the mean reading level of African American students. All of the panelists who dealt with the issue agreed that reading gains occurred. Their estimates ranged from .06 to .26 of a standard deviation which translates into roughly a two to six weeks gain. These gains were generally computed *per study* rather than per year. Interpreting this gain is complex. First, one can think of it as a rough estimate of what is gained in a year of desegregation, since most of the studies included in the core group spanned just one year. On the other hand, there is no evidence to justify multiplying this effect by 12 to estimate gain over a student's entire elementary and secondary career. In fact, there is some counter evidence (Mahard & Crain, 1983). While the small number of studies spanning two years tended to find larger effects than those covering just one, the reverse was the case for the three studies which lasted three years. Further, the majority of the studies in the core covered the first year of desegregation which may differ from later years in important ways, including its impact on achievement.

Cook also urges caution in interpreting these results for the following reason. Although some mean or average gain seems clearly present, other methods of looking at the data do not lead to such an optimistic conclusion. Specifically, the median scores in these reviews, the scores which have an equal number of scores above and below them, were almost always greater than zero but lower than the means. Also, the modal gain scores, the most frequently found scores, were near zero. The explanation for these apparently somewhat contradictory findings is that all of the analyses included some studies with unusually large gains. Such gains contributed substantially to raising the overall means. However, they had a much less potent effect on the medians and modes.

These somewhat technical distinctions are worth making because of their implications for the interpretation of the data. Specifically, the gain in mean reading scores suggests that desegregation, on the average, will bring academic benefits. However, the less impressive results for the medians and modes suggest that not all instances of desegregation will lead to academic gains.

The fact that some schools show atypically large gains highlights the fact that desegregation is a very varied process and that different instances of this process can be expected to have very different outcomes. It also suggests the potential utility of systematically exploring the achievement research to see if certain types of desegregation experiences tend to be associated with particularly large or small achievement gains. This task is difficult to achieve with the NIE-sponsored reviews for several reasons. First, the core group included only 19 studies, and these studies were of quite similar situations. Specifically almost all of them involved just one or two years of desegregation, making comparison between initial and later gains difficult. Similarly, 15 of the 19 core studies were of voluntary desegregation, making comparison between voluntary and mandatory programs problematic. Nonetheless, these reviews and others, especially Mahard and Crain (1983), do give some tentative indications about the characteristics of desegregation programs which may have a more positive impact on academic achievement than others.

One suggestion which emerges repeatedly in the reviews is that desegregation may be most effective when carried out in elementary school, especially in the early elementary years (St. John, 1975; Cook, 1984; Crain, 1984a; Stephan, 1984). Crain (1984a) and Mahard and Crain (1983) present the most detailed discussion of this issue and make the strongest case for this point of view. First, Mahard and Crain (1983) point out that all 11 samples of students they examined which began desegregation in kindergarten and over three-fourths of the 44 groups of students who were desegregated as first graders showed achievement gains. In sharp contrast, roughly 50% of the samples of students in the more advanced grades did so. In addition, the estimated effect size of the changes for the kindergartners and first graders is greater than those previously discussed, being .25 of a standard deviation or roughly equivalent to one-third of a year in school. Thus Mahard and Crain (1983) conclude that the academic "effects of desegregation are almost completely restricted to the early primary grades" (p.125). As discussed previously, Cook (1984) raises several technical issues which somewhat weaken the apparent strength of Mahard and Crain's data. Yet Cook's own analysis of the NIE core studies supports the idea that early desegregation is the most beneficial by demonstrating gains which are largest in the second grade and which tend to decrease markedly thereafter.

There is also some indication that the type of desegregation program may make a difference in achievement effects. Mahard and Crain (1983) present data suggesting that metropolitan desegregation plans may have stronger achievement effects than others. This finding is consistent with the suggestion made by Cook (1984) and Stephan (1984) that voluntary plans may have a greater impact than mandatory ones, since virtually all of the metropolitan plans in Mahard and Crain's sample involved the voluntary transfer of African American students from inner-city to suburban schools. Their findings are also consistent with Bradley and Bradley's (1977) finding that all the studies of open enrollment programs, another kind of voluntary program, reported positive effects.

The search for other variables which influence the impact desegregation has on African American students' academic achievement is greatly impeded by the lack of information about the characteristics of the schools studied as well as the method-ological problems discussed earlier. Thus rather than speculate on the basis of single studies or inadequate groups of studies I will now turn to examining the impact of desegregation on Hispanic American students' academic achievement.

School Desegregation and Hispanic American Achievement
There is little empirical evidence about the impact of school desegregation on the academic achievement of Hispanic American students (Orfield, 1986). During the heyday of empirical work on the effect of desegregation on student outcomes, roughly 1968 to 1975, Hispanic American students were virtually ignored. The extent of the phenomenon is illustrated by the fact that several discussions on the impact of desegregation on Hispanic American students published at that time cite no more than two or three studies (Carter, 1979; Weinberg, 1970, 1977). This lack of attention to how desegregation affects Hispanic American students undoubtedly had a number of causes, including the fact that the courts were still in the process of deciding whether Hispanic American students would be treated as an identifiable ethnic minority group eligible for the same legal protections as African Americans under the *Brown* decision. In more recent years, as the number of Hispanic Americans living in the U.S. has burgeoned

rapidly, a considerable amount of attention has been turned to issues related to the education of Hispanic American children (Alvarez, 1992; Arias, 1986; Carrasquillo, 1991; Duran, 1983; Gonzalez, 1990; Meier & Stewart, 1991; Valencia, 1991). However, with some exceptions which will be discussed below, this work has not focused on the impact of desegregation.

Another factor which makes it difficult to assess the impact of desegregation on the achievement of Hispanic American students generally is that the relatively few studies of this issue which are available deal almost exclusively with Mexican Americans. Although Mexican Americans and other Hispanic American groups certainly share certain aspects of language and culture, there is tremendous diversity within the groups which fall under the label Hispanic American (Arias, 1986; Carrasquillo, 1991; Meier & Stewart, 1991; Orfield, 1986). Thus, it is a mistake to assume that research results coming from the study of one of these groups can be applied automatically to others.

The major published source of information on the impact of desegregation on Hispanic American students is a study conducted in Riverside, California (Gerard & Miller, 1975). This massive longitudinal study included over 1,700 students, 650 of whom were Mexican American. (The district was approximately 10% Mexican American, 6% African American, and 84% white.) The analyses presented in this study are numerous and somewhat complicated. However, the ultimate conclusion drawn is that desegregation did not significantly influence the achievement level of any of the groups, including the Mexican American children.

Several other studies report more positive findings. For example, in a study of over 1,500 Mexican American junior high school students, Kimball (cited in Weinberg, 1977) found that the higher the proportion of white students in the schools he studied, the greater the minority-group achievement. Feshbach and Adelman (1969) studied African American and Mexican American junior high school boys bused to a university-based private school. Not surprisingly, both groups gained markedly in achievement compared to a control group. Mahard and Crain (1980) used data from the National Longitudinal Study of the high school graduating class of 1972 to explore the impact of desegregation on Hispanic Americans. They found a positive correlation between attending predominantly white schools and the achievement scores of Cuban, Puerto Rican, and Mexican American students. Arias (1989) cited in Alkin (1992) concluded that desegregation increased the achievement of Hispanic American and African American students when it raised the average socioeconomic background of the students' peers, but not otherwise. Finally, Morrison's (1972) study found that a group of desegregated Hispanic American children gained significantly more in achievement during their elementary school years than did a control group of Hispanic American peers. It is not clear why these studies suggest positive academic outcomes for Hispanic American students whereas Gerard and Miller's study does not. However, it is important to note that, to my knowledge, there is no social evidence suggesting negative academic outcomes of desegregation for Hispanic American students.

Two kinds of more recent studies lend indirect support to the idea that segregation is implicated in the poor academic performance of many Hispanic American students. First, there are a number of studies which document the adverse educational conditions under which Hispanic American students in segregated schools have often labored (Gonzalez 1990; Menchaca & Valencia, 1990; Orfield, 1988). Second, there are studies which demonstrate a strong inverse relationship between the proportion of the school's student body which is Hispanic American and the overall level of student achievement (Espinosa & Ochoa, 1986; Jaeger 1987 cited in Orfield, 1988; Valencia, 1984). It is important to point out that the existence of such a relationship does not lead inevitably to the conclusion that segregation is harmful academically or that desegregation would help. It could merely reflect the fact that Hispanic American students on the average come from homes which are lower in social class than white students and that social class plays a major role in influencing students' achievement (Jencks et al., 1972). Nonetheless, these studies do document the fact that Hispanic American students, like African American students, tend to be concentrated in schools in which achievement is relatively low, an environmental condition which seems likely to inhibit rather than bolster their achievement (Rumberger & Willms, 1992; Summers & Wolfe, 1977).

In summary, the data on the impact of desegregation on the academic achievement of Hispanic Americans, while extremely fragmentary, are consistent with the information on its impact on African American achievement. Results appear to be either neutral or positive. However, whereas the preponderance of evidence suggests a positive outcome for African Americans, the most recent, extended and sophisticated study of Hispanic Americans does not. Clearly more research is needed before any firm conclusions can be drawn.

One further issue needs to be dealt with before leaving this topic. It is not uncommon for discussions of desegregation's impact on Hispanic Americans to discuss its impact on African Americans and then to either assume or to make explicit assertions that "there is no reason to believe the outcomes (of desegregation) for (Hispanic Americans) differ" (Carter & Segura, 1979, p. 325). This assumption ignores two potentially very important differences. First, a substantial number of Hispanic American children may know little if any English when they first enter school. Thus, many Hispanic American students face a language barrier in schools that is less common for African Americans (Arias, 1986). Second, to the extent that culture influences students' preparation for and reaction to schooling, Hispanic American children may be different from African Americans, as indeed different segments of the population labelled Hispanic American differ from each other (Carrasquillo, 1991).

It is clearly beyond the scope of this chapter to evaluate thoroughly how the linguistic and cultural differences which exist between African American and Hispanic American Americans may effect desegregation's impact. However, it is important to note that constructive thought has been given to the issue of how one can handle the needs of children who are not proficient in English while at the same time avoiding or minimizing racial and ethnic isolation (California State Department of Education, 1983; Carter, 1979; Carter & Chatfield, 1986; Fernandez, 1978; Fernandez & Guskin, 1978; Garcia, 1976; Gonzalez, 1979; Haro, 1977; Heleen, 1987; Milan, 1978; National Institute of Education, 1977; Roos, 1978).

School Desegregation and White Achievement
There are a substantial number of studies on the impact of desegregation on white students' achievement, although nowhere near the number that have looked at African American students' achievement. This situation is hardly surprising since desegregation is often seen as a strategy for improving the achievement of minority group students and there is little reason to expect that desegregation in and of itself will improve the academic achieve-

ment of white students as measured by standardized tests. However, the issue of the impact of desegregation on white achievement is important since one of the major concerns expressed by whites opposing desegregation is that it will undermine their children's academic progress. Whether this concern is based on knowledge about the link between school social class and student achievement level (Coleman et al., 1966) or on racial prejudice, it is sufficiently widespread that the issue merits attention in this chapter.

The major review available on desegregation and white achievement is St. John's (1975). There is also an earlier review of the literature by Weinberg (1970). These reviews were completed over two decades ago. Thus it is reasonable to question their usefulness today since relations between whites and African Americans have changed significantly in that time as previously noted. However, extremely little research produced on this topic since the mid-1970s. Therefore, I will present a summary of Weinberg's and St. John's conclusions and then briefly discuss the most important studies relevant to this topic which have been published since those reviews.

After examining dozens of studies, many of which had serious methodological flaws, Weinberg (1970) concluded that "white children fail to suffer any learning disadvantage from desegregation" (p. 88). This finding is consistent with every other summary statement on this issue of which I am aware. For example, Orfield (1978) wrote:

> What is remarkable, however, is the consistency of the finding that the desegregation process itself has little if any effect on the educational success of white students, as measured by achievement test scores. . . . Researchers operating from very different scholarly and ideological starting points support this general finding. (p. 124)

St. John's (1975) review cites 24 studies of the impact of school desegregation on white achievement. Many of these do not meet strict standards of methodological rigor. However, the pattern of results is clear. The overwhelming majority suggest no impact in either direction. When statistically significant effects do appear, they are more often positive than negative. However, the overall pattern is such that St. John (1975) concluded, "Desegregation has rarely lowered academic achievement for either black or white children" (p. 36). This is true not only for studies of situations in which African Americans have been bused to previously white schools but also for the few available studies of situations in which white children were bused to previously African American schools.

The only two major studies of which I am aware of desegregation and white achievement not covered in the Weinberg and St. John reviews do little to change their overall conclusion. The first of these, Singer, Gerard, and Redfearn (1975), concludes on the basis of the massive study in Riverside, California described earlier that desegregation has no effect on white students' achievement. For example, they found that the standardized reading achievement scores of white elementary school students stayed consistent from the pre-desegregation time period to post- measures taken from one to five years after desegregation. The second study, Patchen (1982), also concludes there is little relation between the racial composition of the schools students attend and white academic achievement. Patchen did find some indication that white students who had attended majority African American elementary schools had lower achievement scores in high school than their peers who had attended majority white schools, but the effect was *very slight* (one percent of the variance in such scores). He concluded with regard to high school racial composition that "there were no substantial associations between the average grades or the average achievement scores of whites and the racial composition of their schools" (Patchen, 1983, p. 303), although he did find some decrement in academic effort in whites in majority African American schools.

Post-secondary Educational and Occupational Outcomes of School Desegregation

As indicated earlier, there has been a great deal of research on the impact of desegregation on achievement test scores. However, it is important not to overemphasize achievement scores as an end in and of themselves. They are, at best, fairly weak indicators of college grades or occupational success (Jencks, et al., 1972; Marston, 1971; McClelland, 1973). In addition, there is evidence that they predict academic success less well for African American students than for white students, although this phenomenon may be limited to African Americans enrolled in predominantly white institutions (Fleming, 1990). Such scores have received disproportionate attention because they are widely administered and hence convenient rather than because they are an outcome of premier importance.

In the past decade or so the work of a small group of researchers, most notably Braddock, Crain and McPartland (1984), has opened up a new and potentially very important line of inquiry — the impact on desegregation on later life outcomes for minority students such as college choice and occupational attainment. Braddock and Dawkins (1984) make the case for this line of inquiry by pointing out that desegregation may have long-term social and economic consequences for minorities by providing "(a) access to useful social networks of job information, contacts and sponsorship, (b) socialization for aspirations and entrance into `nontraditional' career lines with higher income returns, (c) development of interpersonal skills that are useful in interracial contexts, (d) reduced social inertia — increased tolerance of and willingness to participate in desegregated environments, and (e) avoidance of negative attributions which are often associated with 'black' institutions" (p.367). (e.g., Braddock, 1980; Braddock & McPartland, 1982; Coleman et al., 1966; Crain, 1970; Crain & Weisman, 1972; McPartland & Crain, 1980).

The evidence concerning desegregation's impact on such outcomes is quite sparse and virtually all of it concerns such outcomes for African Americans, rather than for members of other racial or ethnic groups. Furthermore, almost all of these studies explicitly or tacitly use the word *desegregated* as a synonym for racially–*mixed*. Thus they are generally not studies of the outcomes of specific desegregation programs. Yet I believe these studies are well worth discussing because of the fundamental importance of such outcomes — to minority groups members in particular and to American society in general.

Braddock and Dawkins (1984) point out that school desegregation can influence the *amount* and the *type* of post-secondary education African Americans receive, their academic success in the post-secondary years and their chances of attaining a well-paying job. For none of these outcomes is the evidence so clear cut that the issue of desegregation's impact can be definitively settled. Yet, some data suggestive of positive effects are available.

The data on the impact of desegregation on the amount of post-secondary education African Americans complete has been explored in a number of studies. Crain and Weisman (1972) utilized retrospective data to explore college attendance and completion patterns in a relatively small sample of Northern African American adults. They found that roughly one-third of the African American males from desegregated schools went to college compared to 24% from segregated schools. Segregated and desegregated African American females evidenced much smaller differences in the same direction. College *completion* rates were also higher for African American males and females with desegregated schooling at the elementary or secondary level than for their segregated peers. Crain and Weisman's analysis suggests that these patterns were not due to initial differences in the family background of individuals attending segregated and desegregated schools. Armor (1972) reported positive effects of two small voluntary desegregation programs on college enrollment rates as well as the quality of the institution of higher education in which African American students enrolled, although in one case in which the data allowed exploration of the issue a higher dropout rate for the formerly desegregated students dissipated this enrollment advantage by the end of the sophomore year. Another study with a somewhat limited sample concluded that African American students who had participated in a voluntary desegregation program had higher high school and college graduate rates than a control group of peers who attended segregated schools (Crain et al., 1986, cited in Jaynes & Williams, 1989).

In yet another study, Crain and Mahard (1978) explored similar issues with a database more adequate to the job. Using data on 3,000 African American high school graduates, they replicated the earlier suggestion of benefits of desegregation for those living in the North, finding that desegregation was associated with college enrollment and persistence for these individuals. However, this relationship was not statistically significant for African American students living in the South. It should be noted, though, that another analysis of this same data set using different control variables and exclusion criteria found no statistically significant relationship between desegregation and college attendance in either region (Eckland, 1979).

Braddock and McPartland (1982) utilized this same database merged with later follow-up surveys to explore the same issue. Their results are moderately consistent with Crain and Mahard's. Controlling for family background and the students' academic qualifications, they found a weak trend suggesting a positive impact of early desegregation on enrollment in four-year colleges for African Americans living in the North. However, such a relationship was not apparent in the data for their Southern peers. Since the studies just mentioned constitute, to my knowledge, most of those which deal with the impact of desegregation on the amount of post-secondary education African Americans complete, it seems reasonable to conclude that, although desegregation has no measurable impact on college attainment for Southern African Americans, it appears to have a positive, though weak, effect for those living in the North.

Another issue which these researchers have explored is whether desegregation leads African Americans to be somewhat more likely to attend predominately white colleges rather than predominately African American colleges. There is, of course, some controversy over whether this is a desirable outcome since it is clear that attendance at predominately white institutions poses certain very real problems for African American students which they are not as likely to confront at historically black colleges and universities (HBCUs) (Allen, 1988; Allen, Epps, & Haniff, 1991; Nieves, 1977; Smith, 1981). However, researchers working in this area tend to argue that such an outcome is valuable since attendance at predominately white institutions tends to have positive job market consequences for several reasons. For example, research has documented the importance of desegregated social networks for job attainment (Braddock & McPartland, 1987). In addition, some employers tend to derogate degrees received from HBCUs and prefer African American graduates from white institutions (Braddock & McPartland, 1983; McPartland & Crain, 1980; Crain, 1984a). Such factors may be at least partly responsible for indications that African American graduates of white institutions, especially African American male graduates, earn more than roughly equivalent graduates from African American institutions, (Braddock, 1985).

There are three studies which suggest that desegregation at the pre-college level encourages African American students to enroll in predominately white colleges (Braddock, 1980; Braddock & McPartland, 1982; Dawkins, 1991). The first showed a fairly strong positive relation between attending a desegregated high school and enrolling in a predominately white college. However, the number of students and colleges involved in this study, which was carried out in one Southern state, was relatively small. More convincing evidence comes from a second study based on the data from 3,000 African American high school graduates. Utilizing controls for variables such as the student's social-class background and high school grades, this study found that attendance at predominately white institutions was more likely for students who had prior experience with desegregation than for others. Braddock and McPartland (1982) interpret this as evidence that prior desegregation experience frees African American students to risk attendance at a predominately white institution, the only readily available kind of four-year college available in the North. Finally, Dawkins (1991) uses data from the National Survey of Black Americans to show a positive relation between the racial composition of the high schools respondents attended and the racial composition of the colleges in which they enrolled.

One of the major reasons there is interest in whether school desegregation influences the kind and amount of college education obtained by minority students is that this has an important bearing on occupational outcomes. The first evidence of which I am aware on this topic appeared in studies by Crain (1970) and Crain and Weisman (1972). These reports, based on the same set of survey data, concluded that "Alumni of integrated schools are more likely to move into occupations traditionally closed to blacks; they also earn slightly more money, even after education is controlled" (Crain & Weisman, 1972, p. 161). More recent evidence has been mixed. A recent study by Trent (1991) failed to replicate this finding. However, another recent study by Dawkins (1991) based on the National Survey of Black Americans did find a modest positive link between attending a desegregated high school and later occupational attainment. Although regional and age cohort differences in this effect were apparent with the Southern sample being least likely to show this link, this link was consistently found for the three youngest non-Southern samples. One factor which might be conducive to creating this relationship when it is found is that employers show relatively favorable attitudes toward hiring minority group graduates of suburban high schools (Braddock, Crain, McPartland, & Dawkins, 1986). Thus, desegregation efforts which transfer students from urban to suburban settings would presumably have positive job market consequences for the minority students involved. More recently, several studies have focused on the impact of the racial composition of the *college* African American students attend on their occupational attainment. Although the results vary somewhat from study to study, a recent review of this work concludes "On balance, African American graduates (especially males) of predominantly white institutions seem to receive labor-market advantages over those from predominantly African American institutions (Braddock, 1985, p. 18).

In summary, attending desegregated schools appears to have some positive impact on the kind of jobs African Americans get as well as on the amount and type of college education they undertake. Although the evidence to date is sparse and suggests that these effects are moderated by both region and gender, these outcomes are so crucial for individual's social position and economic well-being that any reliable indication they are influenced by desegregation is of real importance.

The Effect of School Desegregation
on African American Self-esteem

A considerable body of research has explored the impact of school desegregation on the self-esteem of African American children. There is very little comparable data on its impact on the self-esteem of other groups, although a few exceptions to this generalization can be found (Green, Miller, & Gerard, 1975; Sheehan, 1980). However, in the last two decades or so research has suggested that the belief that African American children in segregated environments have low self-esteem, which sparked much of this research, is not well-founded. Although this belief was widespread for a substantial period of time (Cross, 1980), the evidence supporting it appears flawed. First, there were some important methodological problems which characterized many of the studies upon which this conclusion was based (Banks, 1976; Spencer, 1976). Second, Cross (1980) and others have pointed out that the interpretation of the findings from these studies has not been entirely consistent with the data. Finally, the social conditions in which African Americans live have changed substantially in the last several decades, which may well have implications for levels of self-esteem. Reviews of the literature published in the past 10 to 20 years have generally concluded that African Americans show the same or possibly higher levels of self-esteem as whites (Cross, 1980; Epps, 1978; Gordon, 1980; St. John, 1975; Taylor, 1976).

Thus, the attention directed towards the issue of desegregation and self-esteem may have been out of proportion to the problem. It does seem likely that a state-enforced system of segregation might undermine the personal and group self-regard of those subject to such a system. However, recent studies, at least, suggest that lack of self-esteem is not a major problem for African American children. It also does not appear to be a major problem for Hispanic American children (Carter & Segura, 1979), although some researchers have suggested that the self-esteem of Mexican American students may be lower than that of whites (Malry, 1968; Parsons, 1965). Furthermore, there is no strong reason to believe that desegregation under the conditions which many minority children have experienced it would automatically increase self-esteem or regard for their own group. For example, Hare (1977) argues that one might expect to find a short-term increase in personal and academic anxiety associated with desegregation since many minority children enter somewhat hostile environments and/or ones which provide increased academic competition.

The major reviews of school desegregation and African American self-concept or self-esteem generally conclude that desegregation has no clear-cut consistent impact (Epps, 1975; 1978; Stephan, 1978; St. John, 1975; Weinberg, 1977). For example, Stephan (1978) reviewed a total of 20 studies. Five of these found that self-esteem was higher in African Americans in segregated schools and the remaining 15 suggested no statistically significant impact of desegregation. Although some of the other reviews, most notably Weinberg (1977), present a somewhat more positive view, none claim a consistent positive effect of desegregation on African American self-esteem. Although there are almost no data available to test this proposition directly, Epps' (1975) suggestion that desegregation is likely to have a very varied effect on self-esteem depending on the specific experiences which students have seems eminently sensible. The conclusion that low self-esteem is not a problem for African American students, combined with the evidence that desegregation does not have any strong consistent impact on self-esteem, understandably led to a sharp diminution in the amount of research on these topics after the mid 1970s.

School Desegregation and Intergroup Relations
Rationale for Research on this Topic

As previously indicated, the lion's share of the research on the effect of school desegregation has focused on its impact on academic achievement. However, a fairly large body of research has also addressed its impact on intergroup relations, most especially on interracial attitudes. Although many of the parties concerned with desegregated schools tend to be relatively uninterested in how interracial schooling affects intergroup relations, there are some compelling arguments in favor of giving more thought to the matter. First, the fact is that much social learning occurs whether or not it is planned. Hence, I would contend that an interracial school cannot choose to have no effect on intergroup relations. It can only choose whether the effect will be planned or unplanned. Even a laissez-faire policy concerning intergroup relations conveys a message — the message that either school authorities see no serious problem with relations as they have developed or that they do not feel that the nature of intergroup relations is a legitimate concern for an educational institution. So those who argue that schools should not attempt to influence intergroup relations miss the fundamental fact that whether or not they consciously try to influence such relations, schools are extremely likely to do so in one way or another (Schofield, 1982/1989).

Because of the pervasive residential segregation in our society, students frequently have their first relatively extended interracial experiences in schools. Hence, whether racial hostility and stereotyping grow or diminish may be critically influenced by the experiences students have there. While there is still considerable disagreement about whether the development of close interracial ties should be a high priority in this country, there is a growing awareness of the societal costs of intergroup hostility. Hence, unless interracial schools are carefully planned there is the possibility that they will exacerbate the very social tensions that many initially hoped they would diminish.

A number of considerations suggest the importance of turning from an almost exclusive concentration on the academic outcomes of schooling and focusing at least some attention on non-academic outcomes such as intergroup relations. First, the ability to work effectively with out-group members is an important skill for both majority and minority group members in a pluralistic society which is striving to overcome a long history of discrimination in education and employment. In fact, a recent report commissioned by the U.S. Department of Labor concluded that the ability to work effectively in a context of cultural diversity is one of the basic competencies which is required to perform effectively in the U.S. labor force (SCANS, 1991). Many individuals lack this ability (Pettigrew & Martin, 1987). Current population trends make this an increasing important aspect of children's education. Second, Jencks et al. (1972) as well as others have suggested that more attention should be paid to structuring schools so that they are reasonably pleasurable environments since schools not only prepare students for future roles but are also the setting in which they spend nearly one third of their waking hours for a significant portion of their lives. This line of argument suggests that positive relationships within the school setting may be of some value in and of themselves.

Finally, there is the possibility that social relations between students in interracial schools may effect their academic achievement and their occupational success (Braddock & McPartland, 1987; Crain, 1970; Katz, 1964; McPartland & Crain 1980; Pettigrew, 1967; Rosenberg & Simmons, 1971; U.S. Commission on Civil Rights, 1967). For example, Katz's (1964) work suggests that the academic performance of African Americans may be markedly impaired in biracial situations which pose a social threat. The potentially constructive effect of positive intergroup relations on minority group outcomes is highlighted by Braddock and McPartland's (1987) finding that African American high school graduates who use desegregated social networks in their job search are likely to attain positions with a substantially higher salary than are those who use segregated social networks. Perhaps not surprisingly they also work in environments which have, on the average, a higher percentage of white workers. Consistent with these findings, a study of the Hispanic American students involved in the Riverside desegregation study mentioned previously found that those who retrospectively reported having been friends with students of other racial or ethnic background completed more years of schooling and scored higher on a measure of occupational attainment than those who did not (Mercer & Phillips, 1987).

The Effect of School Desegregation on Intergroup Relations
This research on the impact of desegregation on intergroup relations can be roughly grouped into three basic categories. First, numerous studies do things like (a) compare the attitudes of

students in a segregated school to those of students in a similar desegregated school or (b) look at changes in student attitudes and behavior associated with the length of time children have been desegregated. Such studies generally give relatively little information about the nature of the schools studied assuming implicitly that desegregation is an independent variable which has been operationalized similarly in a wide variety of circumstances. Such studies often contain analyses which examine the impact of student background variables like race or sex on reactions to desegregation. However, they generally do not directly address the impact of specific policies or programs on students.

The second basic type of research in this area consists of large correlational studies which attempt to relate a wide range of school characteristics, policies, and practices to particular outcomes. Well-known studies of this kind are Patchen (1982), Forehand, Ragosta and Rock (1976) and a substantial body of work by Hallinan and her colleagues concerning the impact of a variety of classroom characteristics, such as classroom racial composition and size, on intergroup friendship (Hallinan, 1982; Hallinan, 1986; Hallinan & Smith, 1985; Hallinan & Teixeira, 1987a, 1987b).

A third type of research in this area experimentally investigates the impact of particular narrowly defined innovations on intergroup relations within desegregated schools, thus allowing fairly clear conclusions about the causal linkage between these innovations and student outcomes. The large majority of this work concerns various techniques for inducing cooperation between African American and white students on various kinds of academic tasks. (For reviews see Bossert, 1988-89; Johnson & Johnson, 1982, 1992; Johnson, Johnson & Maruyama, 1983; Slavin 1983a, 1983b; Slavin, Sharan, Katan, & Hertz-Lazarowitz, 1985). However, another body of research both demonstrates how the gap in the status associated with the social categories such as African American and white in our society influences children's interaction patterns and explores ways of mitigating the impact of this status differential (Aronson & Gonzalez, 1988; Cohen, 1980; Cohen, Lockheed, & Lohman, 1976; Cohen & Loran, 1995a, 1995b; Cohen & Roper, 1972).

There have been several reviews within roughly the last two decades of the first type of research — work studying the link between desegregation and intergroup attitudes (Amir, 1976; Cohen, 1975; McConahay, 1978; St. John, 1975; Schofield, 1978;

Schofield & Sagar, 1983). Such reviews tend to look at both studies of specific desegregation plans and of interracial schools, often without differentiating between them. Several themes reappear time and time again in these reviews. The first is dissatisfaction with technical aspects of much of the work. It is important to recognize the extent of these problems. For example McConahay (1979) writes:

> In my own review of over 50 published and unpublished studies (on desegregation and intergroup relations) done between 1960 and 1978, I did not find even one true experiment and only four of the quasi-experimental studies had enough methodological rigor to make them worth reporting in any detail. (p. 1) (e.g., Gerard & Miller, 1975; Schofield & Sagar, 1977; Shaw, 1973; Silverman & Shaw, 1973)

The situation has not changed markedly in the years since McConahay wrote these words.

A second theme common to most of the reviews is that the extant research does not allow confident statements that *consistent* effects exist. St. John's (1975) review captures the tone of many of the others in suggesting that the most striking feature of the research is the inconsistency of the findings. Many studies suggest that desegregation tends to lead to more positive intergroup attitudes (Gardner, Wright, & Dee, 1970; Jansen & Gallagher, 1966; Kingsley, 1989; Levi, 1988; Mann, 1959; Sheehan, 1980; Singer, 1966; U.S. Commission on Civil Rights, 1967). Others suggest precisely the opposite (Barber, 1968; Dentler & Elkins, 1967; Taylor, 1967). Still others suggest that desegregation has a positive effect on the attitudes of whites and negative effect on the attitudes of African Americans (McWhirt, 1967) or vice versa (Crooks, 1970; Kurokawa, 1971; Webster, 1961). Finally, some like Lombardi (1962), Trubowitz (1969), and Schwarzwald, Amir, & Crain (1992) suggest no overall effect.

Third, virtually all of the reviews emphasize the wide variety of situations covered by the existing literature. They often point out that not only do the student bodies in the schools studied vary sharply in their age and social class, but that the proportion of students from different racial and ethnic backgrounds has also varied dramatically. Further, they go on to point out that given the variation in particular circumstances it is reasonable, perhaps inevitable, that different instances of desegregation will have

varying effects on intergroup relations. This point is well illustrated by the study by Schwarzwald, Amir, and Crain cited above.
This study found no overall impact of school desegregation at the
junior high and high school level on the latter intergroup attitudes
and beliefs of Israeli soldiers from different ethnic backgrounds
(Western vs. European). However, it did find that aspects of
students' school experience, such as the gap in educational
attainment between students of Western and Middle Eastern
background, influenced affective and behavioral reactions to out-
group members.

Fourth, the reviews tend to concern themselves exclusively
with African American-white relations since so few studies in this
area include Hispanic American or other minority students. The
one major study of desegregation and intergroup relations in a
situation involving Hispanic Americans is the previously mentioned
study of Riverside, California's desegregation experience. Gerard,
Jackson, and Conolley (1975) demonstrated substantial ethnic
cleavage between African American, Mexican American, and white
students even after several years of desegregated schooling.
However, the study did not address the question of whether, even
with such cleavage, attitudes toward out-group members were
more positive than they would have been if the children had
remained in racially isolated schools.

The reviews in this area are also similar to each other in being
literary reviews rather than formal meta-analyses. Thus, the most
recent of them (Schofield & Sagar, 1983) explored the possibility
of advancing the state of our knowledge through formal
meta-analytic procedures. For a variety of reasons discussed in
that paper, a formal meta-analysis did not seem appropriate. Since
very few methodologically acceptable studies of desegregation and
intergroup behavior have been published since 1983, the situation
remains the same today.

Thus, the evidence taken as a whole suggests that desegregation has no clearly predictable impact on student intergroup
attitudes. However, there are at least three considerations which
work against documenting positive social outcomes of desegregation when they exist. First, the dependent variables utilized in
many of these studies are often seriously flawed. For example, the
dependent measures used in almost two-thirds of the studies
considered for meta-analysis in Schofield and Sagar (1983) are
structured so that improvement in minority/majority relations can

only occur if students begin to choose outgroup members *rather than* ingroup members. Thus, they embody a hidden and questionable assumption that intergroup relations cannot improve except at the expense of intragroup relations. To some extent, this assumption reflects the nature of social reality. For example, generally a student can only sit next to a few others at lunch. If African American students begin to sit next to whites more frequently than before they are also likely to sit next to African Americans less frequently. However, there is no reason to think that, in general, attitudes towards out-group members can only improve if in-group members are less valued than previously. It seems perfectly reasonable to argue that students might become more accepting of out-group members and at the same time not change their attitudes towards in-group members. Yet, the "zero-sum" measures used in the majority of studies pick up only the changes in out-group acceptance which occur at the expense of the in-group. Another serious measurement problem is the fact that a great many studies have used sociometric techniques which capture information on who children's best friends are, rather than focusing on less stringent but perhaps more appropriate outcomes such as willingness to associate with out-group members (Asher, Singleton, & Taylor, 1982; Schofield & Whitley, 1983; Asher, 1993).

Second, quantitative research on the impact of desegregation on actual in-school intergroup *behavior* is almost non-existent, although there are quite a few qualitative studies of peer behavior in racially and ethnically mixed schools (Hanna, 1982; Metz, 1978, 1986; Peshkin, 1991; Rist, 1979, Schofield, 1982/89). There is an obvious reason for this. As St. John (1975) has pointed out, "Interracial behavior cannot be compared in segregated and integrated settings or before and after desegregation; it can only be examined if the races are in contact" (p.65). Although one might expect a reasonably strong relationship between attitudes and behavior, a plethora of research in social psychology suggests that behavior by no means follows in an automatic way from attitudes (Liska, 1974; Schuman & Johnson, 1976; Wicker, 1969). In fact, one study of a newly desegregated school concluded that although abstract racial stereotypes were intensified, a negative attitudinal outcome, African American and white students came to behave toward each other much more positively (Schofield, 1982/1989). Further, although it is hard to substantiate this conclusion on anything other than a logical basis, it seems in some ways obvious

that interracial behavior is likely to be changed more by desegregation than intergroup attitudes. Unless a school is completely
resegregated internally, the amount of interracial contact has to
increase in a desegregated compared to a segregated environment.
In contrast, attitudes do not have to change.

There is no guarantee that desegregation will promote positive
intergroup behavior. However, the few studies which exist of
actual behavior in desegregated schools suggest that although
cross-racial avoidance is common (Silverman & Shaw, 1973;
Schofield, 1982/1989), cross-race interaction is usually positive or
neutral in tone (Peshkin, 1991; Schofield & Francis, 1982;
Singleton & Asher, 1977). Thus, it is important to keep in mind in
interpreting the mixed findings of research on desegregation and
intergroup attitudes that researchers have generally ignored
intergroup behavior which may be more malleable.

Third, there is some reason to believe that desegregation may
have positive long-term attitudinal and behavioral consequences
that are not captured in the kind of research discussed here which
focuses on short term in-school changes. Although there are just
a few studies that bear on this point, these studies suggest that in
the long run desegregation may help break a cycle of racial
isolation in which both minority and majority group members avoid
each other in spite of the fact that this limits their educational,
occupational, social, and residential choices. For example, two
studies suggest that increasing levels of school desegregation are
related to decreasing amounts of residential segregation (Pearce,
1980; Pearce, Crain, & Farley, 1984). At the individual rather than
the community level, there is evidence that African Americans who
attended desegregated schools are more likely to report living in
integrated neighborhoods and having white social contacts later in
life (Crain, 1984b; Crain & Weisman, 1972). Another more recent
study (Johnson, 1990) found a positive relation between years of
desegregated schooling and acceptance of residential desegregation
for white high school seniors. However, this same relationship was
not found for their minority group peers.

In a quite different area, employment, there is also evidence
that school desegregation breaks down intergroup barriers. For
example, Green (1981, 1982) collected follow-up data in 1980 on
a national sample of African American college freshmen in 1971.
Individuals who had gone to a desegregated high school or college
were more likely to have white work associates and white friends

as adults. In a more recent paper, Braddock, Crain and McPartland (1984) summarize the results of several national surveys (including Green, 1981, 1982) and conclude that African American graduates of desegregated schools are more likely to work in desegregated environments than their peers who attended segregated schools. Additional support for this conclusion comes from Trent's (1991) examination of data from the 1979 cohort of the National Longitudinal Survey of Labor Force Behavior Youth Survey. Desegregated schooling may not only effect one's propensity to work in racially-mixed settings but also one's reactions to this experience. Specifically, Trent (1991) has concluded

> that black, Latin, and white graduates of segregated schools perceive racially-mixed work groups as less friendly than racially-homogeneous ones . . . . Respondents from desegregated schools make . . . much less of a distinction . . . . This suggests that desegregated school experiences can reduce negative feelings toward co-workers of other ethnic groups. (p.35)

There is little comparable research on the long-term impact of desegregation on whites. However, it seems reasonable to expect a parallel effect. Indeed, two studies have demonstrated that the racial composition of white students' high schools or colleges influences the likelihood that they will work in a desegregated setting later in life (Braddock, McPartland, & Trent, 1984; Trent, 1991). Perhaps this finding is at least partially due to the fact that whites in desegregated schools frequently show a decrease in their often initially high levels of fear and avoidance of African Americans and an increasing willingness and ability to work with them (Schofield, 1981; Collins & Noblit, 1977, Noblit & Collins, 1981). This is consistent with Stephan and Rosenfield's (1978) work suggesting that white students who have increased contact with African American and Mexican American peers in desegregated schools develop more positive attitudes towards members of these groups. It is also consistent with the finding of a NORC survey (cited in Aspira of America, 1979) which found that desegregated white students were more likely to report having a close African American friend, having had African American friends visit their homes, and the like.

Conclusions

What have been the outcomes flowing from the desegregation which has been achieved over the past four decades? First, research suggests that desegregation has had some positive effect on the reading skills of African American youngsters. The effect is not large. Neither does it occur in all situations. However, a modest measurable effect does seem to occur. Such is not the case with mathematics skills which seem generally unaffected by desegregation. Second, there is some evidence that desegregation may help to break what can be thought of as a generational cycle of segregation and racial isolation. Although research in this topic is scant and often marred by unavoidable flaws, evidence has begun to accumulate that desegregation may favorably influence important adult outcomes such as college graduation, income, and employment patterns. The measured effects often are weak, yet they are worth consideration because of the vital importance of these outcomes both for minority group members individually and for our society as a whole.

The evidence regarding the role of desegregation on inter-group relations is generally held to be inconclusive and inconsistent. However, three points which are not adequately addressed by the research literature need to be considered here. First, the abolishing of dual systems and the changes required in systems found to have engaged in other sorts of de jure segregation of necessity have changed certain important aspects of minority/majority relations in this country. The existence and legal sanctioning of governmental policies and practices intended to segregate African Americans were and are in and of themselves statements about intergroup relations. Even if no other specific benefits were to flow from the *Brown* decision, in my view, the abolishing of this sort of governmental sanctioned "badge of inferiority" was an important advance in intergroup relations. Second, as discussed earlier, most studies of desegregation and intergroup relations have not addressed the question of how intergroup *behavior* has changed. They have focused almost exclusively on attitudes because "pre" measures of attitudes are available whereas there is no feasible way to measure intergroup behavior in segregated schools. Yet there are indications that desegregated schooling can provide students with valuable behavioral experience which prepares them to function in a pluralistic society. In fact, some studies suggest that this occurs even when racial attitudes become more negative. In addition, there is some evidence that school desegregation may help to break down longstanding patterns of racial isolation in adult social relationships, housing, and the like.

Finally, it is clear that desegregation can be implemented in very different ways and that these differences have marked effects. The literature reviewed here assesses the impact of desegregation as it has been implemented in the past, often in schools which have actively resisted this change.

Thus, this preceding discussion of research on the effects of desegregation should not be read as an assessment of the potential of carefully structured desegregation to effect positive change. Rather, it is a summary of what has occurred, often under circumstances where little if any serious attention was paid to creating a situation likely to improve either academic achievement or intergroup relations. Seeing racially and ethnically heterogeneous schools as having the *potential* to improve student outcomes and focusing more attention on the actual *nature* of the students' experiences to assure that they are as constructive as possible should make it possible to surpass present outcomes.

References

Allen, W. R. (1988). The education of black students on white college campuses: What quality the experience? In M. T. Nettles (Ed.), *Toward black undergraduate student equality in American higher education* (pp. 57–85). Westport, CT: Greenwood Press.

Allen, W. R., Epps, E. G., & Haniff, N. Z. (Eds.). (1991). *College in black and white*. Albany, NY: State University of New York Press.

Alvarez, M. D. (1992). Puerto Rican children on the mainland: Current perspectives. In A. N. Ambert & M. D. Alvarez (Eds.), *Puerto Rican children on the mainland: Interdisciplinary perspectives* (pp. 3–16). New York: Garland Publishing.

Amir, Y. (1976). The role of intergroup contact in change of prejudice and ethnic relations. In P. A. Katz (Ed.), *Towards the elimination of racism* (pp. 245–308). New York: Pergamon Press.

Arias, M. B. (1986). The context of education for Hispanic students: An overview. *American Journal of Education, 95*(1), 26–57.

Armor, D. J. (1972). The evidence on busing. *Public Interest,* 28, 90–124.

Armor, D. J. (1984). The evidence on desegregation and black achievement. In T. Cook, D. Armor, R. Crain, N. Miller, W. Stephan, H. Walberg, & P. Wortman (Eds.), *School desegregation and black achievement* (pp. 43–67). Washington, DC: National Institute of Education.

Aronson, E., & Gonzalez, A. (1988). Desegregation, jigsaw and the Mexican American experience. In P. A. Katz & D. A. Taylor (Eds.), *Eliminating racism: Profiles in controversy* (pp. 301–314). New York: Plenum Press.

Asher, S. R. (1993, May). *Assessing peer relationship processes and outcomes in interracial and inter-ethnic contexts.* Paper presented at the Carnegie Corporation Consultation on Racial and Ethnic Relations in American Schools, New York, NY.

Asher, R. S., Singleton, L. C., & Taylor, A. R. (1982). *Acceptance versus friendship: A longitudinal study of racial integration.* Paper presented at the meeting of the American Educational Research Association, New York, NY.

Aspira of America, Inc. (1979). *Desegregation and the Hispanic in America* (5 Vols.). Unpublished manuscript, New York. (ERIC Document Reproduction Service No. ED 190270–190272)

Banks, W. C. (1976). White preference in blacks: A paradigm in search of a phenomenon. *Psychological Bulletin, 83*(6), 1179–1186.

Barber, R. W. (1968). *The effects of open enrollment on anti-Negro and anti-white prejudices among junior high students in Rochester, New York.* Unpublished doctoral dissertation, University of Rochester.

Bennett, A., & Easton, J. Q. (1988, April). *Voluntary transfer and student achievement: Does it help or hurt?* Paper presented at the meeting of the American Educational Research Association, New Orleans, LA.

Bossert, S. T. (1988-1989). Cooperative activities in the classroom. In E. Z. Rothkopf (Ed.), *Review of research in education* (Vol. 15, pp. 225–250). Washington, DC: American Educational Research Association.

Braddock, J. H., II. (1980). The perpetuation of segregation across levels of education: A behavioral assessment of the contact hypothesis. *Sociology of Education, 53*, 178–186.

Braddock, J. H., II. (1985). School desegregation and black assimilation. *Journal of Social Issues, 41*(3), 9–22.

Braddock, J. H., II., Crain, R. L., & McPartland, J. M. (1984). A long-term view of school desegregation: Some recent studies of graduates as adults. *Phi Delta Kappan, 66*(4), 259–264.

Braddock, J. H., II., Crain, R. L., McPartland, J. M., & Dawkins, M. P. (1986). Applicant race and job placement decisions: A national survey experiment. *Journal of Sociology and Social Policy, 6*, 3–24.

Braddock, J. H., II., & Dawkins, M. P. (1984). Long-term effects of school desegregation on Southern blacks. *Sociological Spectrum, 4*, 365–381.

Braddock, J. H., II., & McPartland, J. M. (1982). Assessing school desegregation effects: New directions in research. In R. Corwin (Ed.), *Research in sociology of education and socialization* (Vol. 3, pp. 259–282). Greenwich, CT: JAI Press.

Braddock, J. H., II., & McPartland, J. M. (1983). *More evidence on social-psychological processes that perpetuate minority segregation: The relationship of school desegregation and employment segregation* (Report No. 338). Baltimore, MD: Johns Hopkins University, Center for Social Organization of Schools.

Braddock, J. H., II., & McPartland, J. M. (1987). How minorities continue to be excluded from equal employment opportunities: Research on labor market and institutional barriers. *Journal of Social Issues, 43*, 5–39.

Braddock, J. H., II., McPartland, J., & Trent, W. (1984, April). *Desegregated schools and desegregated work environments.* Paper presented at the meeting of the American Educational Research Association, New Orleans, LA.

Bradley, L. A., & Bradley, G. W. (1977). The academic achievement of black students in desegregated schools: A critical review. *Review of Educational Research, 47*, 399–449.

California State Department of Education. (1983). *Desegregation and bilingual education — Partners in quality education.* Sacramento, CA: California State Department of Education.

Carrasquillo, A. L. (1991). *Hispanic children and youth in the United States.* New York: Garland Publishing.

Carsrud, K. B. (1984). *Does pairing hurt Chapter 1 students?* Austin, TX: Austin Independent School District, Office of Research and Evaluation.

Carter, T. (1979). *Interface between bilingual education and desegregation: A study of Arizona and California.* Washington, DC: National Institute of Education. (ERIC Document Reproduction Service No. ED 184 743)

Carter, T., & Chatfield, M. L. (1986). Effective bilingual schools: Implications for policy and practice. *American Journal of Education, 95,* 200–232.

Carter, T., & Segura, R. (1979). *Mexican Americans in school: A decade of change.* New York: College Board.

Cohen, E. G. (1975). The effects of desegregation on race relations. *Law and Contemporary Problems, 39*(2), 271–299.

Cohen, E. G. (1980). Design and redesign of the desegregated school: Problems of status, power and conflict. In W. G. Stephan & J. R. Feagin (Eds.), *School desegregation: Past, present and future* (pp. 251–278). New York: Plenum.

Cohen, E. G., Lockheed, M., & Lohman, M. (1976). The center for interracial cooperation: A field experiment. *Sociology of Education, 49,* 47–58.

Cohen, E. G., & Loran, R. (1995a). Producing equal status interaction in the classroom. *American Educational Research Journal, 32*(1), 99-120.

Cohen, E. G., & Loran, R. (1995b). *The operation of status in the middle grades: Recent complications.* Unpublished manuscript, School of Education, Stanford University.

Cohen, E. G., & Roper, S. (1972). Modification of interracial interaction disability: An application of status characteristics theory. *American Sociological Review, 36,* 643–657.

Coleman, J. S., Campbell, E. Q., Hobson, C. J., McPartland, J., Mood, A. M., Weinfeld, F. D., & York, R. L. (1966). *Equality of educational opportunity.* Washington, DC: U.S. Government Printing Office.

Collins, T. W., & Noblit, G. W. (1977). *Crossover High.* Unpublished manuscript, Memphis State University, Department of Anthropology, Memphis, TN.

Cook, T. D. (1984). What have black children gained academically from school integration?: Examination of the meta-analytic evidence. In T. Cook, D. Armor, R. Crain, N. Miller, W. Stephan, H. Walberg & P. Wortman (Eds.), *School desegregation and black achievement* (pp. 6–42). Washington, DC: National Institute of Education.

Crain, R. L. (1970). School integration and occupational achievement of Negroes. *American Journal of Sociology, 75*, 593–606.

Crain, R. L. (1976). Why academic research fails to be useful? *School Review, 84*, 337–351.

Crain, R. L. (1984a). *Is nineteen really better than ninety-three?* Washington, DC: National Institute of Education.

Crain, R. L. (1984b). *Desegregated schools and the nonacademic side of college survival.* Paper presented at the meeting of the Educational Research Association, New Orleans, LA.

Crain, R. L., & Mahard, R. E. (1978). Social racial composition and black college attendance and achievement test performance. *Sociology of Education, 51*, 81–101.

Crain, R. L., & Weisman, C. S. (1972). *Discrimination, personality and achievement: A survey of Northern blacks.* New York: Seminar Press.

Cronbach, L. J. (1982). *Designing evaluations of educational and social programs.* San Francisco: Jossey-Bass.

Crooks, R. C. (1970). The effects of interracial preschool program upon racial preference, knowledge of racial differences and racial identification. *Journal of Social Issues, 26*(4), 137– 144.

Cross, W. E., Jr. (1980). *Black identity: Rediscovering the distinction between personal identity and reference group identification.* Paper presented at the meeting of the Society of Research and Child Development, Atlanta, GA.

Dawkins, M. P. (1991). *Long-term effects of school desegregation on African Americans: Evidence from the National Survey of Black Americans.* Unpublished manuscript.

Dentler, R. A., & Elkins, E. (1967). Intergroup attitudes, academic performance and racial composition. In R. A. Dentler, D. Mackler & M. E. Washauer (Eds.), *The urban R's* (pp. 61–77). New York: Praeger.

Desegregation Studies Unit. (1977). *Resegregation: A second generation school desegregation issues.* Washington, DC: National Institute of Education.

Duran, R. P. (1983). *Hispanics' education and background: Predictors of college achievement.* New York: College Entrance Examination Board.

Eckland, B. K. (1979). School racial composition and college attendance revisited. *Sociology of Education, 22*, 122–128.

Epps, E. G. (1975). Impact of school desegregation on aspirations, self-concepts and other aspects of personality. *Law and Contemporary Problems, 39*(1), 300–313.

Epps, E. G. (1978). The impact of school desegregation on the self-evaluation and achievement orientation of minority children. *Law and Contemporary Problems, 42*(3), 57–76.

Espinosa, R., & Ochoa, A. (1986). Concentration of California Hispanic students in schools with low achievement: A research note. *American Journal of Education, 95*(1), 77–95.

Fernandez, R. R. (1978). *The political dimensions of bilingual education in the context of school desegregation in Milwaukee: A case study.* Unpublished manuscript.

Fernandez, R. R., & Guskin, J. T. (1978). Bilingual education and desegregation: A new dimension in legal and educational decision-making. In H. LaFontaine, B. Persky & L. H. Glubshick (Eds.), *Bilingual education* (pp. 58–66). Wayne, NJ: Avery Publishing.

Feshbach, S., & Adelman, H. (1969). *A training demonstration and research program for the remediation of learning disorders in culturally disadvantaged youth.* Unpublished manuscript, University of California, Los Angeles.

Fleming, J. (1990). Standardized test scores and the black college environment. In K. Lomotey (Ed.), *Going to school: The African American experience* (pp. 143–162). Albany, NY: State University of New York Press.

Forehand, G., Ragosta, M., & Rock, D. (1976). *Conditions and processes of effective school desegregation* (Report No. PR-76-23). Princeton, NJ: Educational Testing Service.

Gable, R., & Iwanicki, E. (1986). The longitudinal effects of a voluntary school desegregation program on the basic skill progress of participants. *Metropolitan Education, 1,* 76–77.

Garcia, G. F. (1976). The Latino and desegregation. *Integrated Education, 14,* 21–22.

Gardner, B. B., Wright, B. D., & Dee, R. (1970). *The effects of busing black ghetto children into white suburban schools.* (ERIC Document Reproduction Service No. ED 048 389)

Gerard, H., Jackson, D., & Conolley, E. (1975). Social context in the desegregated classroom. In H. Gerard & N. Miller (Eds.), *School desegregation: A long-range study* (pp. 211–241). New York: Plenum Press.

Gerard, H., & Miller, N. (1975). *School desegregation.* New York: Plenum Press.

Glass, G. V., McGaw, B., & Smith, M. L. (1981). *Meta-analysis in social research.* Beverly Hills, CA: Sage.

Gonzalez, G. G. (1990). *Chicano education in the era of segregation.* Philadelphia: The Balch Institute Press.

Gonzalez, J. M. (1979). *Bilingual education in the integrated school.* Arlington, VA: National Clearinghouse for Bilingual Education.

Gordon, V. V. (1980). *The self-concept of black Americans.* Lanham: University Press of America.

Green, D., Miller, N., & Gerard, D. S. (1975). Personality traits and adjustment. In H. B. Gerard & N. Miller (Eds.), *School desegregation: A long-range study* (pp. 167–192). New York: Plenum Press.

Green, K. (1981). *Integration and attainment: Preliminary results from a national longitudinal study of the impact of school desegregation.* Paper presented at the meeting of the American Educational Research Association. Los Angeles, CA.

Green, K. (1982). *The impact of neighborhood and secondary school integration on educational achievement and occupational attainment of college bound blacks.* Unpublished doctoral dissertation, University of California at Los Angeles.

Hallinan, M. T. (1982). Classroom racial composition and children's friendships. *Social Forces, 61*(1), 56–72.

Hallinan, M. T. (1986). School organization and interracial friendships. In V. Derlega & B. Winstead (Eds.), *Friendship and social interaction* (pp. 167–184). New York: Springer-Verlag.

Hallinan, M. T., & Smith, S. S. (1985). The effects of classroom racial composition on students' interracial friendliness. *Social Psychology Quarterly, 48*(1), 3–16.

Hallinan, M. T., & Teixeira, R. A. (1987a). Opportunities and constraints: Black-white differences in the formation of interracial friendships. *Child Development, 58*(5), 1358–1371.

Hallinan, M. T., & Teixeira, R. A. (1987b). Students' interracial friendships: Individual characteristics, structural effects and racial differences. *American Journal of Education, 95*, 563–583.

Hanna, J. L. (1982). Public social policy and the children's world: Implications of ethnographic research for desegregated schooling. In G. Spindler (Ed.), *Doing the ethnography of schooling* (pp. 316–355). New York: Holt, Rinehart and Winston.

Hare, B. R. (1977). Black and white children self-esteem in social science: An overview. *The Journal of Negro Education, 46*(2), 141–156.

Haro, C. M. (1977). *Mexican/Chicano concerns and school desegregation in Los Angeles.* Unpublished manuscript, University of California, Chicano Studies Center Publications, Los Angeles, CA.

Heleen, O. (Ed.) (1987). Two-way bilingual education: A strategy for equity [Special issue]. *Equity and Choice.*

Hilliard, A. G. III. (1990). Limitations of current academic achievement measures. In K. Lomotey (Ed.), *Going to school: The African American experience* (pp. 135–142). Albany, NY: State University of New York Press.

Howard, J., & Hammond, R. (1985). *Rumors of inferiority: Black America and the psychology of performance.* Unpublished manuscript.

Hunter, J. E., Schmidt, F. L., & Jackson, G. B. (1982). *Meta-analysis: Cumulating research findings across studies.* Beverly Hills, CA: Sage.

Jansen, V. G., & Gallagher, J. J. (1966). The social choices of students in racially integrated classes for the culturally disadvantaged talented. *Exceptional Children, 33,* 222–226.

Jaynes, G. D., & Williams, R. M., Jr. (1989). *A common destiny: Blacks and American society.* Washington, DC: National Academy Press.

Jencks, C., Smith, M., Acland, H., Bane, M. J., Cohen, D., Gintis, H., Heyns, B., & Michelson, S. (1972). *Inequality.* New York: Basic Books.

Johnson, D. A. (1990). The relationship between school integration and student attitude toward residential racial integration. *Dissertation Abstracts International, 51,* 2527.

Johnson, D. W., & Johnson, R. T. (1982). The study of cooperative, competitive and individualistic situations: State of the area and two recent contributions. *Contemporary Education, 1*(1), 7–13.

Johnson, D. W., & Johnson, R. T. (1992). Positive interdependence: Key to effective cooperation. In R. Hertz-Lazarowitz & N. Miller (Eds.), *Interaction in cooperative groups* (pp. 174–199). Cambridge: Cambridge University Press.

Johnson, D. W., Johnson, R. T., & Maruyama, G. (1983). Interdependence and interpersonal attraction among heterogeneous and homogeneous individuals: A theoretical formulation and a meta-analysis of the research. *Review of Educational Research, 53*, 5–54.

Katz, I. (1964). Review of evidence relating to effects of desegregation on the performance of Negroes. *American Psychologist, 19*, 381–399.

Kingsley, D. E. (1989). Racial attitudes in Liberty, Missouri: Implications for school desegregation. *Dissertation Abstracts International, 50*, 2811.

Krol, R. A. (1978). *A meta-analysis of comparative research on the effects of desegregation on academic achievement.* Unpublished doctoral dissertation, Western Michigan University. (University Microfilms No. 79–07962).

Kurokawa, M. (1971). Mutual perceptions of racial images: White, black, and Japanese-Americans. *Journal of Social Issues, 27*, 213–235.

Levi, A. (1988). Attitudes and stereotypes of Eastern and Western students in integrated and nonintegrated classes in high schools in Israel. *Dissertation Abstracts International, 49*, 2171.

Liska, A. E. (1974). The impact of attitude on behavior: Attitude-social support interaction. *Pacific Sociological Review, 17*, 83–97.

Lombardi, D. N. (1962). *Factors affecting changes in attitudes toward Negroes among high school students.* Unpublished doctoral dissertation, Fordham University.

Mahard, R. E., & Crain, R. L. (1983). Research on minority achievement in desegregated schools. In C. H. Rossell & W. D. Hawley (Eds.), *The consequences of school desegregation* (pp. 103–125). Philadelphia: Temple University Press.

Malry, L. (1968). *The educational and occupational aspirations of Anglo, Spanish, and Negro high school students.* Unpublished doctoral dissertation, University of New Mexico. (University Microfilms No. 66–8284)

Mann, J. H. (1959). The effects of inter-racial contact on socio-metric choices and perceptions. *Journal of Social Psychology, 50*, 143–152.

Maruyama, G., & Miller, N. (1979). Reexamination of normative influence processes in desegregated classrooms. *American Educational Research Journal, 16*(3), 273–283.

Maruyama, G., Miller, N., & Holtz, R. (1986). The relation between popularity and longitudinal test of the lateral transmission of values hypothesis. *Journal of Personality and Social Psychology, 51*, 730–741.

Marston, A. R. (1971). It is time to reconsider the Graduate Record Examination. *American Psychologist, 26*, 653–655.

McClelland, D. C. (1973). Testing for competence rather than for intelligence. *American Psychologist, 28*(1), 1–14.

McConahay, J. (1978). The effects of school desegregation upon students' racial attitudes and behavior: A critical review of the literature and a prolegomenon to future research. *Law & Contemporary Problems, 42*(3), 77–107.

McGarvey, W. E. (1977). *Longitudinal factors in school desegregation.* Unpublished doctoral dissertation, University of Southern California.

McPartland, J. M., & Crain, R. L. (1980). Racial discrimination, segregation and processes of social mobility. In V. T. Covello (Ed.), *Poverty and public policy* (pp. 97–125). Boston: Hall.

McWhirt, R. A. (1967). *The effects of desegregation on prejudice, academic aspiration and the self-concept of tenth grade students.* Unpublished doctoral dissertation, University of South Carolina.

Meier, K. J., & Stewart, J., Jr. (1991). *The politics of Hispanic education.* Albany, NY: State University of New York Press.

Menchaca, M., & Valencia, R. R. (1990). Anglo-Saxon ideologies and their impact on the segregation of Mexican students in California, the 1920s-1930s. *Anthropology and Education Quarterly, 21*, 222–246.

Mercer, J. R., & Phillips, D. (1987). *Factors predicting adult status attainment of Chicano students: 20 year follow-up.* Unpublished manuscript, University of California, Riverside.

Metz, M. H. (1978). *Classrooms and corridors.* Berkeley, CA: University of California Press.

Metz, M. H. (1986). *Different by design.* New York: Routledge & Kegan Paul.

Milan, W. G. (1978). *Toward a comprehensive language policy for a desegregated school system: Reassessing the future of bilingual education.* New York: Arawak Consulting Company.

Miller, N. (1980). Making school desegregation work. In W. G. Stephan & J. R. Feagin (Eds.), *School desegregation: Past, present, and future* (pp. 309–349). New York: Plenum Press.

Miller, N., & Carlson, M. (1984). School desegregation as a social reform: A meta-analysis of its effects on black academic achievement. In T. Cook, D. Armor, R. Crain, N. Miller, W. Stephan, H. Walberg & P. Wortman (Eds.), *School desegregation and black achievement* (pp. 89–130). Washington, DC: National Institute of Education.

Morrison, G. A., Jr. (1972). An analysis of academic achievement trends for Anglo-American, Mexican-American, and Negro-American students in a desegregated school environment. *Dissertation Abstracts International, 33,* 6024.

National Institute of Education. (1977). *Desegregation and education concerns of the Hispanic community.* Washington, DC: U.S. Government Printing Office.

Nieves, L. (1977). *The minority college experience: A review of the literature.* Princeton, NJ: Educational Testing Service.

Noblit, G. W., & Collins, T. W. (1981). Gui bono? White students in a desegregated high school. *The Urban Review, 13,* 205–216.

Orfield, G. (1986). Hispanic education: Challenges, research and policies. *American Journal of Education, 95*(1), 1–25.

Orfield, G. (1988). *The growth and concentration of Hispanic enrollment and the future of American education.* Paper presented at the National Council of La Raza Conference, Albuquerque, NM.

Parsons, T. W., Jr. (1965). *Ethnic cleavage in a California school.* An unpublished doctoral dissertation, Stanford University. (University Microfilms No. 66–2606)

Patchen, M. (1982). *Black-white contact in schools: Its social and academic effects.* West Lafayette, IN: Purdue University Press.

Pearce, D. (1980). *Breaking down the barriers: New evidence on the impact of metropolitan school desegregation on housing patterns.* Washington, DC: National Institute of Education.

Pearce, D., Crain, R. L., & Farley, R. (1984). *Lessons not lost: The effect of school desegregation on the rate of residential desegregation in large center cities.* Paper presented at the meeting of the American Educational Research Association, New Orleans, LA.

Pearl, A. (1991). Systemic and institutional factors in Chicano school failure. In R. R. Valencia (Ed.), *Chicano school failure and success: Research and policy agendas for the 1990s* (pp. 273–320). London: The Falmer Press.

Peshkin, A. (1991). *The color of strangers, the color of friends.* Chicago: The University of Chicago Press.

Pettigrew, T. (1967). Social evaluation theory: Convergences and applications. In D. Levine (Ed.), *Nebraska Symposium on Motivation* (Vol. 15, pp. 241–315). Lincoln, NE: University of Nebraska Press.

Pettigrew, T. (1969b). The Negro and education: Problems and proposals. In I. Katz & P. Gurin (Eds.), *Race and the social sciences* (pp. 49–113). New York: Basic Books.

Pettigrew, T. F., & Martin, J. (1987). Shaping the organizational context for black American inclusion. *Journal of Social Issues, 43,* 41–78.

Pride, R., & Woodward, D. (1985). *The burden of busing: The politics of desegregation in Nashville, Tennessee.* Knoxville, TN: University of Tennessee Press.

Read, F. (1975). Judicial evolution of the law of school integration since *Brown v. Board of Education. Law and Contemporary Problems, 39*(1), 7–49.

Rist, R. C. (Ed.). (1979). *Desegregated schools: Appraisals of an American experiment.* New York: Academic Press.

Roos, P. D. (1978). Bilingual education: The Hispanic response to unequal educational opportunity. *Law and Contemporary Problems, 42,* 111–140.

Rosenberg, M., & Simmons, R. (1971). *Black and white self-esteem: The urban school child.* Washington, DC: American Sociological Association.

Rosenthal, R. (1978). Combining results of independent studies. *Psychological Bulletin, 85,* 185–193.

Rumberger, R. W., & Willms, J. D. (1992). The impact of racial and ethnic segregation on the achievement gap in California high schools. *Educational Evaluation and Policy Analysis, 14*(4), 377–396.

SCANS (Secretary of Labor's Commission on Achieving Necessary Skills). (1991). *Skills and tasks for jobs: A SCANS report for America 2000.* Washington, DC: U.S. Government Printing Office.

Schmidt, F. L. (1992). What do data really mean? Research findings, meta-analysis and cumulative knowledge in psychology. *American Psychologist, 47*(10), 1173–1181.

Schofield, J. W. (1978). School desegregation and intergroup attitudes. In D. Bar-Tal & L. Saxe (Eds.), *Social psychology of education: Theory and research* (pp. 329–363). Washington, DC: Halsted Press.

Schofield, J. W. (1981). Uncharted territory: Desegregation and organizational innovation. *The Urban Review, 13,* 227–242.

Schofield, J. W. (1982). *Black and white in school: Trust, tension or tolerance?* New York: Praeger.

Schofield, J. W. (1991). School desegregation and intergroup relations: A review of the literature. In G. Grant (Eds.), *Review of research in education* (pp. 335–409). Washington, DC: American Educational Research Association.

Schofield, J. W., & Francis, W. D. (1982). An observational study of peer interaction in racially-mixed "accelerated" classrooms. *The Journal of Educational Psychology, 74*(5), 722–732.

Schofield, J. W., & Sagar, H. A. (1983). Desegregation, school practices and student race relations. In C. Rossell & W. Hawley (Eds.), *The consequences of school desegregation* (pp. 58–102). Philadelphia: Temple University Press.

Schofield, J. W., & Whitley, B. E. (1983). Peer nomination vs. rating scale measurement of children's peer preference. *Social Psychology Quarterly, 46,* 242–251.

Schuman, H., & Johnson, M. (1976). Attitudes and behavior. *Annual Review of Sociology, 2,* 161–207.

Schuman, H., Steeh, C., & Bobo, L. (1985). *Racial attitudes in America: Trends and interpretations.* Cambridge, MA: Harvard University Press.

Schwarzwald, J., Amir, Y., & Crain, R. L. (1992). Long-term effects of school desegregation experiences on interpersonal relations in the Israeli defense forces. *Personality and Social Psychology Bulletin, 18*(3), 357–368.

Shaw, M. E. (1973). Changes in sociometric choices following forced integration of an elementary school. *Journal of Social Issues, 29*(4), 143–157.

Sheehan, D. S. (1980). A study of attitude change in desegregated intermediate schools. *Sociology of Education, 53*, 51–59.

Silverman, T., & Shaw, M. (1973). Effects of sudden mass school desegregation on interracial interaction and attitudes in one Southern city. *Journal of Social Issues, 29*(4), 133–142.

Singer, D. (1966). *Interracial attitudes of Negro and white fifth grade children in segregated and unsegregated schools.* Unpublished doctoral dissertation, Columbia University, Teachers College.

Singer, H., Gerard, H. B., & Redfearn, D. (1975). Achievement. In H. B. Gerard & N. Miller (Eds.), *School desegregation: A long-range study* (pp. 69–87). New York: Plenum Press.

Singleton, L. C., & Asher, S. R. (1977). Peer preferences and social interaction among third-grade children in an integrated school district. *Journal of Educational Psychology, 69*(4), 330–336.

Slavin, R. E. (1983a). *Cooperative learning.* New York: Longman.

Slavin, R. E. (1983b). When does cooperative learning increase student achievement? *Psychological Bulletin, 94*, 429–445.

Slavin, R. E., Sharan, S., Katan, S., & Hertz-Lazarowitz, R. (Eds.). (1985). *Learning to cooperate: Cooperating to learn.* New York: Plenum Press.

Smith, D. H. (1981). Social and academic environments of black students on white campuses. *The Journal of Negro Education, 50*(3), 299–306.

Spencer, M. E. B. (1976). *The social-cognitive and personality development of the black preschool child: An exploratory study of developmental process.* Unpublished doctoral dissertation, The University of Chicago.

Stephan, W. G. (1978). School desegregation: An evaluation of predictions made in *Brown v. Board of Education. Psychological Bulletin, 85*(2), 217–238.

Stephan, W. G. (1984). Blacks and *Brown*: The effects of school desegregation on black students. In T. Cook, D. Armor, R. Crain, N. Miller, W. Stephan, H. Walberg, & P. Wortman (Eds.), *School desegregation and black achievement* (pp. 131–159). Washington, DC: National Institute of Education.

St. John, N. H. (1975). *School desegregation: Outcomes for children.* New York: Wiley.

Summers, A. A., & Wolfe, B. L. (1977). Do schools make a difference? *American Economic Review, 67,* 639–652.

Taylor, C. P. (1967). *Some change in self-concept in the first year of desegregated schooling.* Unpublished doctoral dissertation, University of Delaware.

Taylor, R. (1976). Psychosocial development among black children and youth: A re-examination. *American Journal of Ortho-Psychiatry, 46*(1), 4–19.

Trent, W. (1991). *Desegregation analysis report.* New York: The Legal Defense and Educational Fund.

Trubowitz, J. (1969). *Changing the racial attitudes of children.* New York: Praeger.

U.S. Commission on Civil Rights. (1967). *Racial isolation in the public schools.* Washington, DC: U.S. Government Printing Office.

Valencia, R. R. (1984). *Understanding school closures: Discriminatory impact on Chicano and black students* (Policy Monographs Series No. 1). Stanford, CA: Stanford University, Stanford Center for Chicano Research.

Valencia, R. R. (1991). The plight of Chicano students: An overview of schooling conditions and outcomes. In R. R. Valencia (Ed.), *Chicano school failure and success: Research and policy agendas for the 1990s* (pp. 3–26). London: The Falmer Press.

Walberg, H. J. (1984). Desegregation and education productivity. In T. Cook, D. Armor, R. Crain, N. Miller, W. Stephan, H. Walberg, & P. Wortman (Eds.), *School desegregation and black achievement* (pp. 160–193). Washington, DC: National Institute of Education.

Webster, S. W. (1961). The influence of interracial contact on social acceptance in a newly integrated school. *Journal of Educational Psychology, 32,* 292–296.

Weinberg, M. (Ed.). (1970). *Desegregation research: An appraisal* (2nd ed.). Bloomington, IN: Phi Delta Kappa.

Weinberg, M. (1977). *Minority students: A research appraisal.* Washington, DC: National Institute of Education.

Wicker, A. W. (1969). Attitude versus actions: The relationship of verbal and overt behavioral responses to attitude objects. *Journal of Social Issues, 25*(4), 41–78.

Wisdom, J. (1975). Random remarks on the role of social sciences in the judicial decision-making process in school desegregation cases. *Law and Contemporary Problems, 39*(1), 135–149.

Wortman, P. M. (1984). School desegregation and black achievement: An integrative view. In T. Cook, D. Armor, R. Crain, N. Miller, W. Stephan, H. Walberg, & P. Wortman (Eds.), *School desegregation and black achievement* (pp. 194–224). Washington, DC: National Institute of Education.

CHAPTER 5

BROWN V. BOARD OF EDUCATION AND THE CONTINUING STRUGGLE FOR DESEGREGATED SCHOOLS

Susan E. Eaton and Gary A. Orfield

More than two generations have passed since a unanimous Supreme Court, in *Brown v. Board of Education* (1954), declared intentionally segregated schools "inherently unequal."

Where are we now?

We are in Hartford, Connecticut. Ninety-three percent of the schoolchildren in the public schools here are either Hispanic American or African American. More that two-thirds of Hartford's students live in poverty (Connecticut Department of Education, 1993). A mere six minutes on the highway brings us to affluent, nearly all-white suburban, high-achieving school districts that are just next door but seem a world away.

Or, perhaps we are in Norfolk, Virginia. After winning federal court permission to dismantle a desegregation plan, the city school board here reinstituted segregated elementary schools. In a city where about 40% of students are white, nearly 100% of students in Norfolk's 10 resegregated schools are African American. On average, 93% of the students in Norfolk's "resegregated" schools come from low-income families (Eaton & Meldrum, 1994).

The nation has been quick to celebrate *Brown's* anniversary. However, at the same time, few educators or policy experts today even blink at Hartford's and Norfolk's numerical portraits of racial

117

and economic isolation. Some 40 years after *Brown*, even while we reaffirm the decision as the century's great moral victory, racial segregation both between and within school districts is such an ordinary fixture in American K-12 education that the condition often goes unnoticed, unmentioned, and usually unremedied.

In fact, no matter where we are in America in 1995, East or West, North or South, racially and ethnically segregated schools are a fact of everyday educational life. For the first time since the *Brown* decision, national data show that school segregation is on the rise for African American students (Orfield, 1993). School segregation for Hispanic American students has been increasing steadily for decades (Orfield, 1993).

So how is it that the path since *Brown* has led us here, to places like Hartford and Norfolk and to a trend of pervasive and increasing school segregation? Part of the answer can be found in the legal and political history since *Brown*, a history of progress and retreat to and from the goal of racially integrated education. It is true that *Brown* had substantial impact upon our nation and its educational institutions; it was an important catalyst and legal underpinning for the civil rights movement. When enforced, *Brown* did alter the segregated character of Southern education. The school desegregation that *Brown* made possible, though showing clear signs of erosion, did prove resilient over the years, weathering political attacks better than many predicted.

In 1995, however, *Brown* has been stripped of much of its power and reach by subsequent Supreme Court decisions, by political forces and by cumulative effects of an uninformed public debate. But while *Brown's* proud spirit surely has been dimmed, there are signs that the decades-old struggle for equitable, integrated schools — the struggle triggered by *Brown* — will continue.

The New Segregation: Increasing Racial, Ethnic, and Economic Isolation

For the first time since the Supreme Court declared intentional school segregation unconstitutional, segregation is on the rise for African American students in all regions of the country. Perhaps the most significant shift here is the substantial increase, from 1986 to 1991, in school segregation for Southern African Americans. This turn back toward segregation in the South is particularly alarming because since 1970, the South has had the

highest levels of racially desegregated public education and prior
to 1991 the levels had been improving consistently (Orfield, 1993).

Nationwide, the percentage of African American students in
schools where more than half the students were minorities rose
from 63.3% in 1987–87 to 66% in 1991–92. The percentage of
African American students in intensely segregated schools —
where more than 90% of students are minorities — rose from
32.5% in 1986–87 to 33.9% in 1991–1992 (see Table 1). School
segregation of Hispanic American students continued to increase
from 1988 to 1991, just as it had since data were first collected in
the 1960s. Increased segregation for Hispanic American students
was most rapid in the West (Orfield, 1993).

Table 5.1 Percentage of African American and Hispanic American
Students in Predominantly Minority and more than 90% Minority
Schools. For Selected School Years 1968–69 To 1991–92.

	50% Minority		90% Minority	
Year	African American	Hispanic American	African American	Hispanic American
1968–69	76.6	54.8	64.3	23.1
1972–73	63.6	56.6	38.7	23.3
1980–81	62.9	68.1	33.2	28.8
1986–87	63.3	71.5	32.5	32.2
1991–92	66.0	73.4	33.9	34.0

Note: The information in this table was taken from Orfield (1993).

In spite of the recent increase in Southern school segregation,
the South is still the most racially desegregated region for African
American students. This is partly so because enforcement of
Brown was most vigorous in Southern states that had once had
laws requiring segregated education. Consequently, the percentage of Southern African American students in desegregated
schools increased markedly over the decades. The first substantial

reversal of this trend toward racial desegregation did not surface until 1991, the most recent year for which national data are available (see Table 5.2).

Table 5.2 Percentage of Southern African American Students
in Majority White Schools.
1954–1991

1954	.001
1960	.1
1964	2.3
1967	13.9
1968	23.4
1970	33.1
1972	36.4
1976	37.6
1980	37.1
1986	42.0
1988	43.5
1991	39.2

Note: The information in this table was taken from Orfield (1993).

The Northeast is currently the most segregated region for African American students. For more than a decade, the same four states — Illinois, Michigan, New York, and New Jersey — have topped the list of most segregated states for African American students. Hispanic Americans are least segregated in the Midwest and most segregated in the Northeast.

How Did We Get Here?
The History of Desegregation Since *Brown*

In the decades since *Brown*, trends in school segregation have been shaped by Supreme Court decisions, by demographics and politics. Midway into the 1990s, while we seem wedded to the ideals espoused in *Brown*, powerful forces threaten to perpetuate the trend toward increasing segregation in the nation's schools.

Brown's noble words in 1954 were the progenitor in the movement to break down the separate and unequal educational system in the South. By declaring government sanctioned segregation unconstitutional, the Supreme Court was doing more than just outlawing educational discrimination and racial separation. With *Brown*, the Warren Court laid the crucial foundation as African Americans would later seek equality in all segments of public life. Commenting upon *Brown*'s tremendous significance, writer and historian Richard Kluger (1977), who chronicled the events leading to the 1954 decision, commented:

> The Court had restored to the American people a measure of the humanity that had been drained away in their climb to worldwide supremacy. The Court said, without using the words, that that ascent had been made over the backs of black America — that when you stepped on a black man, he hurt. The time had come to stop. (p. 710)

But soon after the victory, *Brown*'s limits became apparent. In *Brown* and the subsequent *Brown II* (1955) that came just a year later, the Supreme Court offered no clear instructions about how to achieve desegregated schools. Neither did the decisions spell out, in either educational or quantifiable terms, what "desegregation" was. The only instruction *Brown II* offered was that intentionally segregated schools be eradicated with all deliberate speed.

Until the late 1960s progress toward eliminating segregation was predictably slow, as a recalcitrant South tinkered with remedies but clung to its essentially segregated character. The North, with its own form of segregated education, would not face scrutiny from the Supreme Court until the early 1970s.

The Supreme Court did not spell out the terms and requirements of school desegregation until 1968, with its decision, *Green v. School Board of New Kent County* (1968). After 14 years of ambiguity, *Green* finally listed six indicators of a desegregated — or "unitary" — system and ordered districts to eliminate segregation "root and branch." *Green*, for example, required that a desegregation plan must promise to work, the proof being that the school system fully desegregate its student body, faculty and staff, facilities, extracurricular activities and transportation.

By 1969, the Supreme Court in *Alexander v. Holmes County Board of Education* had seemed to grow impatient with the slow pace of school desegregation. The Supreme Court declared that *Brown II*s vague "all deliberate speed" had expired; school districts had to desegregate and had to desegregate now.

Other Supreme Court decisions during this period aided the desegregation effort. For example, in *Swann v. Charlotte Mecklenburg County* (1971), the Supreme Court affirmed school reassignment and busing as acceptable means for eradicating segregation.

The Johnson Administration, meanwhile, had enforced the school desegregation mandates vigorously, threatening to cut off federal monies to districts who did not comply with regulations. The Justice Department filed many new lawsuits, delivering the message loud and clear that desegregation was the law of the land. Such intensive enforcement efforts, which essentially gave the Supreme Court mandates their teeth, would taper off soon after Richard Nixon was elected in 1968. But even Nixon, who consistently expressed his opposition to mandatory school desegregation and busing, was forced to compromise with Congress on some enforcement matters.

In 1973, the Supreme Court finally took up the question of Northern-style school segregation. What to do about the racial separation in Northern schools, a segregation that usually came in a more subtle yet equally pervasive form, had been a nagging question for years. In the *Keyes v. Denver* (1973) case, the Court ruled that not only were the overt Southern segregation mandates unconstitutional, but so were any discriminatory government actions that led to segregated schools. This effectively outlawed the common Northern practices of drawing school attendance zones or building schools along racial lines.

But the effort to break down segregation outside the South would last only a year before civil rights lawyers met resounding defeat in the Supreme Court's *Milliken v. Bradley* (1974) decision. In the *Milliken* case, from Detroit, the Supreme Court confronted an increasingly difficult urban reality.   Since the end of World

War II, white families had been fleeing cities and Detroit reflected this trend.

By the 1970s, the share of white students in Detroit's public schools was shrinking and the pool of African American students was growing, leading the lower courts in Detroit to conclude that within-city desegregation was not feasible over the long term. And so the local school board, plaintiff lawyers, and the lower courts agreed that the only way to remedy the unconstitutional segregation in Detroit would be to include the surrounding and predominantly white suburbs in its desegregation plan. As suburbanites just outside Detroit protested noisily, the *Milliken* case made its way to the Supreme Court. The Supreme Court, however, rejected the city-suburban plan 5–4, thereby declaring that *Brown's* reach stopped at municipal boundary lines. Though metropolitan cooperation between cities and suburbs had a long and successful history in America — there were and still are metropolitan sewer systems, garbage disposal, transportation and parks — the Supreme Court ruled that schools were somehow different. Neither did the Court consider the ways suburban government action, through zoning or other measures, had contributed to the segregated housing patterns in Detroit. Local government control of schools, Justice Burger wrote in his decision, was a deeply rooted tradition that could not be violated for the purpose of desegregation. *Milliken* inspired some resolute dissents, perhaps because the opposing Justices understood the serious consequences of the decision.

The angriest objection came from Justice Thurgood Marshall, who as a young National Association for the Advancement of Colored People (NAACP) lawyer in 1954 had argued *Brown* before the Supreme Court. In his dissent, Marshall challenged *Milliken's* intellectual underpinnings and lamented the power it had to divide African American and white America.

> Desegregation is not and was never expected to be an easy task . . . . Today's holding, I fear, is more a reflection of a perceived public mood that we have gone far enough in enforcing the Constitution's guarantee of equal justice than it is the product of neutral principles of law. In the short run, it may seem the easier of course to allow our great metropolitan areas to be divided up each into two cities — one white, the other black — but it is a

course, I predict, our people will ultimately regret. (*Milliken v. Bradley*, p. 3161)

Milliken sanctioned racial separation between city and suburb and in the years to follow, this division came to characterize Northern metropolitan areas. Within most typical Northern urban districts, such as Hartford and Detroit, who in 1995 have tiny shares of white students, full desegregation has since become all but impossible to achieve.

Meanwhile, in the South, desegregation efforts were continuing. Southern districts were hardly affected by *Milliken*'s constraints, as Southern districts were customarily drawn on county, rather than city or town lines. This meant that not only were Southern school districts larger, but, unlike the North, the districts often incorporated city and suburbs and, consequently, the more racially diverse populations needed to achieve desegregation.

Politically, however, desegregation and "busing" were being battered around by national leaders, beginning with Richard Nixon. Rhetorical attacks on mandatory school desegregation intensified during the Reagan era. Enforcement of desegregation mandates during the Reagan period were not only lax, but the U.S. Justice Department even publicly supported efforts to dismantle mandatory desegregation.

Under the leadership of Assistant Attorney General for Civil Rights William Bradford Reynolds, the Justice Department, the traditional government enforcers of school desegregation mandates, switched sides to support some of the formerly segregated school districts it had once sued (Vergon, 1990). As school administrators went into court in an effort to get out of desegregation requirements, they found themselves a new and powerful ally in the civil rights division of the United States government. Civil rights lawyers and advocates, on the other hand, were in an unfamiliar position; they were forced to fight *against* the civil rights office of the executive branch, an office that, in theory, was supposed to be on the civil rights side.

In the Norfolk case, for example, Reynolds submitted a friend of the court brief in favor of the school district's plan to resegregate city elementary schools. At a press conference in 1986, Reynolds said he hoped the Norfolk ruling would assist other school districts to get out of their desegregation plans and praised the Norfolk plan, saying it would increase parental involvement. (Parental involvement, however, actually declined in the resegregated schools following the court ruling) (Eaton & Meldrum, 1994).

In praising the Norfolk school board, Reynolds said that

> they have come to grips with what I suspect is one of the most important elements of public school education . . . and that's parental involvement with the schools . . . That was a big part of changing this plan and I think that that also will serve as an advantage to all the students in that system, white or black. (Mayfield, 1986, p. 4)

The local leader of the dismantling effort in Norfolk, Thomas Johnson, later said that such clear government support for undoing desegregation encouraged him to start his dismantling effort. "I realized the DOJ (Department of Justice) might go along with a plan to end busing . . . I wouldn't have done it if I thought I would have to fight the U.S. Government" (Eaton & Meldrum, 1994, p. 14). Norfolk in 1986 became the first school district in the country to win federal court approval to resegregate. Under its new school assignment plan, the city school board recreated levels of segregation in some schools that were as high or higher than the levels that existed in the old days of enforced segregation. In 1986, the Supreme Court refused to hear the Norfolk case, allowing the controversial ruling to stand and leaving many questions about school desegregation unanswered.

As the nation moved into the 1990s, it was still unclear what remaining obligations a "unitary" or desegregated school district had for maintaining racial desegregation or how long such obligations would last. One burning question: if a federal court, using the *Green* indicators as a guide, declared a district "unitary," could that school district return to school assignment practices that recreated segregation?

By 1992, the Supreme Court had delivered some long awaited answers. In two decisions, *Board of Education of Oklahoma City v. Dowell* (1991) and *Freeman v. Pitts* (1992), the Supreme Court spelled out the process by which school boards could finally rid themselves of their school desegregation plans. The Supreme Court stamp-of-approval was a signal to many educational leaders and lawyers that federal courts might now allow Norfolk-type plans.

Under *Dowell*, a district could be released from obligation to maintain desegregated schools so long as the district had, for at least a few years, desegregated its students and met other requirements laid out in the aforementioned *Green* decision some 23 years before. In the *Pitts* decision a year later, the Supreme Court ruled that in order to end aspects of a desegregation plan, a school district need not have fulfilled all the *Green* requirements at the same time. This meant that a district might be able to terminate its student desegregation plan without ever having successfully desegregated its faculty.

Pitts and *Dowell*, for the most part, were largely ignored by legal scholars and social commentators, but together they strike a devastating blow to *Brown's* underlying logic and moral spirit. While *Brown* and the important decisions that followed, such as *Green* and *Swann*, viewed desegregation as an end in and of itself, or a goal to which all districts should strive, *Dowell* and *Pitts* pose an altogether different conception of desegregation. Under *Dowell* and *Pitts*, the ultimate goal is no longer racial desegregation; the new mission is to simply minimize court intervention and restore local control. These goals are paramount, even when passive or absent judicial involvement and the "local" control results in segregated schools. No longer is desegregation the noble and moral goal extolled in *Brown*, but a type of temporary sentence "imposed" upon on school districts until they can return to their "natural" segregated pattern.

Dowell and *Pitts* affirmed this philosophy about desegregation, espoused for years by the Nixon and Reagan Administrations, but never before officially authorized by the Supreme Court. In more practical terms, *Dowell* and *Pitts* make it possible even for the Southern states, with their legacy of enforcement and favorable boundary configurations, to turn back toward segregated schooling. With the Supreme Court now soundly in their camp, many school district administrators and local officials are looking to dismantle their desegregation plans and return to "neighborhood schools," a phrase often interchangeable with "segregated schools."

Desegregation's Staying Power

Desegregation has chinks in its armor and the recent Supreme Court decisions may prove powerful levers for creating even more segregation. Nevertheless, even in the midst of intense political attacks during the Reagan era, racial desegregation for African Americans, overall, remained more or less stable and even improved in some regions. This staying power is likely due to the original strong enforcement concentrated specifically upon desegregation of African American students. On the other hand, courts and policymakers have paid little attention to segregation of Hispanic American students and segregation among Hispanic Americans has risen steadily since 1968–69 (see Table 5.1).

Another sign of desegregation's resilience is the increase in public support for the policy and the favorable reviews from families who have actually experienced desegregation. *Dowell* and *Pitts*, which may make it easier for school districts to dismantle their plans for racial desegregation, mean it is all the more urgent for school leaders and policymakers to have the facts about public opinion on desegregation.

Desegregation has been attacked in uninformed public debates so fiercely and for so long that political and educational leaders, their attorneys and the local establishment often believe that neighborhood schools would, without question, enjoy great support within a community. In recent years, the opinions of African American politicians who favor segregated schools have been widely publicized, leading to erroneous assumptions that African Americans have all turned against desegregation.

In one nationally publicized comment in 1993, for example, Cleveland's young African American mayor, Michael White, called for an end to mandatory school desegregation in his city. With an ironic twist of the language in *Brown*, White told the press that one-race schools are "not inherently bad" (Theiss, 1993). Commemorating *Brown*'s 40th anniversary in 1994, the nation's newspapers and magazines were full of stories and commentary that carried as a central thesis African Americans' disappointment with school desegregation (e.g., Lewis, 1994; Sanchez, 1994; Schrag, 1994).

But the story of uniform, growing disenchantment with racial desegregation, even with "busing," does not pan out. National, state or local surveys conducted over the years illustrate a much more complex reality that is far more positive than media reports and common assumptions would have us believe. In fact, public opinion data shows that there is deep and growing support of desegregation, and that support for desegregation remains very strong among families, African American and white, who have actually experienced the policy.

For example, a national Gallup Poll on race in 1994 conducted for *USA Today*, found that 87% of Americans believed the

Supreme Court's *Brown* decision was right, (Gallup Organization, 1994; Edmonds, 1994) a sharp increase from the 63% support in the early 1960s. Change in the South was even more dramatic. In 1954, an overwhelming 81% of Southerners disapproved of the Supreme Court mandating desegregation (Gallup Organization, 1955). Although the South has experienced far more desegrega- tion — and far more coercion to achieve desegregation — than any other region, only 15% of Southerners in 1994 said they thought the *Brown* decision was wrong.

The same poll showed a large and growing majority, 65% of the public and 70% of African Americans, said desegregation "improved the quality of education for African Americans." This percentage of people who held such a view was up from 43% percent when busing began in 1971. Also, in the 1994 poll, 62% of whites and 75% of African Americans said that desegregated schools had improved race relations (Gallup Organization, 1994; Edmonds, 1994). The 1994 Gallup poll also indicated that an increasing fraction of the public believe "more should be done to integrate schools." This number rose from 37% in 1988 to 56% in 1994. Among African Americans in 1994, 84% said they support more efforts.

It is true that there has always been divided opinion among African Americans on the question of busing. But the peak opposition came and passed in the mid-1970s. According to the National Opinion Research Center's General Social Survey, the high point of opposition among African Americans came in 1975 when 53% of African Americans said they opposed busing. However, this opposition declined significantly by 1986, with just 38% saying they opposed the policy (National Opinion Center, 1975–1989).

Some of the most revealing data come from families and school principals who actually had experience with busing. In 1978, 63% of African American parents and 56% of whites said that their experience of being bused for desegregation had been "very satisfactory" (Harris & Associates, 1978). Among those who had the experience, 74% of parents of all races said desegre- gation through busing had been very satisfactory and 21% said it was partly satisfactory. Only one in 20 African Americans said that the experience had been unsatisfactory. Another Harris Survey found that attitudes of families whose children had been bused had become more positive by 1989. Specifically, 64% of whites, 63% of African Americans, and 70% of Asians whose children had been bused said that the experience was "very satisfactory." Only 4% of African Americans, 6% of whites, and 2% of Asians said that the experience was unsatisfactory (Harris & Associates, 1989).

According to a 1981 ABC News/Washington Post Poll, a majority of public high school principals whose schools were involved with busing said they approved of the policy. Specifically, 59% of these principals said they approved of busing "for desegregation" and 27% said they disapproved of the policy.

A January 1992 national Harris poll conducted for the *Boston Globe* asked Americans whether or not they would support busing if it were the only way to integrate schools. In response to this question, whites supported busing by a 48% to 41% majority (Tye, 1992).

In the same poll, African American and Hispanic American support for busing was overwhelming in response to a question that posed a choice between busing and segregation. Also, among African Americans, in the 1992 poll, there was a 79% to 16% split in favor of busing if there were no other way to achieve desegregation. The numbers in favor of the policy were even higher among Hispanic Americans, at 82% to 18%. When asked a different question: "would you be willing to have your own children go to school by bus so the schools would be desegregated?" whites split evenly, African Americans said yes by a 76% to 21% ratio, and Hispanic Americans agreed by a ratio of 60:18 (Tye, 1992, p. 1).

A 1989 Harris Survey found that 67% of African Americans and 38% of whites supported busing in general. When those opposed to busing were asked whether or not they would support busing if white children were bused to top quality schools in the inner city and African American children were bused to equally good schools, support for busing increased to 51% of whites and 79% of African Americans (Harris & Associates, 1989).

The results of these polls suggest that the experience with busing is much more positive than is widely believed. Widespread assumptions about fierce white resistance and African American disenchantment appear to be inaccurate. The goal of desegregation is an important one for many whites, even if it requires changes they otherwise oppose. Offering strong evidence that people think school desegregation is valuable, survey evidence simply does not lead logically to a policy of neighborhood schools.

Metropolitan School Desegregation: The Most
Promising Strategy For Remedying Segregation

Despite *Milliken*, which hinders desegregation efforts by favoring local control unless plaintiffs can meet enormous burdens of proof, some civil rights lawyers managed to win city-suburban desegregation plans, which have proved stable and workable remedies. In such cities as Wilmington (Delaware), Indianapolis (Indiana), Louisville (Kentucky), Milwaukee (Wisconsin), and St. Louis (Missouri), children attend school under metropolitan plans similar to the type the Supreme Court shot down in *Milliken*. For example, St. Louis's voluntary metropolitan plan gives African American families the choice to transfer their children to nearby, predominantly white suburban districts. About 13,500 African American students currently attend these suburban schools. A smaller magnet program attracts about 1,500 white students into St. Louis city schools. The court settlement in St. Louis requires 16 surrounding municipalities named in the order necessary to maintain a racial balance in their district. About 75% of urban transfer students come from low-income families (Uchitelle, 1988).

Though attaining city-suburban desegregation plans is not easy to do through court settlements, the evidence suggests that this is the most promising route to lasting desegregation. Such plans have consistently been associated with the most stable white enrollments and the most contact between whites and non-whites.

The St. Louis plan grew out of a court settlement in the early 1980s. The settlement was reached after the city schools and the NAACP found that a small city-suburban voluntary transfer program would not allow African American students enough opportunity to attend suburban schools. As a result, the city schools and the NAACP joined forces and included the surrounding suburbs in their desegregation lawsuit, arguing that their governments had helped create the blatant segregation of the metropolitan area. The suburbs sought to settle the suit and under the current plan the predominantly white districts must maintain certain racial balances in their schools by accepting city transfers. Plaintiffs won a city-suburban transfer plan in Milwaukee under similar circumstances.

In response to desegregation litigation in Louisville (Kentucky) and Wilmington (Delaware), the federal courts ordered the urban districts merged with the surrounding, predominantly white, middle-class suburban districts. (The Delaware plan has been reorganized into several separate districts, each encompassing parts of the urban and suburban areas.) In both these cases, desegregation has been stable and far-reaching.

Why Metropolitan Desegregation?

White enrollment stabilizes under metropolitan plans because, unlike within-city plans, metropolitan plans take advantage of the white suburbanization that has been occurring since World War II ended. Metropolitan plans have a broader reach than within-city plans, since they include whites and middle-class residents already in the suburbs. This guarantees that if white flight from the city to the suburbs continues, those white and middle-class families will still be included in the school district.

For example, from 1967 to 1988, data from various school districts show that those with metropolitan plans, such as Clark County (Nevada), Indianapolis (Indiana) or Nashville (Tennessee), had relatively high levels of desegregation compared to districts that had other types of desegregation plans or no desegregation plan. These city-suburban districts also had much lower levels of white flight compared with districts with other types of plans (Orfield & Monfort, 1989). Interestingly, some of the most dramatic declines in white enrollment were found in districts such as Atlanta or DeKalb County (Georgia) that do not have a desegregation plan. These data, therefore, challenge the widely held notion that white flight is caused primarily or solely by "busing" or mandatory school desegregation.

Besides practical benefits, there are other motivations that drive metropolitan school desegregation efforts. One is that city-suburban districts create a common interest among city and suburb, between minority and white, and between affluent and the poor. In doing so, the regional plans seek to end the patterns that have concentrated less powerful, politically disconnected constituents in segregated schools.

Further, some research suggests that achievement test score gains for African American students are largest under metropolitan plans. Researchers have attributed the higher relative gains to the fact that metropolitan plans achieve socioeconomic desegregation, as well as racial desegregation (Crain & Mahard, 1982). Studies of a city-suburban desegregation program in Connecticut showed that the low-income African American students who attended the suburban schools were more likely to complete high schools, to graduate from four-year colleges, and to major in subjects and get jobs once closed to minority students (Crain & Strauss, 1985). The more recent work of Wells and Crain in this volume, offer important ideas about the long-term benefits associated with certain types of school desegregation plans. (See Chapter Nine.)

Aside from the practical benefits and encouraging stories from the handful of metropolitan school districts, it is nevertheless important to remember that *Milliken* has made it extremely difficult to win metropolitan desegregation plans through the federal court system. Realizing both the practical benefits and legal challenges, civil rights lawyers in Connecticut attempted to circumvent the *Milliken* constraints by seeking a metropolitan desegregation plan in state, rather than federal court. In *Sheff v. O'Neill*, (1995) the plaintiff lawyers, representing 18 African American, Hispanic American, and white schoolchildren and their families, charged that the concentrated poverty and segregation in the Hartford schools deprives Hartford schoolchildren of the equal education guaranteed in the Connecticut state constitution. Plaintiffs, however, lost their first round in a legal battle in which they had asked the court to join urban Hartford's school district with the 21 suburban districts surrounding the city.

The Hope and Significance of
Sheff v. O'Neill and Similar Efforts

Though Connecticut Superior Court Judge Harry Hammer denied the request for a desegregation plan, plaintiffs have appealed the ruling to state Supreme Court which they hope will rule on points that Hammer simply failed to consider. In his decision, Hammer applied federal law to the state case, concluding that since the plaintiffs had not proved that the state had purposely caused the segregation, then the courts could not mandate a remedy. But the decision, based almost entirely on the writings of a single U.S. Supreme Court justice, the "late" William O. Douglas, is apparently incongruous with the plaintiff argument. Plaintiffs never charged state intention, only that the condition of segregation creates an unequal educational condition for Hartford schoolchildren.

Indeed, plaintiffs originally filed their lawsuit in state court because of the known limitations of federal rulings, such as *Milliken*. In addition, while state courts cannot afford citizens fewer rights than federal law calls for, they can go further than federal courts in offering rights to their citizens. For example, while the U.S. Constitution makes no provision for an equal education, some state constitutions, such as Connecticut's, do. The ruling, then, while disappointing to desegregation advocates across the country, does not mean that the chapter on *Sheff* is closed. It remains to be seen how or whether the Connecticut Supreme Court will take up the arguments originally offered by plaintiffs.

The *Sheff* case is still being watched closely by legal scholars and civil rights activists, as guarantees of "equal" or "adequate" education contained in state constitutions may prove effective levers in obtaining metropolitan school desegregation remedies. What is more, the arguments and logic presented by plaintiffs in *Sheff* articulate some of the still prevalent concerns about the negative effects of school segregation and its usual accompaniment, concentrated poverty. It is this concentrated poverty that most concerns many advocates of racially desegregated schools. If planned well, often across school district lines, racial desegregation plans break up concentrations of poverty that cripple many urban schools. In Hartford, for example, teachers and principals testified at the *Sheff* trial that their schools are overcome by the burdens of poverty and isolation. In a statewide address in 1993, even Connecticut's governor, Lowell Weicker, a defendant in the case, cited school segregation as a serious educational problem and advocated increased desegregation through city-suburban cooperation (American Political Network, 1993).

The profound educational consequences of concentrated poverty are well documented in educational research. High poverty schools are far more likely to have high rates of teacher turnover, to have less qualified teachers and to be burdened with problems related to health and nutrition, family instability, violence, family unemployment, homelessness, inadequate facilities, and a lack of adequate monetary resources.

The most troublesome aspect of concentrated poverty and segregated schooling, according to University of Chicago sociologist William Julius Wilson, is the "social isolation" of children from middle-class opportunity and role models. Children who live and attend school in concentrated poverty, "find themselves in a qualitatively different environment, where the structure of social relations makes it increasingly unlikely that they will have access to the those resources and channels necessary for social mobility" (Wilson & Neckerman, 1988, p. 31).

The cruel irony of the inequity is that the students in these schools are the very ones who rely most heavily upon the schools to help them get out of poverty. These students often lack the family connections, monetary resources or community networks that allow for movement into the mainstream economy and higher education system. Viewed from this perspective, school desegregation should not be seen as an assimilationist strategy, but as a strategy for mobility that seeks to break down a stratified opportunity structure that has confined the poor, through housing policies and historical discrimination, to inferior inner-city schools.

An increasingly common dig at desegregationists in recent years has been "black kids don't need white kids to learn." But that winning populist phrase simply misses the essential point of desegregation. The essential point of desegregation is not for paternalistic whites to "help" African Americans, but to level the playing field of education, by giving poor minority children access to the same high-achieving educational environments and opportunity rich schools that middle-class white children get automatically by virtue of the fact that their parents can afford to live in suburban areas.

Sheff also underscores how conditions of segregation and inequality, while they may be ignored nationally or in local politics, recycle themselves. More than 20 years ago, the same city of Hartford, Connecticut filed an amicus curiae brief to the Supreme Court in support of plaintiffs in the *Milliken* case. Hartford's then city counsel Alexander A. Goldfarb urged the Supreme Court to halt the educational divisions between city and suburb that threatened cities across America.

> During the intervening period from 1954 to the present, state boards of education in Michigan, Connecticut and elsewhere in the nation acted under a policy of complicity and neglect . . . . This led directly to a metropolitan community best described as an expanding core of African American schools surrounded by a ring of white public schools . . . . Having encouraged and reaped the gains of regional growth and development, the State and its suburban surrogates cannot tenably claim that school

districts are unrelated and independent of one another. Such facile rationalization cannot be used to circumvent their clear responsibilities to eliminate racial discrimination in public education. (Goldfarb, 1973, p. 9)

The very same issues haunt the state government 20 years later in the *Sheff* case. So, while *Milliken, Dowell*, and *Pitts* might very well look like insurmountable roadblocks to desegregation, *Sheff* and the successful metropolitan desegregation lawsuits before it suggest that the battle for desegregated schools is by no means over.

Future Directions For Research, Policymakers, and Advocates

Brown's power has been stripped considerably but the struggle to achieve the decision's ideals continues some two generations later. School desegregation is a strategy that seeks not only to bring the races together for improved race relations, but also to break up concentrations of poverty that accompany racial stratification. Metropolitan desegregation plans usually offer the best chance of achieving socioeconomic, long-term, stable desegregation. While the barriers to such plans are formidable, focusing on such remedies may be the most promising strategy for fulfilling the goals of *Brown*. Advocates, therefore, should focus upon efforts that would allow economically disadvantaged urban children to take advantage of the economic growth and opportunity that exist within their own metropolitan area. Such an effort might very well start by documenting the inequalities between a given city and its suburbs.

A precondition for any informed, productive community debate about desegregation is a better general understanding of the history, the goals, the successes, and the public opinion on the issue. The desegregation issue has too long been used as a political punching bag, as a means for racially dividing the electorate, and as fodder for a misled media.

Policymakers, courts and others would benefit from further research on longer term benefits of city-suburban desegregation. Also needed is further research about in-school strategies and policies that seek to maximize benefits of district level desegregation by preventing resegregation through tracking and ability grouping.

Policymakers, meanwhile, should realize that problems of economic and racial segregation, which have profound negative effects upon education, will not resolve themselves. Even when the conditions have disappeared from public debate, it is quite likely that political and legal battles to correct such conditions will surface in time. If local and state governments take action to remedy the conditions now, they may very well avoid being forced to do so in the future. Indeed, even though historical, political and legal forces have converged to disarm *Brown*, the fact remains that minority families and their advocates know that a good education is linked to economic mobility and success. This means the fight for educational access will be with us for years to come, especially when the opportunities lie so very close to home, just across an invisible municipal boundary line.

References

ABC News/Washington Post Poll. (1981).   Cited in search conducted by Roper Center for Public Opinion Research, Storrs, Ct., on contract with the Harvard Project on School Desegregation. On file with the Harvard Project on School Desegregation, 6 Appian Way, Cambridge, MA   02138.

Connecticut Department of Education. (1993). *Strategic school district profile, 1993-94: Hartford school district.* Hartford, CT: Author.

Crain, R., & Mahard, R. (1982). *Desegregation plans that raise black achievement: A review of the research.* Santa Monica, CA: Rand Corporation.

Crain, R., & Strauss, J. (1985). *School desegregation and black educational attainment.* Center for Social Organization of Schools, The Johns Hopkins University. Report No. 359.

Eaton, S., & Meldrum, C. (1994). *Resegregation in Norfolk, Virginia: Does restoring neighborhood schools work?* The Harvard Project on School Desegregation, Harvard Graduate School of Education, Cambridge, Mass., 02138.   (ERIC Document Reproduction Service No. ED 346 082).

Edmonds, P. (1994, May 12). Only real difference: how best to desegregate. *USA Today*, p. 8A.

Gallup, G. H. (1972). *The Gallup poll: Public opinion 1935–1971*, (Vol. 3). New York: Random House.

Gallup Organization, Gallup Poll AIPO (1955, April 14–19). Cited in search conducted by Roper Center for Public Opinion Research, Storrs, Ct., on contract for the Harvard Project on School Desegregation, 6 Appian Way, Cambridge, MA 02138. On file with the Harvard Project on School Desegregation.

Gallup Organization, CNN/USA Today/Gallup Poll (1994, April 22–24). (Study No. 42204501). Report Card #5.

Goldfarb, A. (1974). Brief amicus curiae of City of Hartford, Connecticut to the U.S. Supreme Court. In Support of Respondent Bradley. No. 73–434.

Harris, L., & Associates. (1978). *A study of attitudes toward racial and religious minorities and toward women.* Report to the National Conference of Christians and Jews. (Study No. S2829–B). New York, NY.

Harris, L., & Associates. (1989). *The unfinished agenda on race in America.* Report to the NAACP Legal Defense and Educational Fund. (Study No. 883006–9). New York, NY.

Kluger, R. (1975). *Simple justice: The history of Brown v. Board of Education and black America's struggle for equality.* New York: Vintage Books.

Lewis, M. (1994, May 29). School daze; Classroom desegregation efforts in flux. *The Dallas Morning News,* p. 1J.

Mayfield, M. (1985, February 23). A top Justice official speaks out on ruling in Norfolk busing case. *The Virginian Pilot and Ledger Star,* p. 4.

National Opinion Research Center. (1975–1989). General social survey, cited by Roper Center for Public Opinion Research, Storrs CT, on contract with the Harvard Project on School Desegregation, 6 Appian Way, Cambridge, MA. On file with the Harvard Project on School Desegregation.

Orfield, G. (1993). *The growth of segregation in American schools: Changing patterns of separation and poverty since 1968.* The National School Boards Association. Alexandria, VA. (ERIC Document Reproduction Service No. ED 346 082).

Sanchez, C. (1994, May 17). Many black parents unsatisfied with desegregation. On *All Things Considered, National Public Radio,* Transcript # 1485–4. Washington, DC.

Schrag, P. (1994, May 17). Integration: Is it a tarnished trophy? *The San Diego Union-Tribune,* p. B7.

Theiss, E. (1993, January 27). NAACP objects to White comment; Mayor defends view on one race schools. *The Plain Dealer,* p. 2B.

Tye, L. (1992, January 5). Poll shows wide support across U.S. for integration. *The Boston Globe,* p. 15.

Uchitelle, S. (1988). *School choice: Issues and answers.* Phi Delta Kappan Fastback #348 P.O. Box 789, Bloomington, IN 47402–0789.

Vergon, Charles V. (1990). School desegregation: Lessons from three decades of experience. *Education and Urban Society, 23*(1), 22–49.

Wilson, W. J., & Neckerman, K. (1988). Schools and poor communities. In *School success for students at risk: Analysis and recommendations of the council of chief state school officers.* Orlando, FL: Harcourt Brace Jovanovich.

Table of Legal Cases

Alexander v. Holmes County Board of Education, 396 U.S. 1990 (1969).

Board of Education of Oklahoma City v. Dowell, 498 U.S. 237 (1991).

Brown v. Board of Education, 347 U.S. 483 (1954).

Brown v. Board of Education, 349 U.S. 294 (1955).

Freeman v. Pitts, 112 S.Ct. 1430 (1992).

Green v. School Board of New Kent County, 391 U.S. 430 (1968).

Keyes v. Denver, 93 S.Ct. 2686 (1973).

Milliken v. Bradley, 94 S. Ct. 3112 (1974).

Sheff v. O'Neill, No. CV89–0360977S (1995) Conn. Super. LEXIS 1148.

Swann v. Charlotte Mecklenburg County, 402 U.S. 1 (1970).

CHAPTER 6

"BUSING" IN BOSTON:
WHAT WE COULD
HAVE DONE BETTER

Charles L. Glenn

More than 20 years ago, in September, 1974, the first stage of mandatory re-assignment of pupils for race desegregation was implemented in Boston. The turmoil and violence which ensued that year and the year that followed, when a more extensive second stage was implemented, made Boston a symbol for what many took to be the high cost and ultimate failure of school desegregation as a strategy. The reality is more complicated. In a retrospective story published by the *Boston Globe* in 1994, I was identified as the state official primarily responsible for the first stage of Boston desegregation, and quoted as saying that I would do a number of things differently if I had the chance to do them over. These "second thoughts" are the theme of this reflection.

A Brief Overview of Court-Ordered
Desegregation in Boston
First, though, a brief overview will be presented of what happened to bring on court-ordered desegregation in Boston and how it evolved over the subsequent 20 years. The civil rights movement that began in the South in the late 1950s found its echo in the "Massachusetts Freedom Movement" of the early 1960s, focused above all on the inferior and de facto segregated schools attended by most Negro (as they then were called) children in

Boston and other cities; it was only subsequently that outsiders learned of the school system practices that made much of this segregation deliberate and thus de jure.   Inner-city schools had inferior facilities, since available construction dollars had gone to new residential areas, and their teachers tended to be the least experienced and credentialed because of the seniority system. Jonathan Kozol's *Death at an Early Age* (1967) based upon his teaching in a Boston school dramatized (indeed, over-dramatized) the gulf of misunderstanding and alienation between inner-city pupils and their teachers.

The demands of the National Association for the Advancement of Colored People (NAACP) and the Massachusetts Freedom Movement (in which I, as an inner-city minister, played an active role) extended to a wide range of school improvements, but included also measures to address the racial isolation of African American pupils. The demands, and especially the last, were rejected by the Boston School Committee, with one member announcing, "We don't have inferior schools in Roxbury, we just have inferior pupils!" Many months of demonstrations and appeals to suburban legislative support later, a law was enacted in 1965, giving the State Board of Education authority to require school systems with majority-minority schools to develop and implement plans to reduce "racial imbalance."

Half-hearted Desegregation

The Boston School Committee adopted several such plans over the next few years, relying primarily upon voluntary transfers by minority pupils and building new schools (with 65% state funding) in racial fringe areas where both white and African American pupils could walk to school. Very little was accomplished; according to the transcript of a closed meeting of the Committee, one member said that "foot-dragging and shilly-shallying" had worked very well up until then, and he saw no reason why the state should not continue to be taken in by such tactics.

I was appointed director of the state's efforts in early 1971, after serving for a few months as urban education coordinator. As it happened, several of the large new schools for which state funding had been provided were about to open, and among my first measures was to require specific plans for the desegregated enrollment of these facilities. As school was about to open in

September 1971, however, a crucial School Committee vote was reversed to allow white parents reluctant to send their children to school with "the colored" to continue to send them to several "white schools" instead; this resulted in heavily-minority enrollment in the new Lee School, though it was within walking distance of what was then a predominantly white area. With that, the fat was in the fire: it was evident that the School Committee would back down on all of its other commitments whose effect would be to require any white children to attend desegregated schools, even those in their own neighborhoods.

Subsequent investigations indeed uncovered a massive pattern of escape, facilitated by the school system, of white pupils from their *neighborhood schools* in racially changing areas to all-white schools in other areas, together with manipulation of attendance zones and elementary/intermediate/secondary feeder patterns to protect havens of all-white enrollment.

The State Moves to Enforce Desegregation

Fast-forwarding over two years of legal action, in 1973 the State Board ordered Boston to develop a comprehensive racial balance "short-term" plan affecting all schools to which pupils could be assigned on an desegregated basis from within a reasonable distance (a mile and a half for elementary and two miles for intermediate pupils). When the Committee failed to do so, the State Board, as required by law, directed me to prepare a plan that could be implemented immediately without — as in the past — waiting for the completion of often delayed construction projects. With the help of consultant Professor Jack Finger, my staff and I developed an assignment plan based upon data on the number, grade and race of pupils living in each of some 800 "geocodes". This state developed plan affected only about half of the schools in the city, since it was devised within constraints of transportation distance and contiguity of attendance districts (Massachusetts Research Center, 1975).

Hearings were held on the state plan in March 1973, and in June the State Board ordered that it be implemented in September 1974, with the intention that Boston use the intervening time to seek modification of details and to prepare for orderly pupil transfers and preparation of staff and facilities. For example, it became apparent that certain schools were not appropriate for the uses to which they would be put under the state plan, and that a few assignment patterns should be changed because of traffic conditions.

Unfortunately, the School Committee chose to fritter away that time with legal appeals, ordering its staff in the meantime to do nothing that might increase their readiness to implement the plan effectively; after all, a major basis for appeal was that the plan was simply unworkable. Incredibly, all modifications of the plan to make it easier to implement or more effective were rejected. When the appeals failed, therefore, the system was forced to implement a plan with many imperfections that could have been corrected, and with only a few weeks — rather than 18 months — of preparation.

The last throw of the dice for the Boston School Committee and that of Springfield, facing a similar mandate at the same time, was to persuade the state legislature to repeal the law upon which the racial balance order was based. The state's Supreme Judicial Court ruled that a desegregation plan, once adopted, would have to be implemented anyway; to fail to do so would itself be unconstitutional. "Even when steps toward desegregation are made voluntarily rather than pursuant to constitutional mandate," the Court wrote, "any subsequent State action which would cause a return of the preexisting segregation would itself be an act of de jure segregation."

Meanwhile, in June 1974, a suit that had been brought in federal court in March 1972 resulted in a finding that Boston had violated the constitutional prohibition by official action to segregate minority pupils. "At least 80% of Boston's schools," Judge W. Arthur Garrity wrote, "are segregated in the sense that their racial compositions are sharply out of line with the racial composition of the Boston public school system as a whole." This segregation had not arisen from residential patterns alone, but from deliberate actions and neglect on the part of the School Committee and its staff. Judge Garrity ordered that the state plan be implemented in September — as it would have been in any case as a result of the Supreme Judicial Court's order — pending development of a more comprehensive desegregation remedy to meet federal standards. (For an account of the legal process, see Adkins, McHugh & Seay, 1975; Massachusetts Research Center, 1976.)

Chaotic Implementation

Implementation in September, 1974, was chaotic, as a result of the lack of preparations and the refusal of the School Committee to consider modifications that would have improved the plan, even those approved and urged by the state. "Boston's readiness for desegregation was marginal . . . . Planning over the summer was haphazard" (United States Commission on Civil Rights, 1975, p.xxi). A large-scale boycott of schools by white pupils kept more than 10,000 out of school for the entire year, with little effort by school authorities to enforce the mandatory attendance law. More than the sporadic incidents of violence in a few schools, this inactivity by school authorities undermined the effort to put desegregated education on a normal footing. There was a "leadership vacuum"; the mayor made no secret of his opposition to the desegregation plan and the school superintendent did not have the stature or conviction to rise above the constraints placed upon him by the School Committee. Mayor White described his role as a "broker" between the various parties, sometimes referred to as "the extremists on both sides" (as though supporting the court's mandate made one an extremist). White deplored violence in the streets, but did not call for making desegregation work (United States Commission on Civil Rights, 1975, p.29).

Judge Garrity was drawn into making more and more administrative decisions for the school system because its leadership — under orders from the School Committee — refused to take any initiatives to implement desegregative assignments and the administrative measures required to support them. Each time this occurred it created an additional excuse for school system staff at all levels to assert their lack of responsibility for the results of their actions. The court's interventions encouraged a sort of rigid and resentful passivity which prevented, in far too many schools, the problem-solving enthusiasm needed to deal with the merging of African American and white pupils who had previously been schooled apart.

Even the police force became part of the problem. Because the police officers' union took a public position in opposition to school desegregation and helped to finance a legal challenge to the court's order, white opponents were encouraged to defy the court and African American pupils and their parents had reason to doubt the adequacy of the protection they would receive (Lupo, 1977).

In contrast, Springfield, Massachusetts implemented an equally-comprehensive racial balance plan the same month with no significant difficulties or disturbances, because the system, seeing the inevitability of it, had taken ownership of the process and made it work. As proof of the initial success of the Springfield plan, the school system reported that there was 89% attendance the first day of school. While in Boston elected officials were either running for cover or predicting that blood would run in the streets, the elected and community leadership in Springfield insisted that no disturbances of the education of children would be tolerated. Television news around the world carried images of racial conflict in Boston, while in Springfield the police presence was not needed after the first morning of "busing." "A Tale of Two Cities," state Education Commissioner Greg Anrig called it.

Even worse was the situation in Boston the following year, when a new plan developed by court-appointed experts undid the desegregative assignments of 1974 — over my privately-expressed objections — moving many children a second time, and reaching out to almost every section of the city (Dentler, 1991). It was in 1975–76 that the most dramatic confrontations took place in South Boston and elsewhere, and many began to consider the school system a lost cause.

The dozen years that followed were marked by relative stability of pupil assignments, but general incoherence of educational policy as a succession of superintendents each sought to make a mark. The state office that I directed put about $5 million of state desegregation funds into Boston each year (and smaller amounts into 15 other cities), and many individual programs and even schools showed promise, but the system as a whole seemed capable of absorbing and finally neutralizing all efforts at significant improvement. Sparks of energy and creativity would be nourished into little wavering flames, only to die away without spreading. Hundreds of capable teachers and administrators simply left the system in discouragement.

The Bottom Line

One thing *was* a success: the school system was desegregated in the formal sense required by the law. In 1970–1971 Boston had been a highly segregated system: only 23% of the public schools had enrollments within 20 percentage points of the city-wide average; by 1983–1984, 87% of the schools had enrollments within that range. Unfortunately, these desegregated schools by no means reflected the make-up of the wider society. White students went from being around 70% of the system-wide enrollment to being under 30%, largely because of population changes in the city.

The population change was already occurring rapidly before implementation of desegregation. Each year, twice as many white pupils graduated from 12th grade as entered first grade, and the proportion of "non-white" pupils had risen from 16.4% in 1960 to 32.5% in 1970. I later summarized this trend as follows:

> If racial proportions had continued to change at the 1960–1970 rate, the 1983 enrollment would be 53% "non-white." Black enrollment is in fact 48% of the total in 1983–84, and has declined in recent years . . . . The major enrollment increase has been in "other minority" students. (Glenn, 1984, p. 24)

Some have described this precipitous enrollment change as resulting from "white flight," though careful monitoring of the enrollment of parochial and suburban schools over this period found little evidence of where such flight of pupils might have gone. Indeed, a study by my office of enrollments in the two largest nearby suburbs (Newton and Quincy) found white enroll-ment declining as rapidly there as in Boston. This change seems to have been a regional feature (at least in areas of older housing stock) of declining birthrate and an aging white population that no longer had school-age children. After all, other cities like Chicago and Philadelphia that experienced no serious desegregation problems have undergone much the same racial shift in their schools.

On the other hand, abundant anecdotal evidence suggests that many individual pupils — white and African American alike — may have been encouraged to drop out of school altogether as a result of the disruptions and tensions of these difficult years. Others who might have been academically marginal in any case had their energies further distracted from schoolwork by the periodic eruptions in several of Boston's high schools.

What were the positive educational results from the court-ordered desegregation? Those are by their nature hard to measure, even for those intimately involved with school improvement efforts. It is of course a very complex picture, involving at most points more than 120 individual schools and countless programs.

My own impressions derive in part from the fact that over the entire period from 1971 to the present I have had my own children (seven in all) attending the Boston public schools, and so have watched the system with all the hope and anxiety of a parent, as well as with the hope and anxiety of the state official with overall responsibility for urban education.

Briefly stated and without the necessary qualifications, I would say that Boston's public schools have been running hard and improving in countless ways, thanks to many fine teachers and administrators and substantial outside resources, but that they are if anything further behind in delivering on their basic mission than they were 25 years ago. On most measures the schools are far better than when Kozol wrote his exposé, but somehow all the efforts don't add up to a first-rate education and few of the initiatives seem to result in permanent improvement.

There seem to be two reasons for this disappointing result of so much effort and expense. In the first place, societal changes have made the task facing schools, and particularly urban schools, considerably more difficult than it was even 20 years ago. The hollowing-out of civil society in inner-city neighborhoods, described by William Julius Wilson (1987) in *The Truly Disadvantaged*, was intensified by and in turn intensified the catastrophic decline in stable, two-adult families. Moreover, the culture of violence and alienation presented by youth oriented media, have by all accounts presented schools with challenges that simply cannot be met within the framework of less than six hours of contact time and perhaps three of actual instruction per day. It seems likely that we need a very different kind of school that can have as intensive a socializing effect as do elite boarding schools, an idea advanced by James Coleman more than 20 years ago (Glenn, 1994).

In the second place, large school systems may simply be dysfunctional in relation to the demands of effective education. They operate (indeed, arguably they *must* operate) in accordance with bureaucratic rationality to avoid arbitrary decision making, abuse of power and unequal treatment based upon bias, favor or corruption. Routinized procedures may be a very good thing at the Registry of Motor Vehicles or the IRS, but they work against creating really good schools, and they tend to reward compliance over effectiveness, much less initiative, among teachers and principals. This is perhaps especially the case when the political environment in which the school system functions (and of which its leaders must be keenly aware) is highly polarized. In such cases, a premium is inevitably placed on detailed hierarchical control so that no embarrassing mistakes will be made at any level in the system. The problem is compounded when a school system goes through frequent changes in the superintendency, as in Boston, each leading to disruptive periods of administrative reorganization during which few significant decisions are made.

In short, educational results in Boston have not miraculously improved as a result of desegregation; indeed, they may on average have grown worse. In fairness, much the same may be said of other Northern cities that have not desegregated in any significant way. As with racial change, trends that observers of Boston tend to attribute to the tumultuous desegregation process reflect closely what has happened elsewhere without that history. This is, of course, neither a consolation nor an excuse.

How the Process Could Have Been Improved

What are my "second thoughts" about desegregation efforts in Boston? What would I do differently if I could do over my own part, as the responsible state official, in the whole episode?

I would try much harder, if I could turn the clock back, to keep open communication with local officials, especially during the early stages of the process. Our approach to Boston school authorities was, as I see it now, too concerned with creating a public record in which we were always "right" and they always "wrong," and not enough with behind-the-scenes problem solving. The fact that our position was ultimately vindicated by the courts does not remove a lingering doubt about whether it has been vindicated by history. Our distrust of the Boston School Committee's intentions was based on its past record, and we had to avoid being put off with promises, as my predecessors had been. Nevertheless, we should have found supplemental "back channels" — perhaps through the mayor's office or business leadership — to communicate our expectations and work for solutions.

Once the case came under the jurisdiction of the federal court, it became even more difficult to negotiate solutions to the problems that continually and inevitably arose. The fact that appeals of the desegregation orders continued for several years encouraged the School Committee to maintain a posture of being forced into every implementation measure and of refusing to allow its staff to solve problems. The message conveyed to us at the state in 1974–1975, and undoubtedly to the federal court's experts subsequently, was: we'll carry the plan out exactly as you wrote it; wherever there's ambiguity, we'll choose the more disruptive alternative. We predicted that desegregation wouldn't work, and we're going to prove that we were right!

To be honest, there was rigidity on both sides. Once the full legal battles were joined, my own actions were very much controlled by how they would affect our prospects of winning in court. In order to comply with a provision of the law requiring the state to "advise" school districts that failed to come up with effective strategies for desegregation, my office made recommendations in a highly formal way that must have seemed unbearably smug as well as naive to our counterparts in the school system.

That we were later able to work collaboratively with good success in other Massachusetts cities facing desegregation mandates may be partially attributable to the scare that local officials in those communities had been given by observing the breakdown of negotiations in Boston. I may have been perceived as possessing more power in reserve than in fact was the case. After all, it seems likely that federal judges might also have looked to Judge Garrity's experience with Boston before deciding to take on other Massachusetts cities that were recalcitrant about desegregation.

We also learned from the Boston experience the importance of working with a plaintiff group, something that had not been anticipated when the 1965 racial imbalance law placed upon the state education agency the full burden of serving as advocate for and articulator of the issues of racial justice. As I wrote in 1983 as part of a report prepared by the Education Commission of the States, this involvement of plaintiff groups

> allows the state to mediate and interpret the conflicting interests of minority groups and school systems, rather than to serve as a surrogate for the interests of parents. The presence of minority parents who can articulate goals clearly and realistically produces a better plan at a lower cost to the state's on-going relationships with the school system. The second factor [in greater success] is the importance of agreeing at the start on expectations regarding the nature and impact of the plan. Such agreement, generally expressed in a list of principles used to assess every proposed option,

provides a common point of reference for negotiations. These principles set the rules by which all parties agree to play, and they provide assurance that special concerns will receive serious attention.

Gradually, the new state approach has become easier to implement. Each superintendent who has gone through the new process has emerged a stronger leader [i.e., none lost their jobs!] and ready to boast about how his schools have improved while desegregating. And while enforcement efforts in Boston and Springfield carried high political (as well as budgetary) costs for the state education agency [because of retribution by legislators], there is now a renewed support in the legislature for state desegregation efforts which are perceived as benefiting school systems . . . . In 1983, the racial imbalance law was broadened to include additional communities and the appropriation increased by $1.3 million. (Winslow, Andrews, Bray, Glenn, & Lines, 1983, p. 25)

Over the dozen years that followed implementation of racial balance plans in Boston and Springfield, we were able to persuade more than a dozen other cities to develop comprehensive plans on a "voluntary" basis: that is, through negotiation and without ending up in court. These plans, because they were locally owned, were implemented with much greater success than had been the case in Boston.

The success of desegregation in Springfield cannot be attributed to the benefits of hindsight. I keep on the wall of my office a newspaper photo of myself staring grimly at that school system's leadership during one of our early meetings, an apt reminder of how difficult those discussions were. I attribute the positive turn that the process in Springfield eventually took to the wise and principled leadership of Superintendent John Deady. It is no exaggeration to say that it was the confidence which we at the state came to have in his *character*, and the trust which he already enjoyed in Springfield, that made it possible for the plan to work. These factors allowed his very competent staff to develop, and us to accept, a desegregation plan fitted to the circumstances of his school system in a way that no plan developed by the state could have ever been. The Springfield School Committee, as adamant as that in Boston, refused to adopt Deady's plan, but it was a simple matter for us to adopt it as our own and to require that it be implemented. Having developed the plan, the school system leadership was committed to ensuring that it was a success in every detail of implementation.

I may be naive in suggesting that agreement could have been reached on an effective desegregation strategy in Boston, given the rhetorical virulence and refusal to consider the slightest compromise of several political figures, (most notably Louise Day Hicks and John Kerrigan) who for a time wielded enormous influence. They seemed willing to bring the whole system crashing down, and very nearly did, rather than make the slightest concessions to the agenda of the African American leadership and of the State Department of Education. After a time, school department officials were forbidden to meet with me; instead, there were full-scale and highly polarized public meetings of the State Board of Education and the Boston School Committee, with all local television channels in attendance. It seems likely, however, that informal channels could have been opened by the mayor and business leadership, and concrete steps worked out to make progress in areas on which the spotlight of media attention had not been turned. We'll never know.

A Different Kind of Plan

The other major change that I would make is in the nature of the desegregation plan that we developed for Boston, and that was implemented in September 1974. The underlying premise of that plan, I now understand, was a profound mistrust of ordinary parents and a determination to require them to overcome their prejudices and fears and send their children to the schools that we selected for them, in order to serve the common good. We were arrogant, and we were wrong. Don't misunderstand me: racial desegregation is a very good thing, and we should seek it in our schools by every legitimate means. For nearly 40 years, I have lived in an desegregated Boston neighborhood, attended desegregated churches and for 23 of those years have sent my children to desegregated public schools. But racial desegregation, like any legitimate end, should be sought by legitimate means, and simply substituting our "expert" judgment for that of parents was wrong.

How would I do it if I could do it over? I would seek to base school assignments so far as possible upon well-informed parent choice. This would in turn have the effect, if done right, of encouraging diversity and school-based decision making and of weakening the stifling effect of a hierarchically organized school system. Treating everyone in similar formal circumstances the same is one of the virtues of bureaucracy, but it is antithetical to the suppleness and responsiveness of good education. A system that must promote parent choice in order to achieve race desegregation will not find its efforts successful unless it can learn to allow decisions about the character and organization of each school to be made by those directly involved, both staff and parents.

Including a few magnet schools, as occurred in the second-stage Boston desegregation plan implemented in 1975, does not have the same effect. Having a few such schools accommodates the most engaged teachers and parents, but at the expense of depressing the energy level and the prospect for improvement of other schools even further. The reports I prepared for the Federal District Court

> revealed many problems with the way the process of providing information and encouraging choices was handled. In particular, there seemed little expectation that individual schools (apart from the magnet schools) would develop distinctive themes and encourage parents to take advantage of the possibilities for choice. (Glenn, 1987, p. 11)

At one point, for example, my office provided funding for a "recruitment specialist" to work with under-selected schools, but long delay in making an appointment rendered the position useless.

In 1989 Judge Garrity permitted the school system to implement a new approach to desegregation developed by Michael Alves, my long-time assistant for desegregation planning, and Professor Charles Willie. This plan was based upon a model developed originally in Cambridge and subsequently employed with good results in six other Massachusetts cities. Known as "universal controlled choice," this assignment strategy abolishes school attendance districts and requires all parents with children entering the system or a new level of schooling to indicate preferences that are then accommodated to the extent consistent with school capacities and racial guidelines.

> Controlled choice is . . . a means of maximizing the impact of choice for school improvement and for educational diversity while taking care to avoid the negative side-effects upon poor and minority children so

> often associated with unrestricted choice...and should be
> distinguished from calls for unrestricted market forces
> in education. (Glenn, 1990, p. 3; see Glenn, 1991, for a
> fuller account)

Four well-staffed parent information centers were established in Boston, at state expense, and the staff of each school were helped to develop materials explaining their programs to prospective parents.

While desegregation remained an objective and a requirement, the role of compulsion was greatly reduced with this new system. For example, only about five percent of children each year are assigned to schools that their parents have not expressed a willingness to accept. Of course, having offered parents a choice, the pang of disappointment is all the keener for those who do not receive their preferred assignment. This is particularly true for middle-class parents who, in the past, had almost a monopoly on applications to the magnet schools. In Boston, African American and "other minority" parents are actually more likely than white parents to be given the school assignment they seek for their children (Glenn, 1992).

This is not to suggest that controlled choice has been an unmixed success in Boston. Several of the elements required to make it an effective means of empowering parents and improving schools were very slow to develop, in part because they ran counter to the highly centralized control and distrust of initiative that is characteristic of any bureaucratic organization. In January 1990, for example, the Chair of the State Board wrote of the Board's "intense disappointment over the delays that put effective implementation of further modifications in jeopardy." The primary areas of inadequacy had to do with information to parents and school improvement efforts — sticks as well as carrots — for schools that were not attracting pupils. Both encountered stubborn resistance at all levels of the school system, perhaps because they assumed that more power could be given to parents both to decide among and also to make demands upon schools (Glenn, 1990).

Summing Up

My "second thoughts," then, have to do primarily with the overly rigid process by which a desegregation plan came into being, and the overly rigid nature of the plan itself. I wish that we had taken a "messier" approach, seeking areas of agreement with school officials rather than operating in a climate of mistrust, and working with rather than against the desire of parents and teachers to make decisions about how children are educated. I wish we could have found a way to say to parents and teachers in Boston (as, more wisely, we *did* in other cities), "create the sort of school you want most, provided that parents of both black and white children are persuaded to entrust them to your school." I am now convinced that many (though by no means all) of those who resisted and sabotaged the desegregation effort would have reacted very differently to a situation in which interracial cooperation had its rewards in improved schooling and more responsive schooling for their children.

There was another missed opportunity of a different nature. We should have used the desegregation crisis to push for fundamental and comprehensive changes in the school system. There were some behind-the-scenes discussions along these lines. For example, in our frustration over Boston's intransigence on piecemeal reforms of vocational, bilingual, and special education, I tried several times to persuade Massachusetts Commissioner Anrig to file legislation to simply break up the Boston school system into three or more smaller systems comparable to other cities we were working with more fruitfully. Ideally, these districts would have extended into contiguous suburban areas, as they did in Wilmington, Delaware. But the political cost of such proposals seemed too high.

Similarly, we included a variety of sweeping educational reform measures in the recommendations provided to the Boston School Committee in late 1972, as part of the process of putting pressure on them to authorize their staff to develop a desegregation plan, as had been done in Springfield. When they refused to do so and we were forced to develop a plan for them, the educational reforms somehow dropped out of the picture and we produced what was exclusively a student assignment plan concerned "to make the numbers come out right." The fact that we had only two weeks to complete that massive job may be some excuse, but I continue to feel that a great opportunity was lost. If we could somehow have designed the assignment plan in such a way that it required significant educational and organizational changes, the latter would have been included in what was subsequently ordered by the state and federal courts.

Lost opportunities, but also opportunities to learn from our mistakes. I console myself that other Massachusetts cities found the desegregation process an opportunity for educational reforms and for as much community energizing as (inevitably) community tensions, for expanded diversity as well as enhanced fairness to all children.

Patiently seeking solutions through a variety of channels, putting the power of parent and teacher choice to work, and using the desegregation crisis to press for fundamental reforms are lessons learned in Boston that we have been able to take across the Commonwealth and to a dozen cities elsewhere in the nation.

References

Adkins, J. F., McHugh, J. R., & Seay, K. (1975). *Desegregation: The Boston orders and their origin.* Boston: Boston Bar Association.

Dentler, R. A., & Scott, M. B. (1981). *Schools on trial: An inside account of the Boston desegregation case.* Cambridge, MA: Abt Books.

Glenn, C. L. (1984). *Desegregation in Massachusetts: 1983 annual report.* Quincy, MA: Massachusetts Department of Education.

Glenn, C. L. (1987). The new common school. In *Creating the new common school*, Quincy, MA: Massachusetts Department of Education.

Glenn, C. L. (1989). Putting choice in place. In J. Nathan (Ed.), *Public schools of choice.* St. Paul, MN: Minnesota, Institute for Learning and Teaching.

Glenn, C. L. (1990). *Controlled choice in Boston: The first year.* Quincy, MA: Massachusetts Department of Education.

Glenn, C. L. (1991). Controlled choice in Massachusetts public schools. *The Public Interest*, 103.

Glenn, C. L. (1992). Do parents get the schools they choose? *Equity and Choice, 9*(1).

Glenn, C. L. (1994). Schooling and the family crisis, *Revista Española de Pedagogía* (Spain), *51*, 196.

Kozol, J. (1967). *Death at an early age.* Boston: Houghton Mifflin.

Lupo, A. (1977). *Liberty's chosen home: The politics of violence in Boston.* Boston: Little Brown.

Massachusetts Research Center. (1975). *Balancing the public schools: Desegregation in Boston and Springfield.* Boston: Author.

Massachusetts Research Center. (1976). *The courts and desegregation.* Boston: Author.

Ross, J. M., & Berg, W. M. (1981). *"I respectfully disagree with the judge's order: The Boston school desegregation controversy.* Washington, DC: University Press of America.

United States Commission on Civil Rights. (1975). *Desegregating the Boston public schools: A crisis in civic responsibility.* Washington, DC: U.S. Government Printing Office.

Wilson, W. J. (1987). *The truly disadvantaged.* Chicago: University of Chicago Press.

Winslow, H., Andrews, R., Bray, J., Glenn, C., & Lines, P. (1983). *State desegregation initiatives in a period of transition.* Denver, CO: Education Commission of the States.

CHAPTER 7

THE HARTFORD DESEGREGATION CASE: IS THERE A JUDICIAL REMEDY FOR RACIALLY ISOLATED INNER-CITY SCHOOL DISTRICTS?

Richard Fossey

> Whether . . . segregation came about through the change of historical boundaries or economic forces beyond the control of the state or whether it came about through private decisions. . . what matters is that it is here and must be dealt with.

Governor Lowell Weicker (Jacklin & Pazniokas, 1993)

Introduction

Forty years after the Supreme Court's decision in *Brown v. Board of Education*, it is worth remembering that the Court buttressed its decision with social science research on the evil effects of racial isolation. The Court was persuaded that feelings of inferiority that could last a lifetime would be generated if African American children were assigned separate schools solely because of their race.

The Court's conclusion, that racial isolation harms children, did not depend on whether the isolation was intentionally caused. Nevertheless, it has subsequently been made clear that federal courts will only desegregate schools if they find that children have been intentionally segregated by race. As Eaton and Orfield discuss in Chapter Five, a distinction has been made between de jure and de facto segregation. De jure segregation results by law or deliberate act of school officials and is unconstitutional. De facto segregation results from housing patterns or other factors and is not remedial in the federal courts.

As a result of the distinction between de jure and de facto segregation, the federal courts have been unable to fashion effective desegregation plans for many of the nation's racially isolated urban school districts. In many urban areas, inner-city school districts with overwhelmingly African American and Hispanic school populations are surrounded by predominately white suburban school districts. Unless district boundaries were deliberately drawn to segregate children by race, which is seldom the case, the courts will not require suburban districts to participate in regional desegregation plans with inner-city school systems.

This chapter describes *Sheff v. O'Neill*, a lawsuit filed by schoolchildren living in metropolitan Hartford, which attempted to erase the distinction between de jure and de facto segregation. Abandoning all reliance on the U. S. Constitution, these children argued that racially isolated schools violate the Connecticut Constitution and must be desegregated, whether or not the racial isolation was the result of intentional government acts. They asked the court to develop a regional school desegregation plan that would encompass more than 20 school districts.

The *Sheff* plaintiffs lost their case at the trial court level, and the case is now on appeal. But regardless of the final outcome, *Sheff* will surely be a major milestone in the nation's long journey toward desegregated public schools. Forty years after *Brown* decreed an end to segregated schools, *Sheff* is a fresh attempt to make *Brown's* promise a reality for thousands of African American and Hispanic school children. If the Connecticut Supreme Court authorizes a cross-district desegregation plan, *Sheff* may mark the beginning of a fresh effort to desegregate schools on a regional basis. If such a plan is rejected by the court, *Sheff* will symbolize a growing judicial tolerance for large concentrations of impoverished African American and Hispanic school children attending racially isolated schools.

An Overview of *Sheff v. O'Neill*

Hartford school children, like school children in many urban school districts, are mostly African American or Hispanic. Like inner-city school children across the nation, they attend racially isolated schools that are surrounded by suburban, largely white school systems. In 1993, 93% of Hartford's students were African American or Hispanic; but nearby suburban districts had student enrollments that were 90% non-Hispanic white. In Connecticut as a whole, 80% of the state's minority students were enrolled in 18 districts; while 136 of the state's 166 districts had minority enrollments of 10% or less (Peirce, 1993).

In 1989, 17 schoolchildren from the Hartford area sued the state of Connecticut in an attempt to end the racial isolation of Hartford schools. In *Sheff v. O'Neill*, the children asked Judge Harry Hammer to develop a regional desegregation plan that would change the racial composition, not only of the Hartford school system, but of 21 surrounding suburban districts as well. They wanted Judge Hammer to redraw district boundaries to achieve racial balance or to order some other action to bring about racially balanced schools on a regional basis.

In April, 1995, Judge Hammer issued his long-awaited decision in *Sheff*, ruling that the state of Connecticut was not required to correct educational inequities that it had not caused. In a 72-page opinion, Judge Harry Hammer ruled that racial isolation of Hartford schoolchildren was the result of social and economic forces, not governmental action. Judge Hammer refused to impose any desegregation plan that would extend beyond the boundaries of Hartford, ruling that coercive desegregation strategies such as this were ineffective.

The *Sheff* plaintiffs quickly appealed, and the Connecticut Supreme Court accepted the case for expedited review. Oral arguments before Connecticut's highest court took place in late September 1995, where the plaintiffs renewed their plea for a regional desegregation plan for the metropolitan Hartford area.

Background of the Sheff Case

Unlike most desegregation lawsuits, *Sheff* was filed in state, not federal court; and the plaintiffs relied entirely on the Connecticut Constitution for relief. The *Sheff* plaintiffs' primary goal was to obtain a court-ordered regional desegregation plan for the Hartford metropolitan area. By filing in state court, they avoided the impact of federal case law that probably would have prohibited a multi-district desegregation plan for the Hartford region.

Specifically, by filing in state court, the *Sheff* plaintiffs made an end run around *Milliken v. Bradley* (1974) or *Milliken I*, in which the U.S. Supreme Court had rejected a court-ordered desegregation plan for the Detroit school system and 53 nearby districts. Federal courts had no authority to order such relief, the Supreme Court ruled, unless it were shown that district boundaries had been deliberately drawn to segregate children by race.

According to the Supreme Court, a multi-district desegregation plan for the Detroit area would make the district court the "school superintendent" for "a vast new super school district." In the Supreme Court's opinion, this was a task that few federal judges were qualified to undertake.

Moreover, the Supreme Court expressed a strong regard for the concept of local control in public education.

> Boundary lines may be bridged where there has been a constitutional violation calling for interdistrict relief but the notion that school district lines may be casually ignored or treated as a mere administrative convenience is contrary to the history of public education in our country. No single tradition in public education is more deeply rooted than local control over the operation of schools; local autonomy has long been thought essential both to the maintenance of community concern and support for public schools and to quality of the educational process. . .

As a result of the *Millikin I* decision, in cases involving de facto desegregation rather than desegregation created by law, federal courts were foreclosed from developing desegregation plans that crossed district boundaries. Three years later, in *Milliken II* (*Milliken v. Bradley*, 1977), the Supreme Court endorsed "educational compensation" remedies for such situations, which usually consisted of additional state money and special programs as a way of redressing the effects of past segregation in a district (Feldman, Kirby, & Eaton, 1994).

In *Sheff*, the plaintiffs argued that the education provisions of the Connecticut Constitution prohibited school children from becoming racially and economically isolated, no matter how that isolation came about. Even if the segregation had resulted by accident or by forces outside the state's control, the plaintiffs contended that the Connecticut Constitution compelled the court to develop a remedy. That remedy, they maintained, should be a regional desegregation plan that would change the racial composition, not only of the Hartford system, but of the 21 largely white suburban districts that surrounded Hartford.

Besides being a state rather than federal lawsuit, *Sheff* is also noteworthy for the fact that the state of Connecticut, the defendant, had an exemplary record for fighting race discrimination both in the schools and the workplace. In extensive findings of fact, Judge Hammer sketched the state's history of racial tolerance going back more than 100 years. Moreover, more than 30 years before *Sheff* was filed, Connecticut education leaders had recognized that school children in some Connecticut cities were becoming increasingly isolated by race; and they had taken a number of steps to address the problem (Integration proposals over 30 years, 1995).

Nevertheless, in spite of these efforts, the condition of children in Hartford had dramatically deteriorated. In 1970, the school system was 71% white, and only 32% of its 9th graders dropped out of school or transferred to other districts before graduating. Twenty years later, 93% of the district's enrollment was African American or Hispanic; and 55% of its 9th graders failed to graduate with their Hartford classmates (Christensen, 1993). In 1993-94, only 11% of Hartford students scored adequately on all three parts of state mastery tests, compared with 48% statewide. Almost three quarters of Hartford's students lived in poverty in one of the nation's most affluent states (How Hartford fares, 1995). In 1988, 67% of Hartford children were born to unwed mothers, up from 10% in 1960 (Christensen, 1993).

Judge Hammer's Ruling

Sheff v. O'Neill was filed in April 1989. Plaintiffs were represented by the Connecticut Civil Liberties Union, and consisted of 15 African American, Hispanic, and white Hartford school children and two white school children from the neighboring town of West Hartford. The case went to trial in January 1993, but Judge Hammer did not render his final decision until April 1995, six years after the lawsuit was filed.

Although plaintiffs submitted extensive evidence and testimony to support their case, their legal theory was simple. The Connecticut Constitution, they argued, guaranteed Hartford school children a minimally adequate education. This they were not receiving, as evidenced by scores on state mastery tests. Educational inequalities between Hartford's minority students and suburban white students were the result of state educational policies that had permitted de facto segregation of Hartford and surrounding suburbs. The state was constitutionally obligated to desegregate the districts on a regional basis, the plaintiffs maintained, regardless of how it had come about.

On April 19, 1995, Judge Hammer released a lengthy opinion summarizing the evidence, particularly with regard to state efforts to desegregate Connecticut schools. Based on this evidence, Judge Hammer ruled that racial isolation of Hartford schools was not caused by state action, but was the result of residential segregation and other factors beyond the state's control. Quoting a federal court decision, Judge Hammer concluded that "racially balanced municipalities are beyond the pale of either judicial or legislative intervention"; and he granted judgment in favor of the state (Sheff v. O'Neill, memorandum of decision, 1995).

Shortly thereafter, plaintiffs appealed; and the Connecticut Supreme Court directed Judge Hammer to supplement his decision with findings of fact. Judge Hammer complied; and on June 27, 1995, he submitted 161 separate fact findings (*Sheff v. O'Neill,* Findings of Fact, 1995). It is in this pleading that Judge Hammer's reasoning and the evidence he relied on becomes most clear.

First, Judge Hammer's fact findings showed that he was influenced by Connecticut's long history of local control in the field of education. Although he noted that Connecticut education had always been a colonial or state government responsibility, a tradition of local control could be traced back to the early eighteenth century. Judge Hammer was aware that the plaintiffs' request to redraw school district boundaries or change school attendance patterns in 21 districts would alter a practice of local school governance spanning almost 300 years.

Second, Judge Hammer was favorably impressed by the state's long history of combating racial segregation. Drawing on the trial testimony of a Connecticut historian, Judge Hammer sketched the state's record on race issues back to the mid-nineteenth century. In 1868, the state legislature had passed an open enrollment law, opening the schools to all children without regard to race, creed, or color. About the same time, the legislature abolished tuition in the public schools, making them accessible to all children without regard to socioeconomic status. In 1905, Connecticut abolished racial discrimination in public accommodations. It outlawed employment discrimination in 1936; and in 1943, the state created the nation's first civil rights commission (Findings nos. 17-19).

More importantly, Judge Hammer also found that Connecticut had actively promoted school desegregation for many years. Connecticut was one of only seven states that had spent its own funds on school desegregation programs without being under court order (Finding no. 46). Since 1966, the state had contributed financial and technical support for Project Concern, a voluntary interdistrict transfer program designed to promote school desegregation in the state's urban areas. According to the Judge, Project Concern and METCO, a similar project in Massachusetts, may be the longest continually operated desegregation programs of their type in the United States (Finding nos. 48-49).

Judge Hammer further noted passage of a racial imbalance law in 1969, at a time when Connecticut's urban schools were less racially isolated than they were in 1995. The state had also taken urban school problems into account in its funding formulas. It awarded more money to school systems with high percentages of children from low-income families and to districts with large numbers of children who scored below the remedial standard on state mastery tests (Finding no. 64). Since 1970, the state had provided technical assistance for intradistrict magnet schools, which were believed to help reduce racial imbalance and improve overall school quality.

Finally, Judge Hammer's fact findings recorded that Governor Lowell Weicker, speaking 11 days after the *Sheff* trial began, had publicly acknowledged racial and economic isolation in Connecticut schools and had urged the state legislature to act. In June 1993, the legislature had responded to Governor Weicker's plea by passing legislation to encourage voluntary intradistrict cooperation to reduce racial isolation (Finding no. 86).

Judge Hammer then shifted his attention to the state's responsibility for school conditions in Hartford. "Students in the Hartford schools are racially isolated," he acknowledged, " and are likely to become more isolated in the future" (Finding no. 42).

Furthermore, this racial isolation was coincident with poverty and low standardized test scores.

Plaintiffs had argued that Hartford children's low standardized test scores provided proof that education in Hartford fell below constitutionally permissible minimum standards. They further argued that the low academic achievement was attributable to racial isolation, which the state was constitutionally obligated to correct.

But Judge Hammer disagreed. He ruled that poverty, not racial isolation, was the principal cause of low academic achievement in Hartford. It was inappropriate, he added, to use state mastery test results to draw conclusions about the quality of education in Hartford. On the contrary, Judge Hammer cited evidence to show that the Hartford education system was working well, given the background and socioeconomic status of Hartford students. Hartford teachers were no less qualified than suburban teachers, Judge Hammer noted (Finding no. 120); they were relatively well paid (Finding no. 67); and they were dedicated to providing quality education (Finding no. 121). In fact, he observed, some of Hartford's special education classes were among the best in the state (Finding no. 124). Hartford's teacher training program was based on the "effective schools" concept, which was specifically designed to meet the needs of urban and minority children.

In short, Judge Hammer ruled, the state of Connecticut was providing Hartford school children with a minimally adequate education, in the sense that their education gave them a chance to be successful in life (Finding no. 132). Hartford children did not do as well as suburban children on state mastery tests; but in Judge Hammer's opinion, that was not the fault of the education system. "Teachers and educational administrators have no control over where their students live or the conditions under which they live," Judge Hammer reasoned. "[N]or can they be expected to attend to their physical and psychological health needs. . . ." (Finding no. 141).

Judge Hammer concluded his Findings of Fact with several pessimistic observations. First, he wrote:

> There are no educational strategies . . . that can fully deal with the complex social issues that produce in-

equality and undermine education because substance abuse, hunger, parental neglect, crowded and substandard housing and inadequate employment opportunities disproportionately attack minority children in our state and divert them from educational opportunity (Finding no. 142).

Second, Judge Hammer observed: "There are no existing standards or guidelines that educators, social scientists or desegregation planners can . . . recommend in order to achieve the proper racial, ethnic and socioeconomic balance" for the schools of metropolitan Hartford (Finding No. 157). Citing some of the experts who testified in the case, Judge Hammer stated flatly that mandatory student assignment plans or other coercive means of achieving desegregation either failed or had unacceptable consequences (Finding No. 159).

Finally, Judge Hammer wrote, meaningful integration could only be achieved by building affordable suburban housing for the purpose of breaking up urban ghettos and by making urban schools more attractive to suburban families (Finding No. 161). In other words, the plaintiffs' proposal for a court order directing Hartford and suburban districts to reconfigure district lines or take some other mandated action to achieve racial balance simply would not work.

Sheff's Legal Significance

Judge Hammer's decision, with its bleak conclusions about school desegregation, was appealed and may be reversed by the Connecticut Supreme Court. Regardless of how that court decides, *Sheff* will not be legally binding outside Connecticut. The dispute hinges on an interpretation of the Connecticut Constitution, not federal law.

Nevertheless, if the *Sheff* plaintiffs are successful, they will have vindicated a legal theory for avoiding the Supreme Court's *Milliken* decision, which restricts federal courts from ordering interdistrict desegregation plans in most circumstances. If the Connecticut Supreme Court ultimately authorizes a regional desegregation plan for Hartford and 21 surrounding towns, *Sheff* might encourage courts in other jurisdictions to rely on their state constitutions to craft regional desegregation plans for metropolitan areas in their states.

Indeed, the *Sheff* plaintiffs are not the first parties to rely on state constitutional principles to argue for a court-ordered regional desegregation plan. In a 1979 case, the California Court of Appeals ruled that California courts can order interdistrict desegregation plans as a remedy for racially imbalanced schools, even if some of the affected districts played no part in creating the problem (*Tinsley v. Palo Alto Unified School District*, 1979). According to the California court, *Milliken* provided no guidance for enforcing the California Constitution, which obligated school districts to eliminate *Tinsley* was essentially nullified by a constitutional amendment, approved by voters in 1979, prohibiting state courts from implementing school-assignment or pupil-assignment plans that went beyond the scope of what a federal court would impose.) Likewise, the New Jersey Supreme Court, ruling before *Milliken*, held that the state commissioner of education had the power to merge two school districts to avoid racial imbalance. Local government boundaries "may readily be bridged," the New Jersey Supreme Court said, to enforce racial and educational policies embodied in the state constitution (*Jenkins v. Township of Morris School District*, 1971, p. 629). That decision involved the prospect of merging two districts that existed side-by-side within one community. But in a 1992 opinion, a New Jersey appellate court made clear that the state board of education also had the power to "regionalize" several unrelated districts to improve racial balance (*Englewood Cliffs v Englewood*, 1992).

In spite of these precedents, however, *Sheff* is charting new territory. None of the earlier state court decisions involves desegregation plans as large as the one the *Sheff* plaintiffs envision — a metropolitan desegregation plan that would manage student enrollment in 22 districts. *Sheff's* demand — that a *state* court disregard local boundaries to shape a large-scale desegregation plan — is unprecedented in reported court cases.

If the plaintiffs are successful, *Sheff* will almost certainly encourage others to bring similar suits on state constitutional grounds. Such a development would follow the precedent set in school finance litigation after the U. S. Supreme Court's *Rodriguez* decision (*San Antonio School District v. Rodriguez*, 1973). In *Rodriguez,* the Supreme Court ruled that per-pupil funding disparities among Texas school districts were not remedial under the U.S. Constitution, foreclosing future school funding challenges in the federal courts. Plaintiffs then began attacking inequitable school financing schemes under the education clauses of their state constitutions. Taking their lead from the California Supreme Court's *Serrano* decision (*Serrano v. Priest*, 1971), courts in more than a dozen states have invalidated education financing formulas that were deemed unfair (Underwood, 1994). In each of these cases, the courts relied on state constitutional provisions as the basis of their decisions.

Persuading State Courts to Adopt Regional Desegregation: Is It Realistic?

Plaintiffs may find, however, that persuading state courts to create regional desegregation plans is more difficult than convincing them to address school funding inequities. For many state courts, the injustice of school funding disparities was fairly apparent; because of differences in communities' taxable property wealth, some districts were able to spend more money on schools than others. Furthermore, the remedy was also relatively straightforward; in essence, courts ordered state legislatures to develop new funding formulas that would provide more equitable funding among districts. Although state legislatures often had great difficulty developing politically palatable funding formulas (Sparkman & Hartmeister, 1995), that was the legislatures' problem, not the courts'.

The problems of racially isolated urban schools are much more complicated than school funding inequities, however; and the best strategy for solving those problems is by no means certain. Enforcing regional desegregation plans would be a massive judicial undertaking, involving thousands of students and school employees, next to which the school-funding litigation would seem small by comparison. For example, the Detroit-area desegregation proposal which the Supreme Court rejected in *Milliken* would have involved as many as 700,000 school children and 50 school districts.

Plaintiffs might also find state court judges politically disinclined to approve regional desegregation plans, particularly in regions where local control is a strong civic value. For example, a regional desegregation plan to diminish racial isolation of the Boston schools could involve more than 40 suburban towns.

Would a Massachusetts state judge order a regional desegregation plan that diminishes local control in Acton or Concord — towns that have managed their schools more or less autonomously since before the American Revolution?

We should also remember that in many states, state court judges are elected. Unlike federal judges who are appointed for life, many state judges must face the voters at regularly-scheduled elections. In these jurisdictions, it would take extraordinary political courage for a state court judge to decree a regional desegregation plan that would affect pupil assignments in the affluent suburban districts that surround most inner-city school systems.

Developing Regional Desegregation Plans:
Some Policy Considerations

Apart from the viability of *Sheff's* legal theory or the willingness of state judges to alter the character of local school governance, regional desegregation plans raise major policy issues. Does it make sense, 40 years after the *Brown* decision, for courts to expand the scope of judicial segregation remedies in an effort to break the racial isolation of inner-city schools?

There are good arguments that the courts should engage in such a task. Forty years after *Brown,* the evidence is irrefutable that the Supreme Court's promise of desegregated schools remains unfulfilled in the inner cities. Hartford's racially isolated schools are typical. In Washington, DC, 90% of the student enrollment is African American; in Atlanta, the figure is 91%; in Baltimore, it is 82%; and in New Orleans, 87% of the student body is African American. During 1986–1987, a majority of the schools in 9 of the nation's ten largest districts had enrollments that were at least 80% minority. Of the 47 member districts of the Council of the Great City Schools, only nine have student enrollments that are predominately white. These 47 districts enroll 36% of the nation's public school African American students, 30% of its Hispanic children, and 21% of its Asian American children (Council of the Great City Schools, 1994, p. 4).

Moreover, in all urban districts where there are high concentrations of African American or Hispanic students, high rates of poverty are also present. Student performance in urban schools almost invariably lags behind student performance in the suburbs, and dropout rates are high. Although it is impossible to compare graduation rates among the inner-city schools because of variations in measurement techniques, on-time graduation rates are generally low, hovering around 50% (Fossey & Garvin, 1995; Burch, 1992). In many of these districts, an African American eighth-grader's chance of graduating from high school is only about 1 in 2.

So far, few court-ordered desegregation plans cross district boundaries; and plans developed for a single urban district have been largely ineffective. Again and again, urban districts have come under federal court desegregation orders only to have their white and middle-class students melt away to surrounding towns. If we are truly going to desegregate the public schools, something else must be tried. In fact, regional desegregation plans may be the only way desegregated schools will become a reality.

Nevertheless, before implementing large-scale multi-district desegregation plans, we should realistically assess the difficulties involved in such an undertaking and the likelihood of success.

Difficulty of Supervising "Super Districts"
First, we cannot ignore the problems associated with judicial management of "super districts," problems which the Supreme Court identified when it rejected a regional school desegregation plan for metropolitan Detroit (*Milliken I*). Wholly apart from the logistical problem of transporting vast numbers of students, the Court saw a number of political and administrative difficulties.

> Some of the more obvious questions would be: What would be the status and authority of the present popularly elected school boards? Would the children of Detroit be within the jurisdiction and operating control of a school board elected by the parents and residents of other districts? What board or boards would levy taxes for school operations in these fifty-four districts, if this were deemed requisite? What provisions would be made for financing? Would the validity of long-term bonds be jeopardized unless approved by all of the component districts as well as the State? What body would determine that portion of the curricula now left to the discretion of local school boards? Who would establish attendance zones, pur-

chase school equipment, locate and construct new schools, and indeed attend to all the myriad day-to-day decisions that are necessary to school operations affecting potentially more than three-quarters of a million pupils?

Of course, not every regional desegregation plan would be as large as the one that had been contemplated for Detroit. But most of the Supreme Court's questions apply to every regional desegregation plan, and certainly one as large as that which the *Sheff* plaintiffs seek. It would be naive to argue for regional desegregation without providing realistic answers to the questions raised by the Supreme Court in *Millikin I.*

Necessity for Developing Accountability Standards

Second, as the Harvard Desegregation Project pointed out in a 1994 report, previously approved court-ordered desegregation plans sometimes had no clear guidelines for determining success. After examining desegregation plans in four districts, the Project concluded that there was "no evidence whatsoever that the expensive programming and extra money [called for in the desegregation plans] redressed the harms of desegregation or provided an equal educational opportunity" (Feldman, Kirby, & Eaton, 1994, p. 5).

The districts that the Harvard report described had implemented *Millikin II* remedies, where "educational compensation" money was the prime component for redressing harms caused by segregation. Presumably, regional desegregation plans like the one contemplated in *Sheff* would require much more actual desegregation than those plans required. Nevertheless, the Project's report illustrates the danger of implementing desegregation plans which have no clear goal for improving educational outcomes for dis-advantaged students and no accountability mechanism to determine whether any benefits will be realized. The report's authors recom-mended that courts appoint educational experts to help design effective desegregation plans and a panel of professional independent monitors to make sure the plans are carried out (Feldman, Kirby, & Eaton, 1994, p. 10).

Assessing the Need for More Financial Resources

Third, before committing financial resources to regional desegregation programs, we should recognize that our racially isolated urban schools are not always short of money. Per-pupil funding in Hartford, for example, was over $8,600 per year during 1992-93, higher than the state average. Hartford received 62% of its budget from state revenues; almost twice as much as the average district received (How Hartford schools fare, 1995). This pattern is fairly typical. Massachusetts' racially isolated school districts — Lawrence and Holyoke, for example — receive relatively high levels of state financial assistance; and per-pupil funding for some, Boston in particular, is above the state average. New Jersey's racially-isolated urban districts are also well funded. The New Jersey department of education recently took control of three of them, based on evidence of mismanagement, corruption, and low student performance (McLarin, 1994). Lack of money was not their primary problem.

Urban school systems might argue that they need more money to deal with the high number of children living in poverty — 74% in Hartford in 1992 — and additional funding, targeted wisely, might improve educational outcomes for some of these systems (Ferguson, 1992). Nevertheless, it would be a mistake to develop regional desegregation plans under the assumption that every inner-city school system has a shortage of financial resources or that committing more money will bring good results.

Addressing Mismanagement and Corruption

It would also be a mistake to develop interdistrict desegregation plans without addressing the mismanagement and corruption that sometimes exist in many inner-city districts. We seldom read about wholesale corruption in wealthy, white communities — Marin County, California, for example, or Wellesley, Massachusetts. Most serious abuses are discovered in inner-city districts, where school populations are overwhelmingly African American and Hispanic.

Although little research has been done in this area (Fossey, 1995), newspaper reports confirm that it is a significant problem. In Washington, DC, for example, auditors recently discovered that district officials had hired hundreds of employees, including teachers, with criminal arrest or conviction records (Strauss, 1995). New York City has been plagued with mismanagement or corruption concerning asbestos inspections (Marks, 1993), custodial services (Flamm, Loughran, R., and Keith, 1992), school supplies (Bloomfield, 1995), and child abuse reporting (New York City Board of Education, 1994). According to news reports, other urban districts have similar problems (Primetime Live, 1995).

Stopping fraud and abuse in urban school systems may be as critical to improving schools for minority students as desegregating them. The Supreme Court's decision in *Brown v. Board of Education* was intended to improve the life chances of African American children. Desegregating inner-city schools will not achieve that goal unless the schools that African American children attend are well-run and staffed by honest and conscientious educators.

Conclusion

Our racially isolated urban school systems — with their high rates of poverty, high dropout rates, and substandard student performance — are a national disaster. Desegregation efforts so far have failed to disperse this isolation. New efforts will not succeed until the destinies of white suburbs are welded to the destinies of Hispanic and African American inner-cities. Regional desegregation plans for metropolitan schools show promise of breaking up urban concentrations of impoverished, racially isolated children, but the federal courts have been constrained by *Milliken I* from ordering such plans in most circumstances.

The *Sheff* plaintiffs tried to break this log jam by suing in state, not federal, court. They argued that the Hartford school system's racial isolation violates the Connecticut Constitution; and they asked a state judge to order a regional desegregation plan that would include Hartford and 21 surrounding towns. If the *Sheff* strategy works, either in Connecticut or in another state's court, great progress might be made toward fulfilling the promise of *Brown v. Board of Education*, now more than 40 years delayed.

On the other hand, regional desegregation plans may provide one more opportunity for disillusionment. If they disrupt suburban school systems without achieving desegregation or improving life chances for African American and Hispanic students, these plans may further weaken public support for urban schools.

Therefore a regional desegregation strategy should not be pursued unless some precautions are taken. First, the problems of administering regional desegregation plans that the Supreme Court identified in *Milliken I* should not be minimized. A court will need extensive administrative and logistical support to successfully implement such a plan. Second, the goals of regional desegregation plans should be clear from the outset; independent monitors should determine whether the goals have been met; and the educators who implement these plans must be held accountable for results. Third, we should recognize that some of our inner-city schools are well-funded; in those districts the challenge is determining how best to spend the resources that are presently available, not how to find more money to fund desegregation efforts. Finally, corruption and mismanagement that exists in some urban districts must be rooted out if efforts to improve the quality of education for African American and Hispanic children is going to achieve the results we desire.

Obviously, the stakes are enormous. Over the long term, the nation cannot prosper with large populations of racially isolated, impoverished, and poorly educated children dwelling in our major cities. All signs show that this class is growing. If regional desegregation plans fail to improve this situation or if some alternate effective strategy is not devised, the nation's well-being will certainly be imperiled.

One thing is certain. More than forty years after the *Brown* decision, African American children in many of our inner cities are as segregated from white children as they were in 1954. If we are unable to change this situation, we must face the fact that *Brown's* promise of equal educational opportunities for all children has been irreparably broken.

References

Bloomfield, D. C. (1995, September 22). Decentralize now. *New York Times*, p. A-ll.

Burch, P. (1992). *The dropout problem in New Jersey's big urban schools:Educational inequality and governmental inaction.* New Brunswick, NJ: Rutgers, Bureau of Government Research.

Christens, J. (1993, March 15). Weicker watch: Connecticut Governor Weicker'splan to integrate schools across the state. *National Review.*

Council of Great City Schools. (1994). *National urban education goals: 1992-93 indicators report.* Washington, DC: author.

Feldman, J., Kirby E., & Eaton, S. (1994). *Still separate, still unequal: The limits of Milliken II's educational compensation remedies.* Cambridge, MA:Harvard Project on School Desegregation.

Ferguson, R. F. (1991).   Paying for public education: New evidence on how and why money matters. *Harvard Journal on Legislation 28,* 465–498.

Flamm, S. R., Loughran, R. A., & Keith, L. (1992, November). *A system like no other: Fraud and misconduct by New York City school custodians.* New York: New York City Office of the Special Commissioner ofInvestigation.

Fossey, R. (1995, October 25). Corrupt, mismanaged, and unsafe schools: Where is the research? *Education Week,* p. 31.

Fossey, R., & Garvin, J. (1995, February 22). Cooking the books on dropout rates, *Education Week,* p. 48.

How Hartford schools fare. *Hartford Courant,* April 13, 1995, p. A15.

Integration proposals over 30 years. (1995, April 13). *New York Times,* Section B, p. 6.

Jacklin, M., & Pazniokas, M. (1993, January 7). Weicker calls for integration;School regions sought to end racial imbalance. *Hartford Courant,* p. A1.

Marks, Peter. (1993, August 8). Asbestos tests were faked, officials say. *NewYork Times,* p. 37.

McLarin, K. J. (1994, July 23). New Jersey, denouncing local management, prepares to take over Newark's schools. *New York Times,* p. 10.

New York City Board of Education (1994, October). *Final Report of the Joint Commission of the Chancellor and Special Commissioner for the Prevention of Child Sexual Abuse.*

Peirce, N. (1993, February 28). A governor gleefully tackles income tax, school disparities. *Dallas Morning News,* p. 5J.

PrimeTime Live. (1995, May 3). *Reading, writing and rip-off.* ABC News.

Sparkman, W., & Hartmeister, F. (1995). The Edgewood saga continues: The Texas school finance system is constitutional. *Education Law Reporter 101,* 509–529.

Strauss, V. (1995, April 14). Board to urge schools to fire workers with serious records. *Washington Post*, p. C1.

Sullivan J. A. (1986). Equal protection in the post-*Milliken* era: The future of interdistrict remedies in desegregating public schools. *Columbia Human Rights Law Review 18,* 137-167.

Underwood, J. (1994, November 19). School finance symposium. National Organization on Legal Problems of Education. San Diego, CA.

Table of Legal Cases

Butt v. State, 842 P.2d 1240 (Cal. 1992).

Englewood Cliffs v. Englewood, 608 A.2d 914 (N.J. Super. A.D. 1992).

Jenkins v. Township of Morris School District, 279 A.2d 619 (N.J. 1971).

Milliken v. Bradley, 433 U.S. 267 (1977).

Milliken v. Bradley, 418 U.S. 717 (1974).

San Antonio School District v. Rodriguez, 411 U.S. 1 (1973).

Serrano v. Priest, 5 Cal.3d 584, 96 Cal.Rptr. 601, 487 P.2d 1241 (1971).

Sheff v. O'Neill, CV89–0360977S, Memorandum of Decision (Judicial District of Hartford, April 12, 1995).

Sheff v. O'Neill, CV89–0360977S, Statement of Facts (Judicial District of Hartford, June 27, 1995).

Tinsley v. Palo Alto Unified School District, 154 Cal. Rptr. 591 (Cal. Ct. App. 1979).

CHAPTER 8

BLACK COLLEGES AND DESEGREGATION:
AN INTRODUCTORY OVERVIEW

Charles Teddlie and Kofi Lomotey

Section II, The Impact of Desegregation on Black Colleges, contains three of the six chapters in this volume that consider the impact of the *Brown* and the *Hawkins* decisions on historically black colleges and universities (HBCUs). These six chapters can be briefly summarized as follows:

1. Chapter Two (from Section I) — The authors of this chapter provide an historical overview of the impact of the *Brown* and *Hawkins* decisions on HBCUs, especially across three time periods (1964–74, 1975–84, 1985–present). Enrollment figures for HBCUs from the beginning of the twentieth century through 1995 are reported in this chapter. It also contains comments on the threats that desegregation has posed to HBCUs in terms of the loss of students and the potential merger/closure of institutions.

2. Chapter Seventeen (from Section III) — The author of this chapter discusses the failure of the news media to accurately and completely cover higher education desegregation issues, such as the recently adjudicated Mississippi case. An interesting aspect of this chapter concerns the sometimes adversarial relationship between the NAACP and the administrations at HBCUs, which was also discussed in Chapter Two.

3. Chapter Nine — The authors of this chapter present particulars regarding the November, 1994 adjudication of the longstanding Louisiana higher education desegregation case from

their point of view as administrators at Southern University (an HBCU directly affected by the case).

4. Chapter Ten — The author of this chapter is the President of an HBCU who was called as an expert witness regarding the Mississippi higher education desegregation case, in which the closure of HBCUs was considered.

5. Chapter Eleven — The author of this chapter (reprinted from an earlier article appearing in *Education and Urban Society*) discusses at length the unique role that HBCUs have played in the education of African Americans. Information from this chapter allows the reader to place the Louisiana, Mississippi, and Alabama court cases in the context of the larger issue of the continuing role of HBCUs in the education of African Americans as we approach the twenty-first century.

6. Chapter Twenty (from Section IV) — The author of this chapter presents an overview of the future of HBCUs and proposes an intriguing solution to the ongoing problems faced by these institutions.

Taken together, the information contained in these six chapters provides a unique set of perspectives regarding the evolving role of HBCUs in educating African Americans. With the resolution of the higher education cases in the South, some general conclusions can be made regarding the future of HBCUs, but as these chapters attest, there are many unresolved issues.

Turning to the particular chapters in this section, Delores R. Spikes (the President of the Southern University system) and James Meza (a former board member of the system) explore in Chapter Nine the impact of the *Brown* decision on the Southern University system. According to these authors, 40 years after the *Brown* decision, educational opportunities at predominantly black institutions are still not comparable or equal to that of predominantly white institutions. In relation to this point, they note that one year after the *Brown* decision, Louisiana spent three times as much money at Louisiana State University as it did at Southern University. Spikes and Meza conclude that the impact of any desegregation court rulings, settlements or legislation should minimally: (a) provide opportunities for success in higher education for African Americans, (b) clearly indicate through policy and practice that African Americans and their institutions are not subordinate or inferior, and (c) provide representative African American input into higher education public policy.

Spikes and Meza refer to the unresolved issue of the land grant status of Southern University in Baton Rouge (SU-BR), a city that also serves as the home for another land grant university (the predominantly white Louisiana State University). As noted in Chapter Two, President Spikes was recently rebuffed by the Louisiana Board of Regents in her efforts to get a new land grant center (together with other programs) at SU–BR. This controversy is a good example of the continuing difficulties that HBCUs face in getting quality graduate programs developed in states in which the predominantly white universities are often Research I or II institutions and have a virtual monopoly on many of these programs. Waltman in Chapter Twenty addresses this issue by proposing a separate system for all HBCUs administered by a federal governing board.

Another particularly fascinating part of the Spikes and Meza chapter is the recounting of the negotiations that occurred during the desegregation case in Louisiana. At one point in these negotiations, the Southern University Board of Supervisors (the only predominantly African American *system* of higher education in the U.S.) was willing to go along with the creation of a single board of higher education in the state, thus eliminating their unique role as a separate board. This did not occur, however, as the Governor's counsel later called stating that "the deal was off" with no further explanation. Details of these negotiations were not made public at that time, nor carried in the state newspapers, thus providing more evidence for the conclusions from Chapter Seventeen regarding the failure of the news media to accurately and completely cover higher education desegregation issues.

Frederick S. Humphries (the President of Florida A & M University, an HBCU) addresses the impact of the Mississippi desegregation case on HBCUs in Chapter Ten. He notes that during segregation, Mississippi state officials deliberately built inferior facilities and provided inadequate resources for African Americans to ensure that individuals and institutions would not miss the point — blacks were not equal to whites. He further indicates that "this perception of inferiority is the hidden frame of reference used to justify the state's plan (*U.S. v. Fordice*, 1992) to close Mississippi Valley State, constrain Jackson State University and deprive Alcorn State University of its autonomy." Humphries concludes that such a plan shows a disrespect for HBCUs and their culture, dampens the ambitions of black students and further perpetuates the perception of inferiority of programs, institutions, and all things initiated by or associated with African Americans.

This theme of the real or imaginary "inferiority of educational opportunities" at HBCUs is echoed throughout this volume. It was first addressed in Chapter Two, where the authors noted that NAACP attorneys made use of the "separate and unequal" argument in their efforts to desegregate graduate and professional education in the decade following World War II. The tendency for some educators to lump all HBCUs into one, usually unflattering, category was also discussed in that chapter. The theme is picked up in Chapters Fourteen and Fifteen of this section in which the Presidents of two HBCUs contend that states have historically failed to provide HBCUs with the resources necessary to be on an equal basis with predominantly white state institutions.

In Chapter Sixteen, Antoine M. Garibaldi (the Vice President for Academic Affairs at Xavier University of Louisiana, a private HBCU) explains the role HBCUs have played in educating African American students. He begins by noting that although HBCUs represent less than 3% of all colleges and universities in this country, and enroll less than 20% of all African American college students, they still graduate a disproportionately high number of African American students. He further indicates that HBCUs provide a supportive environment in which African American students who come from varied socioeconomic backgrounds with average abilities can succeed.

In conclusion, Garibaldi suggests that: (a) the academic enrichment provided through tutoring and remedial assistance, (b) their faculty's close monitoring of students' academic progress, (c) the small class sizes, and (d) the promotion of graduate and professional opportunities at HBCUs facilitate resilience in African American students and raise their academic expectations and abilities. He further suggests that many institutions of higher education can learn from the successful programs of HBCUs and that HBCUs should be recognized for the contributions they have made to society, and in particular, to the lives of African American youth.

Colon (1991), in a similar vein, related five functions that HBCUs continue to play in African American higher education:

1. *Pedagogical* — HBCUs have a history of taking students with inadequate educational backgrounds and transforming them

into successful college students through remediation, guidance and support.

2. *Psycho-social* — HBCUs provide African American students with a hospitable, nourishing environment as opposed to the alienation and isolation which face many of them at predominantly white institutions.

3. *Cultural* — HBCUs serve as repositories for African American culture and as centers for research and writing regarding this culture.

4. *Economic* — HBCUs traditionally provide African American students with a more affordable college education experience than predominantly white institutions.

5. *Political* — HBCUs have produced generations of African American leaders and continue to promote forums for exploring solutions to community problems.

Garibaldi was an expert witness in the Alabama higher education case (as indicated in his updated introduction to this chapter in this volume). Thus, this volume contains contributions from key players in three of the most important higher education desegregation cases in the U.S.: Alabama (Garibaldi, an expert witness), Louisiana (Spikes and Meza, officials at the foremost HBCU in the state), and Mississippi (Humphries, an expert witness and an official at an HBCU in another Southern state). Their perspectives in this section of the volume are illustrative of the importance that many high ranking African American educators place on the continuing and expanding role of HBCUs.

The Garibaldi chapter (Chapter Eleven) also presents information that was discussed extensively in Chapter Two regarding the enrollment and graduation rates at HBCUs. There is a discrepancy between the methods that Garibaldi and the American Council on Education (ACE) have used in calculating HBCU enrollment and graduate data. As noted in Chapter Two, Garibaldi's analyses included African Americans enrolled in all institutions of higher education, including two-year colleges. Thus, the aforementioned conclusion that HBCUs enroll less than 20% of the total number of all African Americans in college is based on a denominator that includes the large number of African American students enrolled at two-year institutions. The most recent ACE publications use in the denominator only those African Americans enrolled in four-year institutions. The Garibaldi method would indicate that HBCUs enroll a smaller percentage of the total number of African American undergraduate students than the ACE method. This discrepancy is potentially important in policy terms, because the Garibaldi estimate indicates that HBCUs produce a disproportionate share of undergraduate degrees, while the ACE figures indicate a production proportionate to other types of institutions.

While there is some debate regarding these overall figures, there is little doubt concerning another conclusion that Garibaldi makes in Chapter Eleven: HBCUs continue to educate a disproportionate share of African American students who have academic and/or economic disadvantages and little access to other institutions of higher education. For these students (many of whom have low college entrance test scores and low high school grade point averages), their choice for higher education comes down to HBCUs or two-year institutions, which often are dead-ends for students wishing to complete a bachelor's degree. The HBCUs, on the other hand, provide these students a nourishing environment in which their chances for attaining a bachelor's degree is much better than is the case with other alternatives available to them.

References

Colon, A. (1991). *Black studies and historically black colleges and universities: Towards a new synthesis.* Unpublished manuscript.

CHAPTER 9

THE IMPACT OF THE *BROWN* DECISION ON THE SOUTHERN UNIVERSITY SYSTEM

Delores R. Spikes and James Meza, Jr.

Historical Perspective Through the Filing
of *U.S. v. Louisiana* in 1974

Article 231 of the Louisiana Constitution of 1879 set the agenda for publicly supported segregated higher education in the state of Louisiana (L.A. Constitution, 1879):

> The General Assembly shall also establish in the city of New Orleans a university for the education of persons of color; provide for its proper government, and shall make an annual appropriation of not less than five thousand dollars nor more than ten thousand dollars for its maintenance and support. (p.168)

The Supreme Court's *Plessy v. Ferguson* (1896) decision gave credence to the state's intent and action relative to separation of the races in colleges or universities by declaring that separate but equal accommodations were not violative of the Fourteenth Amendment. The state of Louisiana was apparently comfortable, then, in relocating the Southern University created by Article 231 of the 1879 Constitution to Scott's Bluff (Scotlandville, Louisiana), just north of Baton Rouge, in 1914. Louisiana State University was only a few miles to the south of the relocated Southern University, but was for whites only. When branches of Louisiana State University were established in New Orleans and

Shreveport, branches of Southern University followed in the same cities — as late as 1959 and 1964, respectively. This was, of course, following the *Brown* decision of 1954.

Meanwhile, the Louisiana legislature had created other institutions exclusively for white students. However, the funding patterns for the African American schools (Southern University and Grambling State University) were by no means comparable or "equal" to that of the predominantly white institutions. (Grambling State University was originally Lincoln Parish Training School and later Grambling College and a junior college until 1948.) One year after *Brown v. Board of Education* (1954), Louisiana spent three times as much per student at Louisiana State University as it did at Southern University (Samuels, 1991).

While the *Brown* decision gave impetus to efforts to tear down the walls of de jure segregation in higher education, the decision itself was not to have the potential sweeping effects of a Supreme Court ruling applied to higher education until its citation in *Ayers v. Fordice* (1992). At this writing, it is yet too early to surmise what the long-range effects of *Ayers* will be, although some have written on the subject from their broad and long-time study of desegregation in higher education and close attention to the desegregation of higher education in Mississippi (Blake, 1991). (See Chapters Two, Nine, and Ten for other discussions of the *Ayers* case.)

Brown gave further impetus and encouragement to a move-ment that would end de jure and de facto segregation in all areas of public life. The Civil Rights Act of 1964 was an outgrowth of this movement and of increasing consciousness in the matter of race among larger segments of the American people. Title VI of the Civil Rights of 1964 asserted that:

> No person in the United States shall, on the grounds of race, color or national origin, be excluded from partici-pation in, be denied the benefits of, or be subjected to discrimination under any program or activity receiving Federal financial assistance.

The United States Department of Health, Education and Welfare (DHEW) charged in 1969 that Louisiana was in violation of Title VI of the 1964 Civil Rights Act because the State operated a racially segregated system of public higher education and directed the state to submit a desegregation plan.

On February 16, 1973, the court in *Adams v. Richardson* (1973) ordered DHEW to secure acceptable plans for higher education desegregation from Louisiana and nine other states within 120 days of the court's order or to commence enforcement action against those states under the provisions of Title VI. Among the nine other states named in the *Adams* case were Mississippi, Georgia, Florida, and North Carolina.

The original intent of the *Adams* case certainly was not to place the burden of desegregation on historically African American colleges and universities. One intent was to enhance sufficiently and significantly African American colleges so as to attract other race students, thereby serving as a means of desegregation.

The state of Louisiana did not submit a plan for desegregation of higher education as required by DHEW. Accordingly, on March 14, 1974, the United States Department of Justice filed suit against the State of Louisiana for maintaining and operating a dual system of higher education. Specifically, the United States complained that Louisiana was maintaining Grambling State University and Southern University as predominantly African American institutions, while simultaneously maintaining other public universities and colleges in the state as predominantly white institutions. More specifically, the United States maintained that Louisiana had failed to provide financial support and approval on an equal basis for Grambling and Southern universities for new academic program implementation, physical facilities and for overall general enhancement. Further, the United States maintained that Louisiana, through its governors, followed a practice of appointing predominantly white persons to serve on the Board of Regents, the Board of Trustees, and the Louisiana State University Board of Supervisors, while appointing predominantly African American persons to the Southern University Board of Supervisors — thereby maintaining racially dual governing boards. The suit was dormant until 1979.

Louisiana Higher Education Consent Decree Between
the State of Louisiana and the United States
In 1981, the State of Louisiana (inclusive of Southern University and Grambling State University, along with other, predominantly white, public universities and all higher education governing boards of Louisiana) entered into a consent decree with the United States (*United States v. Louisiana*, 1984). This consent

decree was to erase vestiges of the dual system under which the Justice Department declared Louisiana continued to operate. This was to be done in a prescribed period of time — six years.

Under the consent decree, historically African American institutions were to be significantly enhanced through the implementation of new academic programs, new capital outlay projects, faculty development and the overall general enhancement of existing programs. The original consent decree document set forth goals for other race presence at historically African American institutions and for what is described in the formal consent decree document as proximate institutions in relation to these African American institutions. The predominantly African American institutions (PBIs) and their proximate, predominantly white institutions (PWIs) are:

PBIs
Southern University — Baton Rouge
Southern University — New Orleans
Southern University — Shreveport
Grambling State University
PWIs (Proximate)
Louisiana State University — Baton Rouge
University of New Orleans
Bossier Parish Community College
Louisiana Tech University

The consent decree specified new academic programs that would be implemented at PBIs in the state. Most of these programs were developed and implemented exclusively by the respective PBIs during the six-year period of the decree. Some were specified to be offered on a dual or cooperative basis with the proximate institution.

Ideally, the programs that were offered as cooperative or dual degree programs were to attract other race students to the campuses of both the PBIs and the PWIs. These programs were especially important because the other race students who took courses at their proximate institution contributed to the other race student goals on that particular campus. The new academic programs that were offered by Grambling and Southern were also designed to attract other race students.

The consent decree stipulated that certain new construction and renovation projects were to be identified for PBIs. Again, the intent was ultimately to enhance the PBIs to the extent that other-race students would want to enroll at Southern University or Grambling State University. A number of capital outlay projects were prioritized and submitted for funding during the period of the consent decree. In terms of actual buildings completed during and shortly after the consent decree, the numbers were dismally low.

Very few capital outlay projects were completed by the end of 1987 within the Southern University System. It is perhaps also significant to note that during the period of the consent decree and the existence of a consent decree capital outlay program, little or no non-consent decree related construction was approved or funded for Southern University. So, in one sense, the consent decree capital outlay programs, which were to enhance the existing capital outlay programs, *became* the capital outlay programs for both Southern University and Grambling State University. Some buildings that were crucial to the success of specific consent decree programs and are crucial to the success of programs in general were not completed until 1993–94. As of this writing, some $47 million (adjusted for inflation) in consent decree projects for Southern University remain unfulfilled.

Another important component of the consent decree program was the Faculty Development Program. This program allowed Grambling and Southern University faculty members, who were not holders of the terminal degree, to pursue the doctorate in their respective areas. Participants received leave with pay not to exceed a three year period. The PBIs felt that this component of the consent decree was a success. At Southern University at Baton Rouge alone, during the six-year consent decree period, over thirty faculty members participated in the program, representing fifteen disciplines. More than one-half of that number had received the terminal degree by 1989.

One gets mixed reviews when assessing the total impact of the consent decree on Southern University. On the one hand, some high quality programs were added and persist to this day. Physical facilities that started construction after the signing of the consent decree in 1981 are still not compatible overall to the goals envisioned at that time. Southern University argued that its consent decree programs were never funded to insure high quality development during the six-year period. Budget requests, based on Board of Regents' guidelines, were systematically reduced by the Regents' staff, with little or no rationale provided to the university. Southern University further contended that some of the new academic programs offered under the consent decree proved to be a drain on existing programs and resources such as faculty, staff, equipment, and services. While this was brought to the attention of the Regents, no specific relief was ever provided.

Although there were many shortfalls in the implementation of new programs, there were some successes. Since their inception, the School of Nursing at Southern University (Baton Rouge) and the graduate Social Work program at Southern University (New Orleans) have been and are today excellent programs which have attracted other race students at rates of 30% or higher. Ironically, while programs at Southern University described as high-demand, limited enrollment programs (such as baccalaureate, registered nursing [R.N.], and law) attracted white students, similar programs at predominantly white schools have not been as successful in attracting significant proportions of African Americans.

The impact of these professional education programs can be traced to the fact that although intended as a policy directive to increase desegregation at Southern University, the enhanced programs have also served to educate African Americans in ever larger numbers. However, an examination of recent demographic data in enrollment trends disproves the contention that the enhancement of Southern University only benefitted a larger pool of African Americans. Although larger numbers of African American students enrolled in these enhanced programs at Southern University, it is apparent that the significant number of white students would not have enrolled there without the enhancements.

Monies were allocated to Southern for general enhancement for a six-year period. Unfortunately, Southern University was forced to use these funds to offset consistent budget reductions in the overall appropriations for all state universities. General enhancement, therefore, never took place and could not have under the existing rather severe budgetary restrictions.

In summary, some basic reasons as to why the consent decree was not as effective as it could have been are as follows: consistent underfunding for program development, failure to complete capital outlay projects in a timely fashion, "supplanting" of regular appropriations (for example, inability to use enhancement funds for enhancement because of budget reductions), and perpetuation of negative attitudes and views.

In retrospect, the outcomes of the consent decree would have been more substantial if there was more diligence and persistence on the part of Southern University. This could have occurred through the Consent Decree Monitoring Committee and through Counsel, addressing specific failures on the part of the state to live up to its commitment as stipulated in the consent decree and demanding that these failures be corrected at the time of occurrence. These more aggressive actions might have resulted in some definitive steps being taken to eliminate many of the problems and obstacles cited during the course of the consent decree.

Overall, the efforts of all of the participants in the consent decree fell somewhat short in terms of effective monitoring and follow-through with prescriptive measures to correct problems as they occurred.

After the Consent Decree

The consent decree was to expire December 31, 1987, but provided that the plaintiffs could request the United States District Court (for the Eastern District of Louisiana) to conduct a hearing for the purpose of determining whether the defendants had fully implemented all provisions of the decree. On December 29, 1987, the United States District Court requested an evidentiary hearing to determine if the consent decree had, in effect, been fully implemented. On December 31, 1987, Southern University filed a motion charging the State of Louisiana with failing to comply with the consent decree. The District Court denied both motions for an evidentiary hearing.

On March 30, 1988, the parties were directed by the District Court to prepare summary motions on whether a racially segregated system of higher education existed in Louisiana, and the parties complied. On August 2, 1988, the three-judge panel of the United States District Court issued a summary judgment finding Louisiana liable in operating a segregated system of higher education in violation of Title VI. The District Court also declared that the consent decree had failed to end racial discrimination in higher education in Louisiana and therefore concluded that the consent decree had ended as of December 31, 1987.

The District Court issued its own guiding principles for a plan for desegregation that it would find acceptable. These principles or features included:

1. A reduction in the number of senior colleges and the duplicity of programs, especially where proximate institutions were involved.

2. The creation of an open-admissions community college system.

3. The institution of higher minimum entrance requirements for senior colleges.

4. The creation of a single governing board for higher education.

Of interest was the fact that the District Court had permitted no argument or evidence that would have supported its plan. In fact, Counsel for Southern University deposed at least one expert witness whose scholarly work negated the position taken by the District Court on the single governing board issue.

Louisiana Governor Charles "Buddy" Roemer appointed a twenty-member task force to draw up a desegregation plan by November 18, 1988. This task force failed to agree on a plan. Then, on December 2, 1988, Dr. Paul Verkuill (Law School Dean at William and Mary) was appointed Special Master and commissioned to recommend a remedy to the Court. The Special Master's Final Report and Proposed Order was submitted to the Court on May 26, 1989.

On July 19, 1989, the United States District Court issued a ruling which abolished the current four-board governing structure for higher education in favor of a single governing board, merged the Southern University Law Center into the Louisiana State University Law Center, created a four-tier classification system for the state's colleges and universities (including a new community college system) and provided for enhancing the historically African American universities "whenever fiscally possible," among other provisions. The order was to be effective August 18, 1989.

Perhaps little known outside of the realm of those directly involved in negotiations prior to the order of July 19, 1989, is the fact that the long-standing lawsuit came close to being settled just prior to Judge Schwarz's federal District Court order. University officials and attorneys for Southern and Grambling State (principally through Grambling State's alumni) had been in marathon discussions with Governor Roemer and his counsel. Governor Roemer had campaigned on and pushed for a single governing board for higher education, a position that was apparently embraced by the District Court. Grambling State University and Louisiana Tech had entered into a Stipulation Agreement, which was acceptable to the District Court. Most, if not all, parties in the case considered, therefore, that if the remaining issues could be resolved (principally the governance issue) then the case could be settled.

When Southern University's attorneys and officials left the Governor's office, it was with the understanding that the Governor and his Counsel had agreed that if the Southern University Board of Supervisors would consent to the single board provision, then the state would agree to:

1. Expeditiously complete the state's commitment to Southern University under the consent decree.

2. Provide sufficient funding for Southern University at Baton Rouge to move — with priority — to Doctoral II status.

3. Guarantee African American representation on the "new" board at some percentage to be agreed upon.

4. Insure that Southern University at New Orleans and Southern University at Shreveport/Bossier City would also continue with enhancements in line with the spirit and commitments of the consent decree.

At a hastily called meeting, the Southern University Board of Supervisors agonized over Southern University's alternatives at this point. They considered the Southern University legal position and wondered why the burden of desegregation had to come again on the "backs of African Americans." They weighed all possible outcomes including settlements, District Court rulings, and appeals. Some recalled what had happened to African American principals, teachers, and students in Louisiana as a result of desegregation of the public schools. One former principal told how he had been removed from his principalship and appointed as an assistant principal to a younger, white principal at another school, and told to "teach" the younger principal.

Board members were anxious because they felt they had few choices based on "true" justice and because they felt that Southern University had to bear the brunt of the decisions being made. They were very concerned about future decisions from the courts, which they perceived as no longer being the allies of people of color who still suffered from discrimination. However, in the end, without formal notification, they decided that Southern University was too important to African Americans for the generations yet to come, and thus the Board itself was willing to take a back seat in favor of a greatly strengthened Southern at all campuses. Then, on a Saturday morning while Judge Schwarz was waiting to receive word from Counsel for the parties who would certify to him that the state was willing to settle, attorneys from Southern University received a call in New Orleans from the Governor's counsel saying that "the deal was off," that the State would not settle. No explanation was offered at that time.

Whether one agrees with its informal decision to settle or not, Southern University's Board had made a bold and courageous move. It had opted, on faith in a system that would guarantee the campuses of Southern and its Law Center long awaited enhancements through a court-ordered mandate, to place itself in the posture of possible oblivion in favor of Southern's historical and expanded missions finally being supported and funded. The Governor's sudden reversal, however, caused the pendulum of that faith to swing to the opposite direction. Never again, to this day, has the Southern Board relented from its current position of opposition to a single governing board for higher education. As we shall see later, however, there were talks of other options for governance.

Returning to the movements in the courts, the District Court, on August 4, 1989 denied Southern University's motion (joined in by the Attorney General but opposed by the Governor) for a stay of the Court's order of July 19, 1989. On August 14, 1989, Southern University's ruling was granted indefinitely by United States Supreme Court Justice Byron White. The District Court issued a remedial order on October 30, 1990, noting that should the Supreme Court issue a finding that overturned the findings of the Fifth Circuit Court of Appeals in *Fordice*, then the District Court's orders would be implemented immediately.

The Supreme Court did overturn the Fifth Circuit (*United States v. Fordice*, 1992) on June 26, 1992, and Judge Schwarz moved immediately to reinstate his earlier order. A show cause hearing was scheduled for September 30, 1992, at which time all parties were scheduled to present any new information or new proposed plans for consideration by the Court in lieu of the Court's earlier order. Legal counsel for all parties to the suit filed a joint motion for continuance. The request was for a sixty-day extension, but a thirty-day extension was granted, with any new proposals or information to be presented on November 2, 1992.

Meanwhile, there were meetings held among higher education officials and others to try once again to settle the case. These efforts failed. Again, the issue of governance was prominent. This time, spokespersons for the Board of Regents and for the Governor (now Governor Edwin Edwards) proposed a multiple-board system based on a tiering of the state's colleges and universities.

The Southern University Board of Supervisors considered the various proposals, but insisted that, given the state's history in the education of minorities, African Americans in particular would have to have representation on the boards in sufficient percentages to enable them to have more than token influence. In the end, not all of the other parties found this condition acceptable. Those discussions also found some engaging in counter proposals to benefit certain institutions without regard to the nature or requirements of the desegregation lawsuit or any settlements thereof. Thus, these talks, too, failed and a settlement was not reached.

We note that once again the Southern University System was called upon to meet in specially called sessions a number of times, and did so primarily because of its sincere effort to do whatever it could to reach some resolution. However, University officials and attorneys were able to develop a proposal for the law centers that did not require merger and which was acceptable to both the Southern University and Louisiana State University boards and to Judge Schwarz. On December 23, 1992, Judge Schwarz reinstated his order, except this time the law center merger was removed.

The United States Justice Department in a Motion for Reconsideration and to Alter or Amend Judgment asked the District Court to make further factual findings in support of its ruling of December 22, 1992 and to clarify and amend specified portions of the order. The Court held that "the factual findings contained in its prior opinion are sufficient to sustain its determination with respect to the State of Louisiana's liability in this matter." The Court further found that the Justice Department's requested clarifications of and amendments to the District Court's remedial plan were either unnecessary or premature in view of the framework and plain language of the court's order. The District Court denied, on January 20, 1993, the United States Justice Department Motion for Reconsideration and to Alter or Amend Judgment.

The implementation date for the District Court's Order was pushed back 35 days from "entry of this order" (that is, from January 20, 1993). On February 4, 1993, the State filed a motion for stay and suspension, pending appeal, of the judgment and order entered by the District Court on December 23, 1992, and all previous judgments and orders reimposed therein. The District Court denied the state's motion for stay and suspension of the judgment and order pending appeal on February 19, 1992. The State of Louisiana and Southern University successfully appealed the District Court's denial of motion for stay to the Fifth Circuit Court of Appeals on March 3, 1993.

Remand of the Case Back to the District Court by the Fifth Circuit

The Fifth Circuit heard oral arguments in June, 1993. Southern University argued (a) that the District Court properly found the state liable for maintaining a segregated public higher education system and, (b) that the District Court erred by applying the *Fordice* standard to a state constitutional provision that was race neutral — the creation of the Southern University Board of Supervisors, along with the state's other three higher education governing boards. Southern University's position was that *Fordice* was limited to the evaluation of a constitutional challenge to policies and practices held over from de jure segregation. *Fordice* did not challenge state statutes and constitutional provisions that were race neutral. Thus, absent a showing of discriminatory purpose, the Louisiana constitutional provision creating the Southern University Board of Supervisors and other management boards was unchallengeable from the point of view of desegregation.

The Fifth Circuit ruled in favor of the state defendants and remanded the case to the District Court for trial. In particular, the Fifth Circuit agreed with Southern University's argument and took the issue of four boards out of the case. The Southern University Board of Supervisors no longer had to concentrate its energies on fighting to preserve its existence. With the immediate threat of the dismantling of the four board management system eliminated, settlement on the other critical issues in the case could now be explored. On remand, the District Court set a March, 1994 trial date but urged the parties to participate in settlement negotiations.

What followed was approximately one year of intensive negotiations.

Settlement Agreement

On November 14, 1994 a settlement agreement was signed by all of the parties including Judge Charles Schwarz, Jr., Governor Edwin Edwards and legal representatives of the United States Department of Justice (*United States v. Louisiana*, 1994). The signing of this agreement signaled the end of a lengthy lawsuit of twenty years.

The settlement established a ten-year plan to end the legal battle of whether Louisiana's public colleges are illegally segregated by race. The settlement calls for the state to spend $48 million over the next decade to establish new programs intended to attract other race students at Southern University and Grambling State University. Southern University will receive $34 million of the funds. In addition, the plan calls for $9 million in scholarship monies to be made available for attracting minority students (African American) students to Louisiana State University and other predominantly white public higher education institutions in the state.

The settlement also mandated that $47 million for the next ten years be allocated for capital outlay projects at Southern University. Most of these projects were left over from the 1981 Higher Education Consent Decree (*United States v. Louisiana*, 1981). Another feature of the settlement was a mandate that a community college be established in the Baton Rouge area under the joint management of Southern University and Louisiana State University. Finally, the settlement preserves the Southern University Board of Supervisors and the state's three higher education management boards. It also preserves the Southern University Law Center and all other campuses and entities in the Southern University and A&M College System.

Land Grant Issues Unsettled

Throughout the settlement negotiations, land grant issues surfaced but were never resolved. For the purpose of this discussion, the term "Land Grant Issues" is defined as any issue arising out of and related to the allocation of federal funds and the appropriation of state funds for agricultural research and extension services to designated land grant institutions (First Morrill Act, 1862 & Second Morrill Act, 1890). The State of Louisiana has designated Southern University and A&M College and Louisiana State University and A&M College as its land grant institutions. While both universities are authorized to administer statewide agricultural research and extension programs, Louisiana State University has always received a disproportionate share of federal and state funds. This policy is traceable to de jure segregation and remains a current vestige.

The issues raised by challenging the current land funding proved to be a hindrance during settlement negotiations. Consequently, the parties agreed to settlement of all other issues except land grant, which have been preserved for later resolution.

Impact on Higher Education

It is possible to speculate on the impact from the more general *Ayers* decision and from previous appeals court rulings. First, it is the authors' contention that there will be more issues on higher education making their way to the United States Supreme Court. For one thing, clarifications and rulings will be sought regarding issues such as vestiges of de jure segregation, duplication of programs and acceptable standards or criteria for admission to higher education institutions.

One can expect the vestige issue to be addressed from a variety of sources, including the United States Department of Education, regional and national panels or committees, individuals writing in scholarly journals or in the print media and litigants at state or federal level. There are those, for example, who indicate that in the Southern states, the higher education institutions themselves (African American or white) are vestiges of de jure segregation. Others suggest that the limitations in terms of program growth, as well as facility growth, are vestiges of de jure segregation. The severe underrepresentation of African Americans at the doctoral level, especially in areas of science, engineering, and some of the arts and humanities, is often cited as directly attributable to a long history of the unavailability of these programs to African Americans.

If agreement is ever reached on what constitutes vestiges of de jure segregation in higher education, the more immediate and substantive question is "What do we do to remove the vestiges, as the U.S. Supreme Court ruling demands?" Responses have ranged from the closure of institutions, to merger, to the transfer of programs, and to the differentiation of missions. These are not new proposals and, indeed, some have been tried (for example, the merger of the predominantly white University of Tennessee at Nashville with Tennessee State University, an historically African American university).

But there have not been debates focusing on more novel and less traditionally defined approaches. Regrettably, perhaps due to the nature of the litigation, there has not been much structured public debate at all. At least, there has not been the level of public discussion which an important issue such as this one deserves.

Conclusion

The long history of court and legislative sanctioned policies and practices rooted in racism in the South (and to some extent, nationally), makes it difficult (a) to erase suspicion of African Americans as to whether government can or will propose solutions in their best interest and, (b) to impose upon higher education standards of desegregation that are absent in the larger community (Waltman, 1994). Thus, now and then, some bold proposals are made which can at least provide an opportunity — and perhaps a widening spectrum — for public debate (Waltman, 1994). (See Chapter Twenty in Volume 14 for an expanded version of the Waltman article.)

The Southern University System holds that the impact of any Court rulings, settlements, legislative, or other decisions regarding desegregation should minimally:

1. Provide that access to higher education for minorities — particularly African Americans who comprise 30% of Louisiana's population — and for poor people in general, be enhanced, not diminished. Access here is broadened to mean real opportunities for success once the student is admitted. These opportunities necessarily take into account campus climate, adequate counseling, and academic support services.

2. Clearly indicate through policy and practice that African Americans and their institutions are not subordinate or inferior. This means that traditional views that desegregation is always best accomplished by closing historically black colleges and universities (HBCUs) merging them into historically white institutions, or

limiting them in their role, scope, and mission must give way to other considerations that enable the HBCUs to benefit, not suffer, from the elimination of vestiges of de jure segregation and to become desegregated as full partners in the mainstream of higher education.

3. Provide that representation of African Americans in higher education is proportionate at all levels.

4. Provide that African Americans have meaningful input into public policy and rule-making governing higher education.

5. Provide that a definition of duplication of programs takes into account, not only course content, but the methodology of delivery of instruction, and recognize that, in general, a university will have certain course programs that duplicate another.

The failure of the African American educational leadership to adopt standards such as these to be used in monitoring desegregation activities in the educational arena following the *Brown* decision is, perhaps, one the reasons that made *United States v. Louisiana* (1981) and other cases necessary. The reality which must be accepted in this case is that the entire community, especially the African American community, and not just those comprising the higher education leadership, must be vigilant and proactive to insure that the terms of the settlement are not manipulated as happened in the consent decree. Unlike *Brown*, *United States v. Louisiana*, (1981) should be the standard by which partnership equity and participation in higher education is achieved and measured for all institutions drawing from the same coffers.

References

Blake, E., Jr. (1991). Is higher education desegregation a remedy for segregation but not educational inequality?: A study of the *Ayers v. Mabus* desegregation case. *Journal of Negro Education, 60*(4).

Samuels, A.L. (1991). *Applying Brown to higher education: a case study of United States v. Louisiana.* Unpublished masters thesis, Southern University, Baton Rouge, Louisiana.

Waltman, J. (1994, July 6). Assessing the future of black colleges. *The Chronicle of Higher Education.*

Table of Legal Cases

Adams v. Richardson, 356 F. Supp. 92 (D.D.C. 1973).
Ayers v. Fordice, 112 S. Ct. 2727 (1992).

Brown v. Board of Education, 347 U.S. 483 (1954).

Civil Rights Act of 1964, Tit. VI, Sect. 601 et seq., 42 U.S.C.A. 2000 et seq.

First Morrill Act of 1862, 12 Stat. 503 et seq. 7 U.S.C. 301 et seq.

LA. Const. of 1879, art. 231 (1879).

Plessy v. Ferguson, 163 U.S. 537 (1896).

Second Morrill Act of 1890, 26 Stat. 417 et seq. 7 U.S.C. 321 et seq.

United States v. Fordice, 60 U.S.L.W. 4769 (1992).

United States v. Louisiana, 527 F. Supp. 509 (E.D. L.A.1984).

United States v. Louisiana, No. 80–3300 (USD/ED, November, 1994).

CHAPTER 10

THE IMPACT OF THE MISSISSIPPI DESEGREGATION CASE ON HISTORICALLY BLACK COLLEGES AND UNIVERSITIES

Frederick S. Humphries

Editor's Note:

Dr. Humphries was an expert witness at the recently con cluded *Ayers v. Fordice* case, which was the latest round in the ongoing Mississippi higher education desegregation case. Other chapters in this volume also address the *Ayers* case — Chapters Nine, Eleven, and Twenty.

The first part of this chapter (through the section on the three plans to desegregate Mississippi higher education) was written before the March 1995 *Fordice* decision and reflect the author's point of view as the case was being heard. The last part of the chapter (from the highlights of the court's decision through the end of the chapter) was written after the *Fordice* decision and reflect Dr. Humphries's thoughts after the case's most recent resolution.

The Context of the Mississippi Desegregation Case

The legal victories that made desegregation a household word (e.g., *Brown v. Board of Education of Topeka, Kansas*, 1954; 1955) by enabling us to overcome the separate but unequal realities of a nation divided against itself, present us now with an even greater issue, born in slavery, fostered during the era of segregation and embedded in the minds of those who will decide the future of higher education in the state of Mississippi (Kluger, 1975).

The overriding legacy of segregation is the imprimatur of inferiority that has been stamped on all things initiated by or associated with African Americans. This perception of inferiority is the hidden frame of reference used to justify Mississippi's plan (*U.S. vs Fordice*, 1992) to close Mississippi Valley State University (MVSU), constrain Jackson State University (JSU), and deprive Alcorn State University (ASU) of its autonomy. (This plan, along with that of the plaintiff and the U.S. Department of Justice, will be described in detail later in this chapter.)

When segregation was the law of the land, Mississippi, the poorest of the Southern states, deliberately built inferior facilities and provided less than adequate resources for African Americans (McMillian, 1989). Inferiority was deliberately built into the education system to ensure that individuals and institutions would not miss the point — African Americans were not equal to whites — and the manifestation of that claim was vested in the education programs to provide a visible expression of white supremacy.

African American teachers were paid less than white teachers, African American students received secondhand books while white students received new books and state of the art science laboratories. Although the notion of separate but equal prevailed, the South was unequivocal in its determination to see that excellence was not achieved in any aspect of society for its African American citizens (Egerton, 1995).

In *Adams v. Richardson* (1973), the onus was placed on the states to rectify conditions at historically black colleges and universities (HBCUs) and improve the educational outlook for African Americans not only through the enhancement of these institutions, but also through the provision of access to white colleges. Unfortunately and unwisely, access to white colleges has been considered the defining factor in desegregation cases. We should have learned by now that over the years of desegregation, vis-à-vis elementary and secondary education and higher education that you cannot achieve a happy medium by focusing only on African American students without focusing on the HBCUs.

It is hard to make the case under the rubric of desegregation that while you respect the individual, you have no respect for the individual's institutions.   This is especially true when those institutions have been bridges over troubled waters for generations of graduates who achieved success levels comparable to their white counterparts despite attending a supposedly inferior institution.

Treating predominantly white colleges as the *sine qua non* of higher education institutions underscores the duplicity that lay at the bottom of the actions of the policymakers who support the states' proposals in the *Fordice* case. First you create the impression that you want to create better educational opportunities for African American students by opening the doors of white schools, and then you destroy the HBCUs because they are supposedly inferior.

Consider the psychological baggage such a decision creates in the minds of African American students.   First, they must participate in a decision that has branded their education as inferior, and then they must attend institutions where the majority of the major leadership positions are held by whites.

The sheer force of such a decision affirms the supposed superiority of white people and white institutions while also affirming that there was something in the HBCUs that could be read as inherently inferior, something causal that was not simply the result of a segregated and oppressive society. The next step is to believe that African Americans were there because they could not do any better. However, if you believe that it was the act of segregation that produced the inequalities within the system, then an ethical and equitable desegregation policy would involve rectifying any deficiencies at the HCBUs.

How can a supposedly just society create a win/lose situation under the guise of rectification? HBCUs have served well as bridges over troubled waters for students and alumni who will continue to benefit from the existence of their respective alma maters. Yet African American students are supposed to believe that they are going to be better off in a system where their schools have limited scope and resources.

Why Mississippi HBCUs Should *Not* be Closed

The closing of any HBCU represents an unsatisfactory response to this issue. The proper swing of justice must result in a win-win conclusion where all parties are treated fairly instead of the current state plan, which is more punitive than remedy to the HBCUs and the African American citizens of Mississippi.

The state plan is a fallacious process that cannot pass the litmus test of fairness to African Americans and HBCUs. It will only engender suspicion and hostility. If it is not changed, we can conclude that the artifacts of segregation have prevented state lawmakers from being fair to its African American citizens.

Only in Mississippi do we have a single public university located within the most populated area of the state without that institution being the epicenter of higher education for that region. Despite its location, JSU has no engineering programs, no law school or Ph.D programs and no nursing school although there is a medical complex within the city. State policymakers have already demonstrated their unwillingness to be fair by creating an alternative structure — by adding a nursing program at the Mississippi Medical School — to avoid enhancing program offerings at JSU.

In the Delta, where the human artifacts of the era of segregation will increase significantly if MVSU is closed, state lawmakers ignore the ability and the willingness of MVSU to accept and graduate students who somehow survived what may be the worst K–12 system in the nation. The people who live in the Delta know that closing MVSU will thwart the ambition of African American students. They also know that a fair and just society would strengthen the K–12 programs and improve MVSU's propensity to serve by increasing programs, adding resources and have MVSU serve both white and African American students.

The current state plan demeans students and protects the culprits in the dastardly education process perpetrated on the people of the Delta. How can we close a school that has delivered on its promise to provide lives of quality and substance, a school that told the students of the Delta that they could make it and then worked to make Delta dreams of success come true? Any decision to close MVSU is unacceptable.

The state should be proud of ASU, the oldest HBCU land grant university in the country (Posey, 1994). An institution poised to help African American and white farmers become more productive only recently began to receive financial assistance from the state for its efforts on behalf of African American farmers. And now, when at the moment of its ability to do even more, it is projected to lose its autonomy and comprehensiveness.

You cannot deliver justice to a people by destroying part of their culture.   An indestructible covenant exists between the HBCUs and African Americans who are exalted by these institutions and who exult in them.   It is a covenant that is as much a part of the African American experience in this nation as the African American family and the African American church.

Mississippi, the state where literacy tests and poll taxes were created for the sole purpose of denying African Americans the right to vote, and whose history of race relations is probably the most despicable in the nation, has a great opportunity in the *Fordice* case to demonstrate that it can be fair to its African American citizens.

It is my opinion that the state's plan will result in the subjugation of African American people in Mississippi and delay the fulfillment of the promise guaranteed to all citizens by the Constitution of the United States.   Further, it is a betrayal of the 14th Amendment and no court dedicated to justice should ever ratify the state plan as the vehicle for the rectification of injustice.   It is unacceptable.

HBCUs in Mississippi have been under siege from their beginnings.   These institutions were established in a state whose leaders were selected more more for their abilities to fan the fires of racism than for their ability to promote equal opportunity and the democratic process.

It took a Reconstruction legislature to establish ASU in 1871. The African American citizens of Mississippi had to wait 70 years later before the state used its resources to increase higher education opportunities by assuming control of Jackson College for Blacks, a previously private college that was founded in 1877 as Natchez Seminary.   MVSU was established in 1946 primarily to prepare its graduates for teaching and vocational careers.

On the other hand, during the 80-year period from 1844 to 1924, Mississippi created five public all white institutions of higher learning.   Those included: the University of Mississippi (UM) (1844), Mississippi State University (MSU) (1878), Mississippi University for Women (MUW) (1884, the first public college for women in the United States), The University of Southern Mississippi (USM) (1910), and Delta State University (DSU) (1924).

Although the school age population of African Americans has remained at nearly half or greater than the total white school age population for most of Mississippi's existence, the state had only one institution of higher learning for its African American citizens and five for its white citizens from 1844 to 1940. This historical injustice perpetrated on the African American citizens of Mississippi amounted to taxation without representation.

In 1940, the year the state acquired Jackson College, there were 115,232 African Americans between the ages of 15 and 19, and 114,415 whites of the same age. Clearly, Mississippi leaders refused to acknowledge African American students as intellectual resources and even as individuals who were guaranteed certain inalienable rights as citizens of the state of Mississippi and of this nation. In 1940, ASU and JSU had a combined enrollment of only 551 students.

Today injustice still prevails. Mississippi has declared itself free at last of the vestiges of racial inequality under the guise of supposedly race-neutral polices, where freedom of choice has somehow become synonymous with equal opportunity. Freedom of choice is not free in Mississippi. Under the plan advocated by the state — a plan with no input from the presidents of Mississippi's three HBCUs or the African American community — the state is asked to ignore its own history while planning to destroy the cultural essence of nearly half its population.

The *Ayers* Case and the 1992 Supreme Court Ruling

In 1975, the late Jake Ayers had a dream and decided to make it a reality. A former student at Alcorn State University, Ayers was the father of 10 children. He was a former civil rights worker in the 1960s and he knew first hand of the economic hardships of African Americans in the Delta where its not hard to evoke images of Mississippi plantations and the people who eked out livings as sharecroppers and laborers. Ayers knew how important education was to the children of the Delta and the significance of MVSU as a pathway to a better life. He also knew that the sons and daughters of sharecroppers had a right to attend an institution with adequate resources and facilities.

He decided to fight. On January 28, 1975, Ayers, along with 21 African American students filed a suit (*Ayers v. Mabus*, 1975) challenging Mississippi's dual system of higher education. Ayers was not seeking to dismantle the state's HBCUs. He wanted the state to treat all of its institutions of higher learning with equal respect and equal resources.

Ayers died on August 26, 1986 of a heart attack, but in an interview published in "Notes," a newsletter he edited for the North Mississippi Rural Legal Services, he blamed racism for the states' failure to acknowledge the importance of MVSU. "I don't think the state cares about educating black people. They underfund all black institutions and underpay all black faculties. Black people have to bear the burden for changing conditions in Mississippi".

On December 11, 1987, U.S. District Judge Neal Biggers, Jr., dismissed the lawsuit, but the attorneys for the plaintiffs filed an appeal five days later with the 5th U.S. Circuit Court of Appeals in New Orleans. A three-judge panel overturned Biggers' dismissal. The panel ruled on the basis that race-neutral policies were inadequate to produce desegregation.

The decision by the three-judge panel was appealed by the state's attorney to a full court (16 judges) of the 5th Circuit. The *en banc* court reversed the three-judge panel's ruling, agreeing with the Biggers Court decision which led the plaintiffs to appeal to the Supreme Court of the United States.

The appeal was argued before the Supreme Court on November 13, 1991. The Supreme Court ruled on June 26, 1992 that public higher education in Mississippi represented a segregated system (*U.S. v. Fordice*). The Court instructed the state to remove all vestiges of de jure segregation, unless the state could demonstrate through sound educational reasoning, why any traces of segregation should remain. This case has been extensively studied since it has implications not only for Mississippi, but for other states with vestiges of de jure segregation at the higher education level (e.g., Blake, 1991; Hawkins, 1994a, 1994b).

The Three Plans for Settling *Ayers v. Fordice*

The Supreme Court remanded the case back to the Biggers Court. The lower court was directed to examine admission standards, program duplication, funding, number of institutions and their missions and any other concerns that would result in continued segregation of higher education in Mississippi. Judge Biggers asked the state and the plaintiffs to submit proposals to remedy the findings of the Supreme Court. The next three sections of this chapter describe the plans of the state, the plaintiff, and the U.S. Department of Justice.

The State's Proposal
Mississippi's proposal was prepared by the Commissioner of
Higher Education and his staff and sanctioned by the Board of
Trustees of Institutions of Higher Learning known as the College
Board in Mississippi. The state's plan was worked out behind
closed doors with no input from students, faculty, or the presidents
of the eight universities. The College Board recommended the
merging of MVSU and DSU through the creation of an institution
in Cleveland, Mississippi that would be named Delta Valley State
University. MVSUs old campus at Itta Bena would be closed and
the new college would be an administrative unit of the UM. The
College Board also called for the closing of the UM Dental School
and the Veterinary School at MSU, but later dropped these
recommendations.
ASU would lose its identity and its autonomy by becoming an
administrative unit of MSU. The remaining HBCU, JSU would
become one of the four lead universities in the state with an
enhanced urban mission. The plan originally called for MUW to be
assigned as an administrative unit of the USM, but was later
changed to propose a merger with MUW and MSU.
In a move that could adversely impact African American
enrollment in Mississippi's colleges and universities, the state's plan
would establish common admission standards for all higher
education institutions. The state also planned to put all of these
recommendations into effect without any increases in funding.

The Plaintiff's Plan
All of eight universities in Mississippi would continue as
separate, autonomous institutions with dramatic changes for JSU.
The plaintiff's plan called for a law school for JSU and new high
demand programs that would attract additional white students to
JSU. The most controversial of the plaintiff's recommendations
would move the administration of the UM Medical Center to JSU.
Since both institutions are located in Jackson, this seems to be a
plausible proposal that would result in greater efficiency for the
state.
JSU would also receive the MSU architecture program and
graduate program in public administration, the UM undergraduate
program in engineering, and the Social Work graduate program
from the USM. Additional programs would be transferred to ASU
and MVSU, including all of the technology curriculum currently

at MSU, as well as some of MSUs agriculture and computer science programs. The nursing and criminal justice programs at DSU would be transferred to MVSU.

The plaintiff's plan also called for open admission policies at ASU, DSU, MVSU, and MUW. Prospective enrollees would need only a high school diploma and an ACT score of 10. JSU would have the same open policies for eight years and then raise its standards to match those at UM, MSU, and USM. The new admission recommendations include a five-year period when the professional programs of medicine, law, dentistry, pharmacy, and veterinary medicine would reserve a percentage of seats for graduates of Mississippi's three HBCUs.

The plaintiffs wanted funding to meet the building needs of the three HBCUs including a major building program at JSU. The plan recommended that 40% of state funds for building projects go to the three HBCUs including buildings for a School of Liberal Arts, Social Sciences and Human Services, a conference and banquet complex, and other campus buildings for JSU.

The plaintiffs wanted African American employees at HBCUs to be given job preferences at the predominantly white universities and on the staff of the College Board for the next 10 years. Governor Kirk Fordice's administration would be expected to fill any College Board vacancy with an African American and the next administration would be expected to add at least two African Americans to the College Board. The plaintiffs also asked for a separate board for the three HBCUs.

The U.S. Department of Justice's Plan

MVSU would remain an autonomous institution but ASU would be downgraded from university status to a technical institute. The Justice Department also called for the Medical Center to be turned over to JSU and for all three HBCUs to receive specialization and enhancement programs. However, the Justice Department was willing to let the current College Board remain as the board for all eight universities.

Highlights of the *Ayers v. Fordice* Decision

On March 7, 1995, Judge Biggers's historic decision saved MVSU and MUW as independent institutions as he rejected that part of the state's plan which called for merging the two institutions (Hawkins, 1995). Nevertheless, he left the door open for a possible merger in the future when he ruled that the state's proposal "is unsupported at this time by sufficient research to determine whether it is practical to merge these institutions."

His decision produced a win/lose/unsure situation for Mississippi HBCUs. MVSU's future is still an open question and the new uniform admission standards will have an adverse effect on African American enrollment throughout the system. Judge Biggers ruled in favor of a system-wide admission policy that will rely on ACT scores plus high school grade point averages and class rankings. This decision was a serious blow to the plaintiff's case who believes the tougher admission standards will reduce African American enrollment by more than 35% at Mississippi's HBCUs.

In addition to MVSU's independence, the win side of the equation of Judge Biggers' decision called for $30 million in improvements for JSU and ASU. ASU's endowment will increase by $5 million and its graduate programs will be augmented by a new MBA degree program. JSU will become Mississippi's urban university with a new doctorate program in urban planning, social work and business. Schools in law, engineering, and pharmacy could be added if studies indicate that they are needed.

Why the Plaintiffs Should Continue the Fight

There is much to applaud in the decision of the Biggers Court, but there is still much to be done before equal access to higher education becomes a reality in Mississippi. JSU should have even more doctoral programs and additional funding should be awarded to ASU and MVSU. I am very concerned about the uniform admission policy and its impact on African American enrollment. Although a monitoring committee has been appointed to oversee the recommended changes, a brief look at the recent past is in order to ensure that we do not repeat such inequities in the future.

According to a 1993 report — *Mississippi Universities, A Three Year Plan of Action, Building a System of Excellence* (1993) — that was submitted by the Board of Trustees in November 1993, African Americans will comprise 46% of the traditional college age population in Mississippi by the year 2000. The report indicates that in 1990, in the 18 to 24 year old age range, whites outnumbered minorities by 168,734 to 117,624. However, the report predicts that by the year 2020, African Americans will outnumber whites by 158,963 to 150,404.

To get some idea of the state's future commitment to the education of its African American citizens, it is instructive to look at current support in one especially critical area: the ratio of state appropriations to federal grants and contracts to each of the eight universities in Mississippi. The data in Table 1 clearly demonstrate that Mississippi's three HBCUs cannot rely on the state for its fair share of state taxpayer's dollars.

According to data from the 1993–94 Annual Report of the Board of Trustees (1995), only the five predominantly white universities in Mississippi received more funds from state appropriations than from federal grants and contracts. The three HBCUs actually generated more revenues through federal grants and contracts than they received from the state of Mississippi through state appropriations. Clearly, Mississippi has one of the best educational bargains in the nation in terms of its HBCUs.

Dr. William Sutton, President of Mississippi Valley State University, in a written summary (Sutton, 1994) of the *Ayers* case, emphasized the same disparity in support for Mississippi's HBCUs: "During the 1993–94 fiscal year, the State of Mississippi allocated MVSU approximately seven million dollars of its $24 million budget. This is not a bad return on the investment, economically or educationally."

A Chance to Redeem the American Promise

Mississippi cannot escape its history as the ultimate symbol of apartheid in the United States. But state leaders must work to change the present. The *Ayers* case represents a great opportunity for Mississippi to redirect its resources, transfer major academic programs to its HBCUs, and create an educational environment where all Mississippians, African American and white, can help steer the state toward a more equitable future (Southern Education Foundation, 1995).

Rarely in the history of the struggle for equality has a state had a greater opportunity than Mississippi to redress a social wrong and resurrect a people's faith in justice and fair play. Mississippi leaders can achieve this high moral ground by simply ensuring the permanent autonomy of MVSU and assigning the planning of new law, engineering, and pharmacy schools under the auspices of JSU, an institution with an outstanding record of success in producing minority graduates in nearly every professional field.

Florida A & M University once had a law school but lost it in 1968 when the state of Florida moved it only blocks away to the campus of Florida State University. We are now engaged in an effort to regain the law school so that African Americans will have greater opportunities to participate in the judicial system of this state and nation.

African Americans are 14% of Florida's population but are less than 2% of Florida's lawyers, even though existing law schools have had plenty of time to diversify their enrollments and graduating classes. Only 4% of the judges in Florida are African American. The African American enrollment and graduation rates at existing public and private law schools will not come close to erasing the stigma of this state's ranking last in the production of African American lawyers among the nation's 10 most populous states. That is why we will need more than just resources and facilities to change the future. The most important factors are commitment, compassion, and an environment that demands "excellence with caring."

Why is it important for HBCUs to retain their identities and remain autonomous institutions?

James Madison, the fourth president of the U.S. once said, "the accumulation of all powers, legislative, executive and judiciary in the same hands, whether of one, a few or many, and whether hereditary, self-appointed, or elective may justly be pronounced the very definition of tyranny." This applies to governments, religions and institutions of higher education. If democracy is to survive, diversity must thrive. History has taught us that a free society can only exist when divisions of power exist.

Pluralism is what made the USA a great nation in the beginning and will make us an even greater nation in the future. Once we were a nation of immigrants, today we are a nation of minorities. Regardless of how we came to these shores, we must now work to guarantee that leadership in our colleges and universities reflect the society that we live in.

References

Blake, Jr., E. (1991). Is higher education desegregation a remedy for segregation but not educational inequality?: A study of the *Ayers vs. Mabus* desegregation case. *Journal of Negro Education, 60*(4).

Egerton, J. (1995). *Speak now against the day: The generation before the civil rights movement in the South.* New York: Knopf.

Garrow, D. J. (1988). *Bearing the cross: Martin Luther King, Jr. and the Southern Christian Leadership Conference.* New York: Morrow.

Hawkins, B. D. (1994a). A quest for equality: After nearly 20 years, Mississippi plaintiffs still fighting. *Black Issues in Higher Education,* pp. 10–13.

Hawkins, B. D. (1994b). The trial: Round two for Fordice. Mississippi higher Education Back in Court. *Black Issues in Higher Education,* pp. 12–19.

Hawkins, B. D. (1995). *Fordice* decision: Federal judge rejects closing of Mississippi black college in desegregation plan. *Black Issues in Higher Education,* pp. 6–15.

Kluger, R. (1975). *Simple justice: The history of Brown vs. Board of Education and black American's struggle for equality.* New York: Knopf.

McMillian, N. R. (1989). *Dark journey: Black Mississippians in the age of Jim Crow.* Carbondale: University of Illinois Press.

Mississippi Board of Trustees. (1993). *Mississippi Universities, A three year plan of action, Building a system of excellence.* Jackson, MS: Author.

Mississippi Board of Trustees. (1995). *1993–94 annual report of the Board of Trustees.* Jackson, MS: Author.

Posey, J. M. (1994). *Against great odds: The history of Alcorn State University.* Oxford, MS: University Press of Mississippi.

Southern Education Foundation. (1995). *Report of the Panel of Educational Opportunity and Postsecondary Desegregation. Redeeming the American promise.* Atlanta: Author.

Sutton, W. W. (1994). *The Ayers case and Mississippi Valley State University (MVSU).* Unpublished manuscript.

Table of Legal Cases

Adams v. Richardson, 356 F.Supp. 118 (D.D.C. 1973).
Ayers v. Fordice, 112 S.Ct. 2727 (1992).

Ayers v. Mabus, (1975).
Brown v. Board of Education of Topeka, Kansas, 347 U.S. 483 (1954).
U.S. v. Fordice, 60 U.S.L.W. 4773 (1992).

CHAPTER 11

THE ROLE OF HISTORICALLY BLACK COLLEGES IN FACILITATING RESILIENCE AMONG AFRICAN AMERICAN STUDENTS

Antoine M. Garibaldi

Author's Introduction

The following chapter is a reprint of a 1991 article that was developed for a very important purpose. In 1990 I was invited to serve as an expert witness for the Alabama higher education desegregation case. My areas of expertise included my service as a full-time professor and administrator at an historically black college or university (HBCU) since 1982 and my previous writings on the special contributions and the future of these institutions. The chapter, therefore, focuses both on the role these institutions have played in educating African American students in particular disciplines as well as the special elements of the HBCU campus ethos. Because the court case was primarily concerned with the state's public HBCUs (Alabama State and Alabama A & M) the chapter highlights the accomplishments of more public, rather than private, HBCUs.

This chapter was originally published as "The Role of Historically Black Colleges in Facilitating Resilience Among African American Students" by A. M. Garibaldi, 1991, *Education and Urban Society*, *24*(1), pp. 103–112. Copyright 1991 by Sage Publications. Reprinted by permission.

Since the *Brown* decision of 1954, these institutions have continued to graduate a disproportionately high number of African American students. For a group of institutions which represents less than three percent of all colleges and universities in this country, and enrolls less than 20% of all African American students in college, their success is unprecedented. (See Chapter Two for a further discussion of the calculations of these ratios.) As you read this chapter in light of this volume's discussions on the *Brown* decision, consider what more these institutions and their students might have achieved with funding and facilities comparable to their proximally located, predominantly white public colleges and universities. Despite the initiation of open admissions policies in many states in the mid-1960s, equality of educational opportunity still does not exist in higher education, but HBCUs have continued to persevere despite the incredible odds they face daily.

The Future of HBCUs

The future of HBCUs has been a topic of continuing discussion since the mid-1960s when open admissions and the gradual dissolution of segregated state institutions provided opportunities for African American students to attend the postsecondary college of their choice. This issue has been raised largely on the premise that predominantly white colleges and universities provide sufficient opportunities for African American students to gain access to and attain degrees from these institutions. However, as will be shown later, these institutions continue to play a major role in the disproportionate production of African American professionals and scholars, even though they account for only about one-fifth of the total African American enrollment in colleges and universities today.

As their graduation production indicates, HBCUs are extremely viable institutions. Nevertheless, a variety of factors contributes to the success of their students. They not only facilitate resilience, but they also provide a supportive environment in which African American students who come from varied socio-economic backgrounds and with average abilities can succeed. Although many students who attend these schools come with high ACT and SAT scores, a large proportion of them are admitted with scores lower than the national average on nationally standardized tests but with high school cumulative grade point averages that demonstrate their diligence about learning. HBCUs maximize the latter group of students' potential by providing small classes, regular academic advising by faculty, small group tutoring by peers and instructors, exposure to role models (faculty and alumni), formal opportunities for remedial assistance in the basic skills, and professional and academic internships at businesses and large research universities in their chosen field during the summer. These institutions recognize the wide range of all African American students' abilities, and their faculty teach with a philosophy that all who are enrolled can succeed. Thus, the campus's ethos and the institution's infrastructure foster resilience by reinforcing students' aspirations and by raising their academic abilities. To demonstrate the success that African American students have had in particular fields, this article will highlight some exemplary programs at a few, mostly public, HBCUs, because the majority of African American students are enrolled there and because the continued existence of many of these state-supported institutions is being threatened.

HBCUs were founded after the Civil War exclusively for blacks and are located primarily in the South. Prior to 1945 they enrolled 90% of all African American students pursuing post-secondary degrees. There are 104 HBCUs in this country today, and because they vary in size, type of control, and original missions, these institutions cannot be viewed as monolithic. The majority of the group (57), approximately 55%, are privately controlled and the remainder (47) are publicly supported. Sixteen of the public institutions are land grant institutions, and another 18 are non-land grant schools. Eighty-seven of them are four-year institutions and 17 are two-year colleges. Approximately 84% of all students at HBCUs in fall, 1989 were African American (199,974), 11% were white (26,962), about 3% were nonresident aliens, and the remainder were non-white (NAFEO, 1990). The majority of the group are also small institutions enrolling between 1,000 and 3,000 students. This information is important to understanding the diversity that exists within and among the institutions, even though their original founding purposes were extremely similar.

Questions about whether HBCUs, especially those that are state-supported, should exist cannot be resolved with simple "yes" or "no" responses. Ideally, the viability of any educational institution should be based on its ability to provide a quality education with adequate resources. The performance of its graduates in the larger society is important, but the institution's standards of academic quality are chiefly determined by the regional accreditation agency that gives it the authority to operate. Nevertheless, this question about whether these institutions should continue to operate has rarely been based on substantiated evidence that they are of inferior quality. The latter point is purely perception and not based on factual information.

Today HBCUs are responsible for producing 37% of all bachelor's and 30% of all master's degrees awarded to African American students (Carter & Wilson, 1989). (During the 1980s HBCUs graduated an annual average of 21,000 African American undergraduates and accounted for 4,064 of the 13,867 master's degrees awarded to African American students.) More important, HBCUs still award close to half of the bachelor's degrees received by African Americans in the states where they are located.

Given the success of HBCUs and the tremendous gains that African Americans have achieved in educational attainment since the 1940s, there is great irony in addressing the question of whether these institutions are still needed. It is a serious dilemma for those individuals, African American s and whites, who believe in these institutions' preservation, but who reject segregation. Public and private postsecondary institutions no longer blatantly refuse African American students but instead actively recruit them, as well as other non-white students, given the smaller numbers of 18- to 24-year-old white youth in the population today. HBCUs serve slightly more than 18% of the 1.1 million African American postsecondary students today, but this percentage is misleading because the majority of these institutions have been experiencing sharp increases in their enrollment over the last few years. Thirty percent of African American students are in predominantly white four-year colleges and universities, but more than 45% are enrolled in two-year colleges and universities, where the transfer rate to a four-year institution is barely 10%. Keeping in mind the earlier baccalaureate graduation rate of the small number of HBCUs in this country, these institutions are doing more than their fair share of ensuring that their students matriculate successfully and obtain a degree.

In considering the enrollment status and fiscal health of all colleges and universities, and that of African American state universities in particular, it must be remembered that a variety of external factors have provided challenges that were not present several decades ago. For example, the total number of colleges and universities in this country has increased by sixty percent since the 1950s (from slightly less than 2,000 to more than 3,500 institutions) and enrollment has multiplied five times (from slightly more than 200,000 students in the 1950s to more than 12 million students in 1990). Equal educational opportunity and access, as well as larger cohorts of 18- to 24-year-olds, contributed to this widespread growth during the 1960s and 1970s, but adverse demographic and financial indicators will affect the stability of postsecondary institutions in the 1990s and in the 21st century. Smaller cohorts of students, aging physical plants that require the institution to renovate or build new facilities, tuition costs that doubled during the 1980s, economic policies of the federal government that required students to finance their education with loans rather than grants and other factors have made it more difficult for institutions to survive in an increasingly competitive market. These market pressures are even more critical for African American state universities because of the level of fiscal resources they have traditionally received, coupled with the fiscal capability of the many low-income students whom they serve.

The Historical Role of HBCUs in
Professional Preparation Programs

Many of the above factors are important issues to ponder as one speculates on the future of African American state universities. Their continued existence cannot be discussed without the recognition of those factors. I took those impending serious external pressures into consideration in the preparation of *Black Colleges and Universities: Challenges for the Future* (Garibaldi, 1984). The book was based on the premise that in order for HBCUs to continue, it would be necessary for them to analyze carefully their original missions and to project what other roles they might wish to pursue to maintain a viable position in the sphere of American higher education. The book discusses in great detail such opportunities as the expansion of graduate education on these campuses, global cooperation through international projects of research and faculty and student exchanges, leadership and public policy development, as well as research on education and in the social sciences, science and engineering. All of these are critical issues for American society as well as the communities where these institutions are located. In the next few pages, some of the notable programs and disciplinary areas that HBCUs have developed over their history and still maintain today will be highlighted with the purpose of stressing their continued value in a multiracial and desegregated environment.

Education, Social Sciences, and Business

Given that most HBCUs began as normal schools, the training of teachers has been a fundamental mission for the majority of these institutions. This field of study was critically important up to the 1970s, not only because African American teachers were needed in elementary and secondary schools, but also because teaching was one of those few careers in which blacks could easily obtain a job. However, as more professional opportunities became available to African Americans in the late 1960s and early 1970s, there was a gradual shift away from this discipline. In recent years this trend has continued — as African American students parallel whites in their choice of the top two majors, business and social sciences — even though the HBCUs still are responsible for graduating the majority of African American teachers in this country. In 1981, for example, 13,325 black students received degrees in business; 9,471 received them in education; and 8,091 received them in the social sciences (Trent, 1984). HBCUs awarded 38.9% of the business degrees, 48.3% of the education degrees, and 29.8% of the degrees in social sciences in 1981 (Trent, 1984).

Those percentages, however, have not changed tremendously as HBCUs in 1987 accounted for 56% of undergraduate education degrees (2,421 of 4,253), 39% of bachelor's degrees in business (5,737 of 14,686) and 28% of the undergraduate degrees in social sciences (1,666 of 5,942). But although percentages are similar for those years noted above, only the field of business has realized actual gains in the number of African American undergraduates since 1976 (from 9,489 in 1976 to 14,686 in 1987). On the other hand, African American students received 14,209 bachelor's degrees in education in 1976 compared to only 4,253 in that field in 1987. Similarly, these students received 10,978 social science degrees in 1976 compared to only 5,942 in 1987. Over the 12 year period, the percentage *declines* as African American bachelor's degrees in education and social sciences were 70% and 46%, respectively (Carter & Wilson, 1989).

Each of the three fields above continues to be a critically important area for African American state universities to maintain but none is perhaps more important than the field of education, as the nation's teaching force, which has an average age of 43, becomes older. Moreover, fewer entrants to the profession today are non-white, at a time when the majority of students in metropolitan school districts are non-white. Today's teaching force has slightly less than seven percent African American teachers and that same small ratio is equal to the percentage of *all non-white students* in teacher education programs in this country (Garibaldi & Zimpher, 1990). Southern states, where the majority of African American teachers worked chiefly because of segregated school systems, were fortunate in the past to have 30% or more non-white teachers, but this trend has been reversed as veteran teachers have retired and fewer have entered the profession. Many African American state universities have exemplary undergraduate and graduate programs in this field and they should be not only enhanced, but also expanded if possible to meet the supply and demand needs of this country's 16,000 school districts. African American state universities such as Grambling State University, Norfolk State University, and North Carolina A & T State University, to name just a few, have become noteworthy examples of teacher education programs in this country, and they have been able to share their successful experiences with other colleges of education nationally.

Health Professions and Sciences

Two of the academic areas in which HBCUs have made tremendous contributions to society are the health professions and the sciences. In 1987, 23% of the bachelor's degree recipients in the health sciences (885 of 3,822) were trained at the HBCUs. The majority of the nation's African American physicians and pharmacists have also been trained at these institutions over the years, and that trend continues today. Xavier University of Louisiana, for example, which initiated its pharmacy program in 1927, is the leading producer of African American pharmacists in this country — 25% of a national total of 3,900 — and is a perfect model of a traditionally biracial environment of white and African American faculty and administrators. (State mandate prohibited white students from attending the university until the 1950s.) Since 1927, Xavier's College of Pharmacy, which is one of only

two remaining in Louisiana, has graduated 1596 pharmacists —
1,148 (72%) of whom are African Americans, 319 (20%) white,
and 129 (8%) foreign born. The first white student was graduated
in 1954, and as the preceding data show, a representative number
of white students enroll in the program. This "attraction" to the
program is obviously a function of its long-standing academic
quality (and its near-perfect pass rate on the pharmacy licensing
exam) and also its location in the southern part of the state. (The
other program is in the northern section of Louisiana.) Nevertheless, the university graduated an average of 20 white students
annually during the 1970s even though there was another program
at a predominantly white private institution in the city.   The
opportunity for students of all races to attend has always existed,
but the decision to enroll has strictly been left to the student.

The success of HBCUs in producing African American
pharmacists for this country has been exemplary. Only three other
HBCUs award degrees in this field: Texas Southern University,
Howard University and Florida A & M University. In 1971, 353
of the 618 African American students (57%) enrolled in these first
professional degree programs were at these four HBCUs
(Blackwell, 1981). In 1979, there were 958 African American
pharmacy students (about 4.2% of the total enrollment) and 54.3%
of these students were enrolled in the four programs at the
HBCUs. As Blackwell (1981) observes, "Although these institutions are historically black universities, founded when blacks were
excluded by law from enrolling in traditionally white institutions,
their schools and colleges of pharmacy in 1980 are considerably
more desegregated than any of their white counterparts" (p.157).
Blackwell further noted that only the University of Maryland,
among predominantly white institutions located in the "Adams
states," ranked among the top six with respect to the enrollment of
black students in 1979. (The actual number of pharmacy students
who matriculated there was 31.)

Another area in which HBCUs have been leading producers
of graduates has been in the field of engineering. There are only
six HBCUs with schools of engineering — Howard University,
North Carolina A & T University, Prairie View A & M University,
Southern University, Tennessee State University, and Tuskegee
University — but these institutions accounted for 65% of all
undergraduate degrees (1,553 of 2,356) awarded to African
American students in that field in 1987. They also graduated 26%

of all African American students who received master's degrees in 1987 (110 of 419). (Three more HBCUs also have engineering programs that have been developed over the last few years: Hampton University, Morgan State University, and a joint program now exists between Florida A & M University and Florida State University.)

The field of engineering has been one of the growth areas for African American students and it ranks third highest (behind business and social sciences) in the number of bachelor's degrees awarded to this group of students in 1987. (There were 1,370 engineering degrees received by African Americans in 1976, 2,039 in 1985 and 2,356 in 1987. This represents a 72% increase when comparing the number of students in the years 1976 and 1987.) However, the reader must recognize also that these increases of African American graduates in engineering are due largely to several innovative and cooperative programs based at HBCUs that do not have engineering schools.

Commonly referred to as "3 plus 2" or "dual degree engineering" programs, the HBCUs prepare the student in the first three years with basic sciences, mathematics, and liberal arts courses. After successful completion of the three-year program, the student transfers to an engineering school of his or her choice to complete training in a specialized area of engineering. Each institution has cooperative agreements with several engineering schools across the country, predominantly white as well as HBCUs black, but the student may also elect to attend another engineering school. In those instances in which dual degrees are available, the student receives a bachelor of arts degree from his host institution when he or she successfully completes the engineering program. These programs have proliferated among the HBCUs in recent years and have been excellent examples of cooperation with predominantly white institutions that want to increase the number of African American students on their campuses. Such programs can be easily replicated at many postsecondary institutions, especially four-year schools.

Graduate Education

As noted earlier, HBCUs play a pivotal role in the advanced degree preparation of African American students. Although only about one-third of these institutions have master's degree programs, they were responsible for producing 37% of all African

American master's degree graduates in education (1,935 of 5,250), 21% of these students in business (586 of 2,810), 26% in public affairs and services (406 of 1,553) and 26% in engineering in 1987 (110 of 419)— to cite a few select fields (Carter & Wilson, 1989). Fewer of them have doctoral programs, but they do produce slightly less than one tenth annually of their share of doctoral degrees, the majority of which are in education. These accomplishments are noteworthy and should be expanded to maximize the graduate education opportunities of African American students. Cooperative programs here between historically black, state and large research universities are also prime opportunities for expanded development when advanced degree programs may not exist.

First-Professional Programs in Law and Medicine
    The HBCUs have also played a leading role in the production of African American physicians and lawyers throughout their history. Up to 1980, 85% of all African Americans trained as physicians and dentists received their training at the two historically black medical and dental colleges: Howard University School of Medicine and Meharry Medical College (Blackwell, 1981). Over 90% of the African Americans with doctor of veterinary medicine degrees received their training at the only historically black school of veterinary medicine, Tuskegee Institute (now University). And the majority of African American lawyers in this country were trained at one of the four HBCUs with these programs: Howard University, Southern University, Texas Southern University, and North Carolina Central University. Although there have been increases in law school enrollments by African American students over the last two decades, and especially in predominantly white institutions, Blackwell (1981) notes that "each one of these [historically black] law schools is considerably more racially integrated than is any other institution, public and private, in the state or jurisdiction in which it exits" (p. 242).
    In select fields such as medicine, dentistry, and law, as well as the sciences, the size of the institution providing the undergraduate preparation of the students has little relationship to what an institution can accomplish in placing these students into first-professional programs. Xavier University once again, which has barely 2,500 undergraduates, ranked second in the country in the

placement of African American students into medical schools in 1989 (31 students). The leading institution was Howard University (50 students), which has a medical school; also in the second spot was Morehouse College (31 students) which now also has a medical school. Behind Morehouse was another well-known HBCU, Spelman College (28 students), and the others were Berkeley (18), Columbia (18), Northwestern (18), Yale (18), Harvard (17), and Michigan (17).

Despite the fact that science and mathematics are fields in which there is a dearth of young, interested African American students, several HBCUs have proven that their graduates are as competent and well prepared as all other students coming from elite and prestigious colleges and universities. The nurturance that is provided by faculty in and outside class coupled with high standards and a pervasive positive self-concept that conveys the belief that anyone can succeed if he or she works hard enough are the cornerstone of HBCUs' accomplishments in these highly specialized fields. There is no magic in that success, but it is a combination of faculty believing that students have the ability to perform in technical fields and students meeting the challenge of the curriculum. There is a tremendous need for more African American physicians, especially to serve in rural settings, and HBCUs can provide the necessary preparation to make this a reality.

Conclusion

As the previous discussion has indicated, HBCUs, and African American state universities in particular, are still viable institutions in this society. They continue to produce two-fifths of all African American bachelor's degree recipients and one-third of all master's graduates, but they are also influential in providing the undergraduate preparation for these students to enter highly specialized disciplines. The fact that their graduates are able to compete with students from the so-called "best institutions of higher education" in graduate and professional programs should clearly extinguish any perception of inferiority assumed by individuals who are unfamiliar with their past and present accomplishments. Moreover, the fact that they serve a proportionately small segment of the African American student population in higher education but account for twice that proportional share in annual undergraduate degree production is also testament to their ability to retain larger numbers of these students than other institutions that serve similar populations. Clearly the academic enrichment that is provided through tutoring and remedial assistance, their faculty's close monitoring of the academic progress of students, the small class sizes, and the promotion of graduate and professional opportunities facilitate resilience in African American students and raise their academic expectations and abilities. Many institutions of higher education can learn from the successful programs of these colleges and universities, and they should be recognized for the contributions that they have made to the larger society and particularly to the lives of African American youth.

References

Blackwell, J. (1981). *Mainstreaming outsiders: The production of black professionals.* Atlanta, GA: Southern Education Foundation.

Carter, D. J., & Wilson, R. (1989). *Eighth annual status report: Minorities in higher education.* Washington, DC: American Council on Education.

Garibaldi, A. M. (1984). *Black colleges and universities: Challenges for the future.* New York: Praeger.

Garibaldi, A. M., & Zimpher, N. (1990). *Annual survey of teacher education students.* Washington, DC: American Association of Colleges for Teacher Education.

NAFEO. (1990). *Annual fall enrollment survey (1989) of undergraduate, graduate and professional students.* Washington, DC: Author.

Trent, W. T. (1984). Equity considerations in higher education: Race and sex differences in degree attainment and major field from 1976 through 1981. American Journal of Education.